THE LEGACY OF
Fawlty Towers

"I identify those characters who have every reason to avoid each other; and I make it my business to bring them together as soon, and as often, as I can."

Georges Feydeau, 1862-1921.

This book owes many debts – to Marc (and Melanie) for facilitating the thing in the first place; to Melanie (and Marc) for editorial support and advice; to my interviewees who sent me down some very interesting rabbit holes; to my parents for hooking me on *Fawlty Towers, Python, Perrin,* et al; to Stephanie for the loan of cats and outstanding sea view, very definitely between the land and the sky; to Ian and Toby without whom (etc), and to Dan for literally thousands of things.

THE LEGACY OF
Fawlty Towers

JACQUI COLLIER

WHITE OWL
AN IMPRINT OF PEN & SWORD BOOKS LTD
YORKSHIRE – PHILADELPHIA

First published in Great Britain in 2025 by
PEN AND SWORD WHITE OWL
An imprint of
Pen & Sword Books Ltd
Yorkshire – Philadelphia

Copyright © Jacqui Collier, 2025

ISBN 978 1 03612 035 1

The right of Jacqui Collier to be identified as Author of this work has been asserted by her in accordance with the Copyright, Designs and Patents Act 1988.

A CIP catalogue record for this book is available from the British Library.

All rights reserved. No part of this book may be reproduced, transmitted, downloaded, decompiled or reverse engineered in any form or by any means, electronic or mechanical including photocopying, recording or by any information storage and retrieval system, without permission from the Publisher in writing. NO AI TRAINING: Without in any way limiting the Author's and Publisher's exclusive rights under copyright, any use of this publication to "train" generative artificial intelligence (AI) technologies to generate text is expressly prohibited. The Author and Publisher reserve all rights to license uses of this work for generative AI training and development of machine learning language models.

Typeset in Times New Roman 10/13.5 by
SJmagic DESIGN SERVICES, India.
Printed and bound in the UK by CPI Group (UK) Ltd, Croydon, CR0 4YY.

The Publisher's authorised representative in the EU for product safety is Authorised Rep Compliance Ltd., Ground Floor, 71 Lower Baggot Street, Dublin D02 P593, Ireland.
www.arccompliance.com

For a complete list of Pen & Sword titles please contact

PEN & SWORD BOOKS LIMITED
George House, Units 12 & 13, Beevor Street, Off Pontefract Road,
Barnsley, South Yorkshire, S71 1HN, England
E-mail: enquiries@pen-and-sword.co.uk
Website: www.pen-and-sword.co.uk

or

PEN AND SWORD BOOKS
1950 Lawrence Rd, Havertown, PA 19083, USA
E-mail: uspen-and-sword@casematepublishers.com
Website: www.penandswordbooks.com

Contents

Fifty Years of Being Fawlty	7
The Hotel and Inhabitants	20
A Touch of Class	42
The Builders	50
The Wedding Party	56
The Hotel Inspectors	61
Gourmet Night	67
The Germans	73
Between the Wars	80
Communication Problems	84
The Psychiatrist	91
Waldorf Salad	98
The Kipper and the Corpse	105
The Anniversary	112
Basil the Rat	119
Memories	126

Criticism of Fawlty Towers	134
Cultural Inheritance	145
Fawlty Towers – The Play	161
Adaptations and Revivals	168
Bibliography	176
Endnotes	178

Fifty Years of Being Fawlty

> *"Fawlty Towers is probably as good as I can do in the half-hour format. Somehow Connie and I managed to top the first series with the second. There is no way we could top that."*[1]

Fawlty Towers appears in many All Time Greatest polls and lists e.g. first on a list of the *100 Greatest British Television Programmes*, drawn up by the British Film Institute in 2000; in 2017 a panel of 100 comedians[2] voted it the best British sitcom of all time; in 2019, it was named the Greatest Ever British TV sitcom by a panel of comedy experts assembled by the *Radio Times*. It has been sold to and watched in more than 60 countries[3], and it always features in personal recommendations and reminiscences, from the late 1970s to the present day. It is easy to love and has proved surprisingly hard to reproduce. *"As with* Monty Python, *there have been few direct imitators, simply because the original was so strong. From that point of view, it is as if* Fawlty Towers *dropped in from nowhere, charmed the world, then skidaddled"*[4] *(sic).*

Why do a mere dozen episodes of misunderstanding, childish behaviour, and the pure embodiment of rage still engage viewers so much? What do we each see in Basil Fawlty that appeals to us? He is an unpleasant person who treats people around him appallingly, especially his wife and inexplicably loyal employees – yet, somehow, they don't leave him. He remains married, despite the apparent awfulness of that relationship. He runs a successful hotel despite, not because of, his behaviour and that of his support staff. He is a walking conundrum.

For the most part, it seems that he accurately reflects aspects of his viewers – we each have our own inner snobbery, anger and frustration; a desire to succeed and exceed, to impress and be impressive. He embodies our collective fear of failure, of being embarrassed, of being seen to be less than we believe ourselves to be, and less than we hope we could be. He's an Everyman in many ways – but as he is always having a really bad day, made even worse by his own outrageous ego, and enabled or hampered by those around him, we can also find him funny. Comedy is tragedy plus time or separation, or to quote Mel Brooks: "*Tragedy is when I cut my finger. Comedy is when you fall into an open sewer and die.*" Andrew Sachs described[5] the show as *"a tragedy with laughs"*. In every episode we see Basil teeter on the edge of his own personal sewer. Sometimes he falls in, sometimes he's rescued from the brink by the inexplicably loyal Polly, sometimes he's pulled back from disaster by his wife, who would revel in seeing him flounder but has her own reputation and livelihood to think of as well. In any event, we can vicariously experience the tragedy and comedy of his days without risk or cost to ourselves. The adrenaline rushes and dopamine hits are free. And above all else, it's *funny*.

Readers of this book are likely to be reasonably familiar with the show, although not necessarily as familiar as they think. The show is currently [spring 2025] not streaming at all in the UK, and due to the retrospectively difficult nature of certain episodes they are not repeated on broadcast channels as much as some others – particularly *The Germans*, which has always been controversial and is now significantly edited for streaming and broadcast when available. Even the original broadcasts weren't as popular as people might believe. Season 1 had extremely low ratings: 3.7% of the UK viewing public watched A Touch of Class on its first showing in September 1975 – 1,868,500 people – although it had reached 7m by *The Germans,* and it only really took off when repeated the following year. Series 2 nearly didn't happen at all for a number of reasons including the breakup of Cleese and Booth's marriage after ten years; they would eventually separate in 1976 and divorce in autumn 1978. The very last episode was delayed by a full seven months due to industrial action. Average viewing figures were 13 million an episode for series 2 – around a third of the total UK adult population[6] – although this still lagged behind shows like *To The Manor Born,* which attracted around 24m viewers for the end of the first series in November 1979.

John Cleese was well-known to TV viewers from *Monty Python's Flying Circus,* which he had been in from October 1969 to January 1973; he'd been writing for sitcoms and sketch shows for a long time by 1975, and he'd been part of the ensemble cast for nine series of *I'm Sorry I'll Read That Again* 1965-1973 on BBC Radio 2.[7] He was becoming part of an unofficial new comedy Establishment, albeit leaning to what would later be known as the Alternative Comedy, slightly surreal, side of things rather than the Traditional standard sitcom.

In the 1960s and early 1970s, Cleese had written a lot of material with his old university friend Graham Chapman, for *Monty Python's Flying Circus* and other shows. Both wrote, individually, for the traditional-format ITV sitcom *Doctor at Large,* but had not collaborated since the first episode of its predecessor *Doctor in the House* in July 1969 – though they were still writing for the same characters and production team. In the 1971 episode *No Ill Feeling!* (s1e14) Cleese accidentally trialled the *Fawlty Towers* concept. The episode features an obnoxiously rude hotelier, inspired by a real hotelier, of whom more shortly, played by Timothy Bateson. Mr Clifford, who runs the Bella Vista hotel, has a domineering wife, played by Eunice Black, and a short temper, and his hotel has an extremely annoying guest, Mr Davidson, played by Roy Kinnear, who winds up with a trifle on his head. Does this sound familiar? It will.

Despite a successful working relationship with Chapman, Cleese would write less and less with him as time went on, especially as Chapman's alcoholism worsened. Terry Jones, who continued working with Chapman on *Monty Python's Flying Circus*, said[8] that they all knew Cleese was always planning to leave and that it was becoming a relief for John not to have to write with Graham. The team would continue to write films together – *Monty Python and the Holy Grail* (1975), *Monty Python's Life of Brian* (1979), and *The Meaning of Life* (1983) – but Cleese and Chapman would grow further apart even during that time.

Humphrey Barclay, producer of *Doctor at Large,* had told John Cleese there was a series in the hotelier character after that episode aired. When Cleese left *Python* at the end of series 3, in late 1972, he needed a plan for what to do next. According to his friends and family, he had often mentioned wanting to write a show with his wife Connie Booth, so Jimmy Gilbert[9], then Head of Light Entertainment at the BBC, suggested he talk to Connie and get back to him. She recalls that he asked her if she wanted to have a go at writing a pilot, based on the disastrous hotel stay that had inspired the *Doctor at Large* character. Why was he so inspiring?

In May 1970[10], as recorded in Michael Palin's diaries, the *Python* team were filming in Devon, and booked a stay in the Gleneagles Hotel, Torquay. Palin wrote for Monday 11 May 1970 that the Gleneagles, slightly outside the town centre, was bright, clean, and looked efficient. However, things were not going to run smoothly there for the team. Palin noted that the proprietor, Donald Sinclair,[11] viewed them as a major inconvenience and was openly disapproving of his guests' behaviour. He admonished Terry Gilliam, an American, for eating like an American i.e. swapping his fork and knife around. He was astonished that the cast wanted a morning wake-up call at 6.45am, seemingly outraged that this would mean he would have to wake up early as well. He threw Eric Idle's bag or briefcase over a wall because it might have been a bomb – some accounts say it contained a ticking alarm clock, others his dirty laundry – blaming his concerns on trouble with ex-staff. He threw a bus timetable at a guest who had dared to enquire about public transport in the area. The tellers of these anecdotes vary the details slightly between tellings, but the gist is clear – Sinclair found guests a huge impediment to his otherwise simple goal of running a hotel. Graham Chapman[12] called him "*completely round the twist, off his chump, out of his tree*".

Chapman, in particular, found the hotelier's rules on alcohol difficult to cope with as it was impossible to get a drink when he wanted one. "[The Gleneagles had] *a bar which could only be open while the owner was around, since he did not trust any of his other two staff.*" Chapman recorded that the bar was only open during meals and only Sinclair was permitted to serve drinks as he did not trust the other staff to do so; as he was also closely supervising the meal "*getting a drink was out of the question*". Sinclair had effectively locked him out of ever being served.

Palin's diaries add that Sinclair had an air of *"self-righteous resentment"* and was hostile to their post-midnight arrival after a late filming session. Shades of Basil and the wedding party.

The following day Palin, Chapman, and Jones checked out of the hotel – Gilliam and Idle were staying elsewhere in Torquay. Palin records that Mrs Sinclair threatened to bill them all for the full two weeks, even though the rooms were being vacated and she could re-sell them – comparable with Sybil Fawlty writing a bill for a dead guest! Cleese, on the other hand, found the Sinclairs so intriguing that he supposedly urged Connie to come down from London and stay as well, so she could experience the hoteliers for herself. Their first joint collaboration, daughter Cynthia Christine Cleese,[13] would be born exactly 40 weeks later in February 1971, although it would be rather *too* convenient to assume that she was conceived under the roof of the Gleneagles. (Andrew Pixley[14] notes that Booth was due to film for the series herself, on 18 May, so would have joined Cleese regardless of Sinclair's behaviour. It makes a better story for Cleese to *summon* her to witness the situation unfolding, however.)

Cleese is often quoted as saying that there are benefits to writing a sitcom set in a hotel, where anyone can arrive without much explanation. A great range of characters can be introduced, whereas in a more home-based sitcom a writer is limited to family and friends. When those family and friends are well drawn this works very well with few extra characters needed (e.g. *Friday Night Dinner, The Royle Family*), but if they are not then the show must resort to lengthy set up and explanation. It's also a universal experience: everyone knows what it's like to walk up to a front desk. You don't have to have stayed in a hotel to be irritated by inattentive or obnoxious staff.

In 1972 Cleese's former colleague Ronnie Barker wrote[15] a sitcom set in a hotel: *His Lordship Entertains* featured Barker's regular character Lord Rustless opening a hotel (the only surviving episode[16] confirms that they opened 10 days before the show starts). Josephine Tewson plays his secretary/assistant Miss Bates who is *"terribly in love with him"*[17] and David Jason plays the extremely old and daft bellboy Dithers – a little reminiscent of Manuel. The hotel also has an attractive waitress Effie, a cook, and an opening episode entitled *The Food Inspector*. Subsequent episodes featured an attempt to improve the guest experience with a cabaret night, the arrival of a wedding party, and a nubile young woman guest. The *Radio Times* synopsis ran: *"They say you're only as old as you feel and Lord Rustless is no exception. When a well-endowed young lady arrives at Chrome Hall Hotel he is completely captivated"*. Rustless isn't as abrasive as Fawlty, but Barker – entirely reasonably – called it *Fawlty Towers: Mark One* in later years.

Cleese had been married to Connie Booth since 1968 but this was only their second successful attempt at writing new material together, and only their third ever writing collaboration at all, after writing a sketch, *The Princess with Wooden Teeth,* for the German version of *Monty Python: Fliegende Zirkus* in 1972, and adapting fellow actor Bill Owen's[18] theatre script for Anton Chekhov's *Romance with a Double Bass*. This production was filmed in 1974 for cinema release in August 1975 – shown as the first part of a double feature, it would leave cinemas during the broadcast run of series 1 of *Fawlty Towers*. She was keen to write with him and felt it gave them options not open to more traditional writing partnerships – *"as husband and wife, there aren't many places you can't go"*. They made each other laugh. and were unafraid to criticise and rewrite the other's work.

Michael Palin thought that Booth's contribution had often been neglected or played down. He noted that most writers, Cleese particularly, need someone to *"bounce the comedy off"*, to tell you when a joke or plot line doesn't work, and he confirmed that Cleese valued Booth's contribution as significant, something Cleese also confirms in interviews. It is telling that they both still compliment each other's work on the show, even after fifty years. Booth has been at pains to note that the show was a joint creation, while complimenting Cleese, who had an extraordinary facility with language and was a wonderful writing partner. Cleese and Booth were both familiar with the work of Mike Nichols and Elaine May, a 1950s American university 'improv' pairing who recorded albums that influenced a generation of comics, from the Oxbridge Python team to Woody Allen, Steve Martin, Robin Williams, and Jerry Seinfeld. In the UK, John Fortune and Eleanor Bron had worked together on similar material, so a Cleese/Booth attempt would have brought nothing particularly new to the table, they felt.

Booth was slightly familiar to those who had paid close attention to *Python* TV and film, but was not prominently visible to the general public, and was mostly known as John Cleese's wife of seven years. Prunella Scales by contrast had been acting for over twenty years by 1975 and was one of the biggest names attached to the show, from the viewing public's perspective. Andrew Sachs was a minor character actor and very amateur playwright – Prunella Scales had appeared in a radio adaptation of his play *Made in Heaven* in 1971, but although the play had popular appeal, particularly when staged again after *Fawlty Towers*, it was not a critical success. Sachs was to become very popular with the public, albeit always most recognisable as Manuel. The hotel's three long-term residents, Miss Gatsby, Miss Tibbs, and Major Gowen were played by theatre and TV old hands Renee Roberts, Gilly Flower, and Ballard Berkeley. Roberts came from a large theatrical family, and was maternal grandmother to comedy scriptwriter Sam Bain (*Peep Show, Fresh Meat*), although he was only five years old when she first appeared on *Fawlty Towers*. Flower made her film debut in 1932 with the appropriately titled *The New Hotel* and continued acting into her 80s. Flower and Roberts would reprise their roles as the Ladies in an episode of *Only Fools and Horses* in 1983. Berkeley similarly debuted in 1930 and continued acting into his eighties. He would be cast most often as military men and policemen, racking up more than 40 such roles over his career: most notably a retired major in radio soap opera *The Archers,* and of course the retired Major Gowen in *Fawlty Towers.*

The first series featured a number of well-known character actors – the best known to modern audiences would probably be Bernard Cribbins, then on TV regularly as a reader on *Jackanory,* and as the voice of *The Wombles* – he could be heard narrating an episode at teatime on BBC1 the same day as his *Fawlty Towers* episode aired – but also a well-respected theatre, film and TV actor, and comic singer. Robin Ellis would shortly become significantly more famous as Ross Poldark in the first adaptation of the *Poldark*[19] novels, written by Winston Graham and first adapted for BBC TV in 1975-77. David Kelly, a staple of 70s sitcoms and 80s soaps, also appeared, and *Fawlty Towers* would be one of the last performances for veteran Michael Gwynn, who would also appear in *Poldark*. The second series would feature more familiar faces such as Geoffrey Palmer, Derek Royle, Una Stubbs, Elspet Gray, and Joan Sanderson.

Fawlty Towers demonstrates to the viewer a wide range of frustrating but relatable situations, all wildly exacerbated by Basil's inability to deal calmly and rationally with the world around him. Prunella Scales described the show[20] in a nutshell: "*John and Connie were extremely angry about 12 aspects of hotel management and wrote one angry and brilliant episode about each of these items.*" Each episode has at least one simple plot device that the character-driven comedy is hung upon. In the best traditions of farce, however, nothing is allowed to remain simple for long. Paul Davies, in *Class and Other Hotel Matters in Fawlty Towers,*[21] notes that while some commentators and critics correctly draw attention to the principal theme and ramifications in each single episode, many deal with specific hotel nightmares – common themes in real life hotelier stories. This echoes Scales's observation that the show is *fundamentally* about aspects of hotel management, without undermining the idea that it is also about class, snobbery, human behaviour, and other themes. He also notes that sex and sexual behaviour is everywhere in the hotel from Basil's perspective, which illustrates his visceral horror of sex and desire – his or other people's. He has pathological fears that are played for laughs, but they demonstrate the audience's own minor phobias and worries *'turned up to 11'*, to quote *Spinal Tap*. He finds or puts himself in normal situations, where normal people would find a workable solution to most of the problems, but because he is not a normal person, things *will* escalate.

Viewers can sympathise, at least initially, with Basil's modest and entirely achievable ambitions (for a normal person): to hide a gambling win from his disapproving wife, to deal with foreign visitors who don't quite 'get' the hotel or the British way of life, to communicate with an obstinate deaf woman, to impress a peer and some hotel inspectors, to deal discreetly with a death, to cover up and control any number of minor lies and mistakes. When the situation inevitably moves out of his control and his temper rises, the humour increases exponentially. Although you may cringe with second-hand embarrassment, you also want to keep watching, to see for yourself just how bad he can actually turn out to be this time. Comedy always works best when it is relatable, and Basil is immensely relatable – though we don't all see his xenophobia or avarice in ourselves, we might recognise his fear of an irritable spouse or a loss of reputation. And how many of us would – honestly – deal *calmly* with a corpse in our workplace?

Polly and Manuel are characters who have nowhere else to go – Connie Booth and Andrew Sachs were both immigrants to the UK, which informed their writing and performances. While Polly is written as an English woman of indeterminate age and background – although she has old friends who visit, and some semblance of a love-life, she does not appear to have any family – Manuel is a non-native English speaker and immigrant to 1970s Britain, which comes with much implicit and some explicit baggage. He relies on the hotel and on the Fawltys for support and money and has formed a very strong attachment to Basil as a result, even though Basil is foul to him on occasion and barely tolerant the rest of the time. Manuel comes from an erstwhile fascist dictatorship – by 1975 the future King Juan Carlos was acting head of state but General Franco was still nominally in charge. Basil name-checks him during series 1, Terry, the chef, does the same in series 2. Franco would die not long after the end of the first series. While Spain had boomed during the 'Spanish Miracle' years 1955-74, the global oil crisis had severely impacted economic growth and it is strongly implied that Manuel has come to the UK to better his chances and to send money home to his rather large family. Although under post-1973 immigration rules he has freedom of movement without many restrictions, Cleese says in the audiobook introductions that Manuel really should be learning English formally, in order to acclimatise as a resident and employee and to comply with immigration rules – but we do not see any evidence of the Fawltys supporting him in this endeavour, either financially or morally.

Polly is a student attempting to complete an art degree while working – this must be either an Open University degree or a degree at the University of Exeter, an easy commute by train from Torquay. In the original pilot she was a philosophy doctoral student, probably at Exeter. She states clearly to Basil that she is not available outside mealtimes, and she is clearly working during term time and short on money, so for practical reasons she cannot simply leave on a whim. She seems to have very little external support, so may be as reliant on the hotel as Manuel is, in her own way. We never hear about her family, although when her school friend Jean shows up in *The Wedding Party* we see that she is close to Jean's family.

Does Sybil have an urge to leave her husband, as she often urges her friend Audrey to do so? Basil is not as terrible as George appears to be – he doesn't hit her or walk out without reason, and while he is verbally abusive, she gives as good as she gets. Is she trapped by a kind of inertia that keeps her with Basil for lack of other options? Or a fear of divorce? Or is she choosing to stay in the marriage on her own terms, getting as much out of it as Basil is? She certainly keeps an independent schedule, working around Basil rather than with him, and socialising separately from him, although they do have some shared friends. She follows her own patterns of daily life with little regard for his needs – and not much more for the hotel's at times. A question that has arisen in 2024, thanks to John Cleese's most recent return to the question of a revival, is "did Basil stray?" He has proposed a new version of the show where Basil continues to run the hotel with his surprise illegitimate daughter, born after a fling with a guest. This raises some significant questions when we think about a man who appears terrified of sexual intimacy. Was the original character always faithful to Sybil? He certainly seems to want to stray on occasion – he is flattered by Mrs Peignoir, and his gaze is drawn by Raylene's cleavage – but his overwhelming fear of Sybil's wrath, accompanied by his vague bewilderment about sex and an unerring ability to say all the wrong things around women, seems to have held him back in the episodes we see. One popular fan theory is that Basil and Polly have had an affair themselves (see *Communication Problems*). Maurice Gran, a veteran sitcom writer himself, suggests[22] that rather than being an octogenarian hotelier, perhaps Basil Fawlty should become the Major Gowen character in any new show – old, absent-minded, and driving his younger, more capable staff round the bend, while still believing himself to be in charge. The West End show cast the 1970s-80s sitcom star Paul Nicholas[23] in this role, so perhaps Gran is on to something.

Cleese and Booth managed to write the second series during and after their 1978 divorce, which adds an extra layer of interest to the interactions between Basil and Polly when watched 45 years later. The dialogue for both series is highly rated and reviewed by critics and comics alike and loved by audiences. It's immensely quotable and has become part of the cultural collective consciousness – catchphrases people know almost without awareness of the origin. The physical comedy of the show mirrors that of silent comedies, and harks back to *Python, The Frost Report*, etc. The plots echo classic theatrical farce, of which Cleese was a huge fan. He told Andrew Davidson that he was influenced by all the farce he had seen, which included French farces at the National Theatre and Whitehall farces. He loves French farce as it is performed by experts who are completely over the top but simultaneously still believable. Classic farce demands that the audience accepts each new plot twist or chaotic development as plausible, even though they can see the flaws in plans and the inevitable doom that will befall the protagonist. The actors' skill is in convincing the audience that the plan might just work *this time*.

There's a lot to praise about *Fawlty Towers* and, overall, surprisingly little to dislike, although we will come back to that in *The Germans* and later, and there are lots of behind-the-scenes details to discuss. Today's viewers are more media-literate and trope-savvy than the original audience. Commentaries and documentaries have been made, and outtakes and oddities are no longer restricted to an annual *It'll Be Alright on the Night* showing but are widely available on DVD releases, and on YouTube and other sites. Memoirs and articles continue to be published so, while books on *Fawlty Towers* do already exist – and there is a bibliography here – there's always going to be more to discuss.

PICTURE THE SCENE

It is 8.59pm on Friday 19 September 1975, and we are settling down on our tastefully upholstered three-piece suites[24] in our living rooms to watch a new sitcom called *Fawlty Towers* on BBC2. We *may* be sticking with BBC2 after watching *The Money Programme* at 8.15pm, but we are much more likely to have switched over from BBC1 after an hour of comedy with old favourites *Dad's Army* at 8pm and *The Liver Birds* at 8.30pm. The episode, and the show, begins genteelly. A delicate piece of classical-style music – original to the show but convincing enough to fool viewers into thinking it was not – plays over the view of an elegant cream and black Edwardian hotel frontage. The sign says Fawlty Towers, the driveway is clear, no people are visible. We have no real inkling of the kind of show we are about to watch. We know it is a sitcom that includes John Cleese – we can see in the opening credits that it is co-written by him – but is it going to be surreal like *Monty Python's Flying Circus*? A classic sitcom like *Doctor at Large*, which Cleese has been writing for lately? Classist and snobbish like the characters he portrayed in *The Frost Report*[25] – the upper-class educated and tall gentleman[26] looking down on the lower-in-every-sense Two Ronnies, who have been dominating BBC TV comedy for a few years by this time? We may or may not have already seen Cleese in *Monty Python and the Holy Grail*, where Connie Booth played a witch (who was not a duck, or made of wood, but *was* really a witch – it was a fair cop![27]) and Cleese played a range of characters from an aggressive French Knight (that's pronounced ker-nig-ut) to Tim the Enchanter. Avid cinema goers may even have seen Cleese and Booth working together in the Chekhov adaptation *Romance with a Double Bass,* also featuring Andrew Sachs – but it is unlikely we'll have many preconceived ideas about *him.* Prunella Scales, however, we do know. We have enjoyed the gentle comedy of *Marriage Lines*[28], where she played Kate Starling, the lead role. Her on-screen husband George Starling was played by Richard Briers, now entertaining us in *The Good Life.*[29] Both Starling and Tom Good are sedate, almost boring characters, quite different in temperament and behaviour from the man we're about to meet.

If we've dutifully bought and perused the Radio Times[30] or a daily newspaper before broadcast, we will know what the show aims to provide. Prominently displayed on page 3 of the *Radio Times* was a pick for the week:

> **Friday: The Python man returns:** Smile, please – say 'Cleese.' Well, it would have been 'Cheese', but John's grandfather changed his name to avoid unnecessary laughter. Tonight there'll be plenty of laughs as the doors of **Fawlty Towers**, John (*Monty Python*) Cleese's new comedy series, are opened (9.0).

On page 4-6 of the magazine was a three-page spread with photographs of the Cleeses and an interview by journalist Benedict Nightingale,[31] with the header: "*From the* Monty Python *world of dotty improbabilities, John Cleese has emerged as a comic writer and performer of rare originality. Now, with his wife Connie, he has concocted and written a new series which starts this week and in which they will be performing together.*" On page 17, columnist Kenneth Griffith also picked it as a must-watch for the week: *I am already refusing all engagements for Friday evenings.* On page 59 the normal listing – BBC2, Friday at 9pm – was accompanied by a large photograph and almost full cast list, plus a synopsis of the plot: *Basil Fawlty tries to improve the class of the hotel's clientele, with remarkable results.* Typical of 1970s listings, we are given the writers' names, the designer and producer's names, and a credit for the music, as well as the main cast and notable guest stars. In addition, a bracket at the end notes that:

> (Andrew Sachs is in 'No Sex Please – We're British' at the Strand Theatre, London)

A credit that speaks volumes: Sachs was under contract to the theatre and was permitted to film *Fawlty Towers* providing it did not clash with performances.

This was also true of a couple of guest stars over the run of the show e.g. James Cossins, Mr Walt in *The Hotel Inspectors*.

If we have not seen a listing, we only have the show's title to guide us.

We *think* we know what to expect. We may be wrong.

PICTURE THE SCENE - TAKE 2

It is 2025, at any time of day we like, and we are settling down in any room of the house – or outside it – with our portable device, smart TV, DVD or Blu-ray player, to watch a sitcom we think we know something about: a show called *Fawlty Towers*. We know it's about an *awful* man named Basil Fawlty – the title isn't a mystery to us at all. We have five decades of reviews and 'common knowledge' behind us and a vague awareness of the characters, storylines, and problems. 'Everyone knows' that *Fawlty Towers* is "*the greatest sitcom ever*" or perhaps "*deeply problematic in today's light*", depending on which interpretation you've been exposed to most – but are either of those things true? Can both be? As with many popular things, it's very easy to list it as great without thinking, even without rewatching, when asked for examples of great comedy writing or popular shows.

> *Community*:[32]
> **Jeff Winger**: Cheers.
> **Abed Nadir**: *M.A.S.H.*
> **Ian Duncan**: *Fawlty Towers*, game over.

Neither of the other characters in this *Community* scene argues with Duncan's trump card – not even Abed, who is a dedicated and knowledgeable – even *obsessive* – connoisseur of TV sitcoms and comedy tropes. It is simply unchallenged as received wisdom – the greatest comedy of all time is British, like Duncan, and while it also showcases some of the *worst* traits of the British this does not seem to matter. Funny wins. End of conversation.

The show was moderately ground-breaking at the time. Cleese has noted in multiple interviews that the average BBC sitcom has 65 pages of script for 30 minutes (usually 28 minutes with credits but *Fawlty Towers* would run long), and the average *Fawlty Towers* script was 135 pages. Similarly, sitcoms tended to have 200 different camera cuts when shot on multiple cameras in a fixed set, but *Fawlty Towers* had 400. The numbers vary for single camera shows like *The Royle Family*, *Ghosts*, or *The Hitchhiker's Guide to the Galaxy*. These tend not to have studio audiences and so do not have audience laughter to contend with either – the audience would add one or two seconds to the running time of many scenes in *Fawlty Towers* as the actors would not or could not speak over them on every occasion. Bob Spiers, director of series 2, confirms in his commentary the number of camera cuts and the complicated editing required, while John Howard Davies, director of series 1, notes that the sets had to be built in an unusual fashion to accommodate Cleese's height. The show was groundbreaking in production terms, even if it was on the face of it 'simply' another studio sitcom.

Does *Fawlty Towers* work without caveats for a 21st century audience, fifty years after the first broadcast? Yes and no. Some aspects have aged poorly over time, and some need a surprising amount of explanation to be intelligible to younger viewers – cashing a cheque, for instance. Ask around on social media or in gatherings – *when was the last time you wrote a cheque? And the last time you cashed one?* Most people will be hard pressed to answer[33]. Banking has moved on so far that 1975 seems unimaginably antiquated now.

My parents were in their late twenties when it was first broadcast: one a European immigrant and non-native English speaker, a big comedy fan who quoted *Python* and Manuel to me throughout my childhood; the other who didn't mind missing episodes[34] at all. They each had very different readings of the show on first broadcast, and continue to differ today, while my daughter, not born until the start of the 21st century, finds much of it simply *baffling*. She is used to sitcoms where physical violence is frowned upon, and where "Mistakes, Misunderstandings and Coincidences"[35] form the rejected title for a Shakespeare play, not vital plot devices in every episode. Farce is rarely *not funny* but it's not always in fashion, and today's viewers simply don't have the same shared lexicon of comedy that the generations before them did: the more comedy is available to watch, the less we share. The experience of viewing farce improves when you have acquired the knowledge essential to predict the outcome – a 'bit of business' with chairs or plates here, some 'door acting' there. Once you spot the building blocks being placed, the plot points being seeded, the farce builds and builds from there: to a generation used to avoiding spoilers, this emphasis on actively looking ahead in the plot is new and strange, but it can be learned. The more we watch and guess what Basil has not yet seen, the further ahead of him we get, the funnier it will be, because *Basil* doesn't know the rules. He only knows that no matter *what* he plans, God, the universe, or Sybil will inevitably thwart his ambition.

I will elaborate on specific aspects that need annotation for modern audiences as they come up, although some issues will span the entire show. The hotel cannot advertise online, for instance – there's no internet as we'd know it,[36] or email available to the public – so Basil's quest for 'good', suitably classy guests is real and difficult. Everyone in the show is reliant on slow options – post, printed newspapers, printed or hand-drawn maps, scheduled TV and radio broadcasts, and regular opening hours. Even if prospective guests phone ahead – and we know that Basil will then ask them to write to confirm their booking – they have to hope that someone answers the phone and doesn't simply slam it down, shout at them, or ask forlornly: *Que?*

Many plot points rely partially or wholly on aspects of everyday life in the 1970s that can feel alien to modern viewers, or might be resolved quickly with the use of mobile phones instead of landlines. The bank doesn't open outside limited hours, the chef is contracted only for mealtimes, there are strict licensing laws, the hotel locks the door at night (still true of smaller hotels today, admittedly, but surprising if you are used to chain hotels with key cards), the hotel rooms don't have TVs, telephones, air conditioning, or in some cases, double beds and en-suite bathrooms. Other notable 'historic' features aren't plot-dependent but are worth looking out for: the guests mostly travel very light, with extremely small suitcases compared to those of modern travellers. Many guests travel by train and taxi, not bringing their own car to Torquay – and if they have brought a car, luggage space will be much more limited compared to modern cars. The cars themselves look very dated today. The fashions are eye-catching, and not all flattering. Every guest and worker featured – with one single exception – is white; most are British. We'll come back to *that* later.

The Hotel and Inhabitants

Basil Fawlty is a petty, angry, snob. This is the received wisdom, and it's borne out in the show, but he is so much more. He's classist, he's cultured, he's a prude, he's neurotic, and he's proud – but most of all, he's a man living in constant low-level fear. He's from upper-middle class stock, with pretensions of being more. Prunella Scales says that her conception of the characters was that Sybil was not as posh as Basil, and fell for his upper-class upbringing and manner as a way to social climb. Germaine Greer[1] noted that while he obviously wants to be a professional, he is a business owner and keeper of a hotel, which is not a professional occupation. Sybil grounds him when he gets ideas above his station. While Basil doesn't seem to have many hobbies (although we do know that he collects coins from the British Empire[2]), he's a cultured and reasonably educated man who likes listening to classical music and reading novels.[3] He dresses moderately well for a very tall and gangly man, and generally keeps himself well groomed. He speaks Classical Spanish rather badly, possibly some Italian (not uncommon in a music-lover), and barely passable French – but very little German. He cannot type well. He is from Swanage,[4] and did his National Service[5] in Korea, serving in the catering corps although he claims to have acquired shrapnel in a war wound. He is over 40 by the start of the series, whereas Cleese was 35. His great-grandfather was a doctor, and he once contemplated becoming a surgeon. Roger Wilmut[6] notes that Basil has a certain amount of education and appreciation of the arts. A number of previous characters played by Cleese, including John in *I'm Sorry I'll Read That Again* and an unnamed undergraduate in *The Frost Report*, are clearly Basil-prototypes, though as Wilmut adds, it's very unlikely that Basil Fawlty ever went to university. National Service and Sybil probably saw to any ambition he might have had there, even if he had passed all his exams without incident – and we can only imagine how chaotic a young Basil would have been.

Robert Gore-Langton, in a biography of Cleese,[7] describes him as a 'rantipole'[8] character, fond of noisy tweeds and sarcasm, and constantly teetering on the edge of a massive breakdown. Many reviewers and commentators would say the same thing, although Basil rarely actually loses control of *himself* – only of situations. Gore-Langton notes the physicality of Basil: *"the use he makes of his elbows...*

they jut out like the useless wings of a flightless bird". Cleese has described his own appearance as *"a cross between a giraffe and a hovercraft"*. Author Jodi Taylor:[9] [Basil] *terrifies me – he's so tall, and he's so angular, with his body all angles and joints. And when he would come racing along that landing to deal with the latest crisis... the speed at which he moves! And his upper body doesn't move at all, it's just the legs – I find that quite disconcerting! I thought it was because I was short and tall people can be alarming, but it's very reassuring to find that it's not just me!* Comedian and actor Rowan Atkinson[10] focuses on *"the legs"* when reminiscing about the show[11]. If Basil Fawlty had been a small rotund man his impact would have been different.

Basil is a victim of his writers' hard-hearted desire to play with his life: *"sometimes when we would think of what would happen next, we would howl with laughter and then we would think 'oh, poor man!'"*. Cleese is a fan of Henri Bergson[12] and often quotes him: *"Comedy requires a momentary anaesthesia of the heart... humour is a social sanction against inflexible behaviour"*. Viewers *can* have some sympathy for Basil: Jodi Taylor[13] acknowledges *"his complete lack of control over events as they not only unfolded but rushed around him. He would always start out with the best of intentions, and he* was *quite well organised, but – let's face it – the universe hated him, and if a thing could go wrong it would... Events would spiral out of control, crisis piled upon crisis, to the apocalypse at the end, and every episode* always *ended on an apocalypse"*.

Author Elizabeth Sandifer[14] described *Fawlty Towers* as a show about *"how the world drives a basically well-meaning man insane and apoplectic... the continual humiliation of a bumbling man who just wants to better his lot in life... it forces its audience to simultaneously cringe at and enjoy Basil's humiliation"*.

But it is a charitable view at best. The viewer has to avoid feeling *truly* sorry for Basil or he stops being funny – and luckily it's often easy to stop sympathising with him, as he compounds terrible situations with his own bad behaviour and responses. Terry Jones felt that Basil was awful and impossible, that he was a sad character who failed to achieve anything he wanted. Una Stubbs called him a ludicrous person, with over the top extremes of emotion.

Basil has been the subject of much analysis over the last 50 years, including a lengthy review by psychologist Michael Apter[15] who notes in *Fawlty Towers: A Reversal Theory Analysis of a Popular Television Comedy Series*[16] that Basil is prone to making two-edged statements that seem innocuous and pleasant before the more vindictive or offensive meaning is understood: tenderly referring to Sybil as a piranha – a small but deadly fish; agreeing with a guest that her son is highly strung – *"he should be"*. It sounds nice until you realise he's advocating hanging the boy.

Apter explains that Basil is characterised by a set of diametrically opposite traits which are rooted in a fundamental superiority/inferiority synergy – his neither-here-nor-there standing drives his behaviour as he attempts to reconcile conflicting instincts and feelings. Echoing Germaine Greer's point, Apter notes that Basil is a hotel owner – subservient to his guests *by definition*, but also in many ways their social superior as a property and business owner with a large house and land to take care of. But he is not free to simply enjoy the property, he *must* accept the encroachment of guests below his own social class. He is well dressed and well educated, considers himself a professional, and clearly perceives himself as superior to lower class 'uncouth' guests like the wedding guests, the undercover policeman, or the series of travelling salesmen that habitually stay at the hotel.

> *"His superiority and high opinion of himself are exaggerated by means of his private school demeanour and also his physical stature – he is six foot five. He is belligerently full of self-confidence."*

But he is also clearly quite ignorant on a number of subjects. His education has left him lacking in various areas, and his own belief that he does not need to learn hampers him with, for example, any attempt to communicate calmly with Manuel. The faults in his Spanish are somehow twisted to become Manuel's fault, not Basil's, as Basil can admit no weaknesses. Barry Cryer,[17] legendary comic writer: *"Success isn't funny. Failure's funny, and Basil just fails triumphantly every day at some point."*

Stuart Jeffries[18] highlights the British love of *schadenfreude* in comedy: "*British TV comedy was cruel and conservative… Endless death – that was Basil Fawlty's life… a long slow march to the grave with only the light relief of being able to hit [Manuel]."* He argues that we like aspirant characters who cannot escape their ruts for one reason or another – circumstances, accidents, temperaments all prevent the protagonist from escaping, succeeding, or achieving happiness. We revel in their frustration and panic. *"When we watch television we* want *to see a theatre of cruelty… to watch others suffer for our pleasure."* Audiences actively prefer it when things go wrong for Basil, when Manuel suffers his wrath, and when he suffers the wrath of Sybil.

Annjo Greenall, writing in the *Journal of Pragmatics*[19], describes the relationship between Basil and Manuel as one of *linguicism*[20] – Fawlty looks down on Manuel for his imprecise and flawed use of language, without giving him credit for being at least functionally bilingual. It's not as clear as overt racism, but it definitely hinges on his being 'other', and imperfectly so.

She notes that one way of creating humour in comedy is *"the technique of exaggeration or hyperbole"* – we see a lot of issues in the hotel, the characters, and the relationships between them, but crucially we also see "*a blown-up, caricatured, version of the response*". The meaning is clear – where *normal people* would encounter a problem and attempt to solve it, and find themselves able to laugh about the catastrophe afterwards, Basil, and to a lesser extent Sybil, *must* take things to extremes. Greenall talks about Basil's *"high degree of animosity"* which he directs fully at Manuel, and which has a linguistic basis in many of their interactions. While Basil is rude to everyone he encounters, including those he is supposed to like, he reserves a special kind of rudeness for his relationship with Manuel, beset as it is with communication issues. We see his worst behaviour to any non-regular character with Mrs Richards, who also frustrates him with her communication problems; Mr Hutchinson is a close runner-up, because he specifically irritates Basil with his way of speaking. Basil embodies linguicism when dealing with Manuel, and it can be split into two causes: firstly, Manuel's apparent inability to understand simple instructions, though he is often capable when spoken to by other characters – Basil obviously flusters him; secondly, Manuel's failed attempts to express his own thoughts appropriately and coherently. Basil subjects Manuel to a range of abusive behaviours as a result of his frustration and anger with the waiter – he ignores him, he ridicules him, he verbally and occasionally physically abuses him. He has generalised his frustrations with Manuel: he assumes that linguistic inability also translates to a general lack of capacity, thinking that Manuel is *stupid* for not understanding, and not merely encountering a language barrier. Greenall argues that this means Manuel's behaviour gets worse and worse, a kind of self-fulfilling prophecy, as Basil actively expects him to make mistakes and effectively sets him up to fail.

The show *relies* on linguistic jokes like *on-dos-tres/on-those-trays, where's Sybil/where's-the-bill, be civil/Seville*. Manuel's errors are accidental but Basil's responses to them are not. With Polly, Manuel's use of language is better and more fluent, because she makes more effort to understand and will not attack him. Basil knows this: *"tell him, Polly"* and uses it to keep things functioning. Basil also demonstrates linguicist behaviour to the Germans when he realises that they are speaking German to him and not, as he had thought, just gobbledygook. He gabbles an explanation in palpable relief: he had thought there was something wrong with them, although he has a head injury and is – consciously or unconsciously – concerned that there was something wrong with *him* when he failed to understand them.

Basil is physically and emotionally incompetent, and even his supreme self-confidence is being slowly and methodically eroded by years of marriage to Sybil, who both sees through his braggadocio and wears down his vague attempts to be competent, with her constant supervision, intervention, and obvious belief that he cannot be trusted to do anything alone. (She may not be incorrect, but it's undermining all the same.) Tom Salinsky points out[21] that the key to Basil's treatment of Sybil is that he *"can say anything he likes to Sybil provided that the insults never seem to strike home. If Sybil were genuinely to be wounded by Basil's bitter sarcasm, we would lose all sympathy for him as a character."*

Apter notes: *"Finally, he is also that classic comic combination, a bully and a coward."* Basil bullies his staff and as many of his guests as he thinks he can get away with – especially those who he deems to be socially inadequate *"riff raff"*. He is snide and mean to his wife, physically and mentally abusive to Manuel, attempts to dominate Polly, who can usually fight back, at least verbally, and is not afraid to be verbally cruel and occasionally physically violent to his guests.

He is also, however, a coward when it comes to dealing with his wife, and his verbal attacks on her generally come from a position of weakness, not strength. He is afraid of her, and of people who he thinks are better than him or who will expose him in some way. He is terrified of the psychiatrist, who may tell him at any moment that he is not normal; he is visibly uneasy around other doctors and professionals. Cleese notes in audio commentary that Basil's primary motive is to keep the peace, to stop Sybil from being – often justifiably – cross with him.

He often demonstrates conflicting behaviours like those referenced by Apter, sometimes all in the same scene – he is fawningly subservient to the parents of a child who has upset him, while dishing out a verbal snipe to the mother and a physical punishment (a clip round the child's ear) behind their backs.

Paul Davies[22] points out that Basil as a name means Royal, and of course Fawlty is a play on *faulty*. Basil Fawlty is king of his domain – when Sybil lets him be – but he is imperfect, flawed. Barry Cryer describes[23] Basil as *cartoony* and cringy. He is not a character who can be a hero.

John Cleese describes the origin of Basil's character in his autobiography *So, Anyway*,[24] where he discusses the pent-up anger expressed by a classmate, David Rogers – the boy attempted to sharpen a set of compasses[25] with a penknife, so frustrated was he with its poor performance – and explains that another key aspect of Basil is his overwhelming fear. His anger both hides and exacerbates his fear, which leads him to make silly mistakes. Cleese explains that each small mistake leads to panic and over-correction, while a desperate need to be judged as both efficient and sufficient drives him to farcical levels of behaviour. It is classic theatrical farce[26] – first a misunderstanding or error, then a cover up and some poor choices, before the whole ridiculous situation culminates in either discovery or escape, with optional forgiveness and redemption. The hero generally lives to mess up another day, and Basil always does, although he doesn't necessarily deserve to.

Benedict Nightingale, writing in the *Radio Times*[27] in September 1975, described Cleese as a shy man who wanted to overcome his inhibitions but struggled to lose his temper even when insulted. Cleese told him that he knew it was an absurd taboo and that to lose one's temper is only human, but that he had to be pushed to the edge before he could get properly angry and let his emotions out.

In *The Pythons*,[28] Cleese discusses the ratio of 'Basil in Cleese and Cleese in Basil' but notes that it is not just himself in the character. *"Connie and I have always had a thing about suppressed rage... we find it very funny to see people getting really steamed up and not being able to 'blast'."* He confirms that there is a lot of himself in Basil, and a certain amount of his father. Cleese often talks about his father's 'stinginess' and his attempts to avoid admitting it, telling his wife (John's mother) that he had bought *"Norwegian ham... better than the ordinary stuff"* rather than just admitting to saving money by buying a cheaper brand – we will hear more in this vein in *Basil the Rat* as Basil expounds on the benefits of Norwegian veal. And on suppressed anger, at least, a lot of Connie appears in Basil too. But he is surprised that viewers respond so well to this. *"It was a private thing – I never expected it to catch on anything like the way it did."*

Michael Palin noted[29] that Cleese often plays people who are good at bullying and delivering a quick put-down and that this was a continuation of what had happened in *Monty Python's Flying Circus*. He could see elements of Basil Fawlty in characters that John had played in *Python*, where he had been a very physical performer. The very popular *Ministry of Silly* Walks sketch obviously went straight into *Fawlty Towers* – particularly in *The Germans*. It was noticeable that a number of characters played by Cleese in *Python* sketches suffered from *"rising anger"*, going *"suddenly completely berserk"*. Terry Jones similarly highlighted how long John Cleese has spent in therapy, over his entire life – largely because of his own anger. Jones felt[30] that Cleese was using Basil Fawlty as a therapeutic method of coming to terms with his own self, and once he had exorcised all the demons he could leave Basil behind: *"It was as though, the more psychiatric help John sought, the less he needed to express himself with things like* Fawlty Towers ... *the less he felt he needed to be funny."* Cleese is very open and relaxed when discussing anger – he can be seen discussing it very calmly indeed, in archive footage included in the *Fawlty Towers: Re-Opened* documentary. He claims he let out all the anger as Basil Fawlty. Jones cast him as the exceedingly calm but exceedingly deadly Halfdan the Black in *Erik the Viking*,[31] a decade after *Fawlty Towers*. Cleese makes a quiet, polite, but utterly ruthless Viking leader, asking calmly, about an accused man: *"Now I'm not an unreasonable man but... would you behead him? Please?"* The terrified victim shouts *"Take all my sheep! All of them!"* and Halfdan thoughtfully turns to his secretary: *"Oh, that's a good idea. Take all his sheep. Then behead him."* And there is also the threatening: *"throw down your weapons or we'll kill the children."* The villagers comply. *"Right, now we'll kill the children anyway"*. Even without the baggage of Basil one expects him to snap and lose his temper at any moment. The quiet calm – expecting but never quite seeing the storm – is more menacing than the ranting, and this is very effective for the audience. We do see that in Basil at times – there are moments when his ranting becomes quiet, and potentially deadly – but even more so in Sybil.

Gore-Langton notes that John Cleese calls Basil a bastard and claims to hate him. He will not slip into character without very good reason – the 2024 play[32] being one of those reasons – and says about him that *"he's an absolutely awful human being. But the strange thing about comedy is that ... people feel affectionate towards* [awful characters]. *They would loathe him* [in real life]." Gore-Langton describes Basil as *"a sarcastic poet of frustration"*. He feels that *Fawlty Towers* is a comedy of emotion: *"mostly rage and embarrassment and British awkwardness at any breach of social convention. Also* superbly *gloomy in outlook."* Where Hamlet considers suicide, Fawlty is merely – but not quietly – resigned to his fate. He rages against the world but knows that he will go quietly when his time comes, for all his frustration.

John Cleese[33] was well-known to BBC TV audiences by 1975 from his work on *The Frost Report* and *Monty Python's Flying Circus,* and to ITV audiences from *At Last the 1948 Show*[34] (1967), and from *Sez Les* (1969-76), a Les Dawson sketch show. Cinema audiences may have seen him in *And Now For Something Completely Different,* a re-filmed *Python* sketch compilation from 1971, and *Monty Python and the Holy Grail,* released in spring 1975. He had also had a long-running part in *I'm Sorry, I'll Read That Again*[35], a BBC Radio comedy show in which he and Jo Kendall played a married couple, John and Mary, who bear a strong resemblance to Basil and Sybil Fawlty. *I'm Sorry, I'll Read That Again* directly led to the long-running *I'm Sorry, I Haven't A Clue,* and was significant in shaping the careers of The Goodies,[36] Monty Python[37], and many modern Radio 4 comedy shows. He would adapt *Fawlty Towers* for the stage in 2016 and a Feydeau farce, *Monsieur Chasse!*[38], in 2017, and has continued acting into his 80s.

Sybil Fawlty is a keen golfer and reader, who dresses nattily – her taste informed by Prunella Scales's input to the costume department – and often wears a very elaborate wig. She is efficient when doing her own work but loves to delegate, often confusing her husband with conflicting orders. She keeps her temper well despite a lot of provocation, but when she loses it can resort to name-calling and physical violence. She does not like classical music or Irish builders. She grew up living and working in family hotels, according to both Cleese and Scales, and they met when Basil was demobbed after National Service. She is also over 40 (Scales was 43 at the start of the show), which means that – for their generation – Basil and Sybil married relatively late, approaching 30 years old.[39] Even with Basil's two years of National Service, this still raises some questions. If Scales's theory of Sybil's family also being hoteliers is correct, it's likely that either Basil worked for her family before gaining enough experience to open his own hotel and Sybil came along as part of the package, or they both worked – separately – in a variety of hotels before winding up in the same place long enough to open a hotel and be manacled together, as Basil would later put it. Neither of them appear to have wanted children, which is probably just as well.

An exchange frequently retold[40] by Prunella Scales involves Cleese asking her what she thought of the scripts and her confirming that they were 'brilliant'.

>Cleese: *Any questions?*
>Scales: *Yes, why did they get married?*
>Cleese: *Oh God, I knew you'd ask that.*

The couple seem inexplicable even to the actors playing them, but there's an odd sort of attraction between them. John Howard Davies describes Sybil as *"the kind of woman who could make love and paint her nails at the same time"*. Maurice Gran[41] counters:[42] *"I don't think Sybil has sex at all"*. April Walker, who played Jean in *The Wedding Party,* also[43] thinks they never consummated the marriage. Sybil is a woman in utter control of her life and her man, when chaos doesn't intervene. Basil rather likes someone else being in control, as it absolves him from blame. Sybil, like Basil, is also a name derived from Greek, and means prophetess or oracle – Sybil is the font of all knowledge for the hotel or, at least, she'd like that to be the case, and she speaks her mind, warning Basil of impending doom. Basil might be more inclined to suggest that she speaks in riddles which need to be interpreted by a soothsayer. Jodi Taylor describes her as *"a force to be reckoned with"* and believes that *"if you got rid of Basil and Manuel, Sybil and Polly would have been perfectly capable of running the place, considerably better. They were strong women."*

Apter notes that Sybil is a stock character, of a type particularly prevalent in sitcoms: the masculine and aggressive woman. She appears to care for her appearance, dressing well – Scales's suggestions were good ones – and models a traditional 1970s feminine appearance with nail varnish, make-up, elaborate hair. But despite this external femininity, she behaves in ways that were viewed as masculine at the time (and still are to some extent in the 21st century). She is efficient, determined, opinionated, unafraid to lose her temper, ruthless, and Firmly In Charge Of The Hotel no matter what Basil thinks. She makes decisions and is aggressive about pursuing her goals – sometimes passive-aggressively, admittedly, but she obviously knows how to make Basil sweat after so many years of marriage. Apter contrasts the feminine-presenting masculine-behaving Sybil with the masculine-presenting feminine-behaving Basil – he cowers, flaps, gets emotional, and often needs someone stronger than himself to take charge of situations that are getting out of hand. The contrast enhances the comedy. From a modern perspective – Apter was writing in 1982, Cleese/Booth in the 1970s – we might be tempted to think that this is a very clichéd way of achieving comedy, but we still see it over and over in all kinds of 21st century shows. And we must remember that the point of the characterisation is not to demonstrate the gendered cliches of femininity and masculinity, but to portray the subversion, playing out the conflict – and harmony – between the two characters. Between them they have all the traits expected of a traditional pairing, just allocated in a less traditional manner. This may be why they remain in business.

Gore-Langton says that initially Cleese wrote Basil and Booth wrote Sybil, but that they would collaborate more and more on the characters over time. He highlights that Sybil gets the least sympathy from viewers because she is the only character in full control of her own life – Polly, Manuel and Terry are employees, Basil is subservient to her, but Sybil sets her own agenda and goals. Cleese backed up this claim in 1995,[44] saying that when they set out he wrote Basil and Manuel, while Booth wrote Sybil and Polly, but that like any partnership, it evolved as he learned more: while she would pull him up initially, highlighting where the dialogue didn't ring true – *"a woman would never say that"* – and transitioning into a full cross-gender collaborative approach. He says that Basil was a joint concoction even if everyone considered it to be simply Cleese in disguise. There were allegations that he had simply added her name to his to boost her career and their fee, but he denies this – she was good at writing characters and coming up with jokes, and he was bad at writing women before their collaboration. In a piece written for the 2024 theatrical programme Cleese repeats these claims and calls himself the 'carpenter' in the collaboration: the one who plans and structures and puts the script together. He would come up with the ideas and Booth was *"good at moulding the characters and making them more believable"*. If Cleese found his text was predictable or stilted, she would pull him up and point out any out of character or unbelievable lines. *"She was ... [a] moderating force."* Cleese was the typist – presumably better at it than Basil turns out to be – and admits that sometimes he *"could pretend to be putting down* [his co-writer's[45]] *suggestion when ... I was putting down mine."* Comedian and writer Steve Punt observes[46] a *"ruthlessness in John Cleese. He is looking for the flaws – which is the trouble with the question of comedy and offence – it's about flaws. People who aren't flawed aren't funny. It's important that* Fawlty Towers *was co-written with a female writer. A co-writer means any temptation to pull back or soften the character doesn't happen. Sybil has to be a balancing monster – viewed against Basil – to be believable"*.

Prunella Scales[47] was recommended to Cleese and Booth by John Howard Davies, who was widely known to be 'good at casting'. Cleese had seen her in *Marriage Lines*, and trusted JHD's opinion. John Cleese has said on many occasions that the role of Sybil Fawlty was originally offered to Bridget Turner, who turned down the part[48]. Michael Palin records[49] that Prunella Scales told him that she was not happy during filming of the first series, as she was very worried about getting the part right, but he calls it *"a touch of theatrical modesty"* as she was clearly very good once she had gained confidence.

Scales remains grateful to the series. In conversation with Gloria Hunniford[50] in 2000, she noted that *"twelve weeks of work have gone on for years"*. She added that it was gratifying to see that it was still popular and stood up to scrutiny after – then – twenty-five years. Hunniford asked her why she thought there had been so few episodes and she explained her theory: that the Cleeses had been very angry about specific elements of hotel management and experiences, that they had written one episode about each element, demonstrating every frustration and exasperation they could think of, and then stopped – all their rage had been dealt with. Although they were under "enormous pressure" to write a third series, she thought it was right to stop at two. She does not believe there is a single weak episode in the twelve.

Cleese is on record as saying that he and Booth were not sure how to characterise Sybil, and after the first rehearsal they were concerned that Prunella was not what they had had in mind but then as she rehearsed, and when they reflected afterwards, they realised that, fortuitously, she was better than they could have imagined or hoped for. Booth praises Prunella's portrayal of a 'bright' and 'complicated' woman. Scales says[51] that she is the kind of actress who requires a degree of 'looking after' – she *needs* to know that the director believes in her in order to play any part. She confirms that the character was based on *"no particular person"* but on an amalgam of memories and mannerisms that the script suggested to her. She believes that the relationship between Sybil and Basil and *"the conditions which led them to marry"*, a phrase which suggests something more complicated than a standard dating-leads-to-marriage relationship, requires as much thought from the viewer as does the situation of Lady Bracknell or other significant theatrical characters. Sam West, Prunella Scales's son and an actor himself, told her biographer[52] that he thought the relationship between Basil and Sybil was about much more than fear: *"She's obviously an attractive woman, she ... keeps him on his toes ... he helps her to aspire... They probably had a very good sex life at the beginning. These are the sort of things which make this relationship work so that it is not just a comedic one. It is true."*

Prunella would revisit Sybil in November 2007 for the BBC's annual charity telethon *Children in Need.*[53] Mrs Fawlty sweeps into *Hotel Babylon* (a glitzy, soapy drama) as the new hotel manager, gives the hotel a makeover, and populates it with staff from 1970s and 80s sitcoms. She also made a series of Tesco adverts 1995-2004, playing lightly, off the Sybil persona to create Dotty Turnbull and her long-suffering daughter, played by Jane Horrocks. Many of these are still available to watch on YouTube.

Prunella's biographer notes that she is perceived primarily as a comic actress – and her three biggest and most memorable TV parts – Kate Starling (*Marriage Lines*), Sarah France (*After Henry*) and Sybil Fawlty – are all comic parts. However, she played Kate and Sarah for *much* longer[54] than she played Sybil, but Sybil is every viewer's first thought when you say 'Prunella Scales', just as Manuel is the response for 'Andrew Sachs'. Her biographer notes that journalist Julie Cockcroft once called her *"the Terror of Torquay, the shrill harridan who made Basil Fawlty's life such a misery"* but clarified that in real life Prunella was quite the opposite, another example of the diametric opposites Apter highlighted. Reviewers too had a hard time separating Scales from Sybil: the *Daily Record* wrote in 1986 that "*Sybil Fawlty appears on the box tonight... NUDE!"* It inevitably proved very hard for the core cast to move past their *Fawlty Towers* characters no matter how much other work they would go on to do, in comedy, drama, or even as themselves. John Cleese is still introduced as 'creator of *Fawlty Towers*' whether he's talking about comedy, cancel culture, or Conservatism.

Scales, who played many dramatic parts before and after *Fawlty Towers*, thinks that comedy and drama are intertwined and cannot be distinguished: *"if you don't get the laughs in* Macbeth [...] *and Beckett, you are failing the author"*. She believes that different countries and styles of comedy expect different things from women – French comedy allows women to be intelligent, attractive, youthful; American comedy allows pretty and dumb or intelligent and ugly, though rarely both. English comedy does not like funny women *"unless you are post-menopausal or so eccentric as not to be a sexual threat"*. *Fawlty Towers* may be to blame for not allowing her to continue into parts that were 'very attractive or very intelligent' women. Her husband, Timothy West, also an actor, also believed that *Fawlty Towers* may have limited people's view of Prunella, leading her to be typecast. Pragmatically, though, she continues to thank *Fawlty Towers* for *"the repeat fees"* which helped the Wests subsidise their live theatre work for years. And she respects Sybil: *"she was an intelligent and funny woman – and rather sexy in all those chic 1960s and 70s clothes. I consider her a heroine."*

Manuel is a Spanish immigrant from Barcelona, who has arrived in the UK to improve his English and earn money. Manuel's birthday is implicitly around the end of September or start of October – it is celebrated in the episode broadcast on 3 October 1975 – and we do not know how old he is. He represents the influx of European labour[55] that followed the entry of the United Kingdom to the EEC (now EU) in January 1973. We do not learn his surname or much about him other than that he left his mother, five brothers, and a sister,[56] to come to the UK – it is implied that he sends money home to them. He looks up to Basil despite some terrible treatment, and allies with Polly. He can play the guitar. Sachs loved that Manuel *"bounces straight back – he's a great survivor"*. He felt that Manuel was happy with his new surrogate family – *"a child with his parents around him"*. He claimed[57] that he invented some of Manuel's back story: *"there wasn't a sort of Stanislavsky feeling... what was his mother like, where did he come from? Not even that he came from Barcelona. I invented that somewhere along the line. Things were invented all the time."*

John Cleese states in multiple sources that at that time in London restaurants *"you were lucky to get what you ordered; the chance of getting what you ordered was 1 in 6"* as employers had discovered that by *"employing people who spoke no known language they could save a lot of money"*. A Torquay waiter[58] who pronounced 'architect' as 'heart attack' was also an influence. It wasn't necessarily a fault of the staff themselves, and Manuel is not intended to be seen as *stupid* – just out of his depth in a job he isn't being trained for and in a second language he is not being supported to learn. David Nobbs addresses the same issue in *The Fall and Rise of Reginald Perrin*[59] and its follow-up novels, written around the same time as *Fawlty Towers,* while TV shows like *Mind Your Language* mocked language learners (with affection, from some perspectives, but offensively from others).

Manuel is the focus for most of the physical comedy in the show, and almost all the violence is aimed at him. John Howard Davies said that he liked *"violence in comedy. When in doubt, hit somebody"*, a strategy that would lead us directly to violent slapstick comedies like *The Young Ones*[60]*, Bottom,* and *Man Down.* Author Andrew O'Hagan examined the relationship in *Sidekick Stories*[61]*: "the sidekick relationship with the main guy is usually one that's completely dysfunctional but based on love. Why doesn't he just fire Manuel? Of course he wouldn't, because something of his absurdity... his whole life, is dependent on this dysfunctional relationship"*. Actor Tony Robinson,[62] famous for playing another physically and verbally abused sidekick, called Manuel *"one of the greatest comic creations"*.

In s3e5 of *Monty Python's Flying Circus, The All-England Summarise Proust Competition,* there is a sketch (*'Travel Agent'*) featuring Michael Palin as a travel agent and Eric Idle as a potential traveller who rants at Palin about the tourism experience of Brits abroad, drinking their Watney's Red Barrel and attending cabaret evenings, as *"adenoidal typists from Birmingham with diarrhoea and flabby white legs try to pick up hairy bandy-legged wop waiters called Manuel"*. This sketch is credited to the entire Python team so it's unclear whether this was just their preferred name for Spanish waiters or if Cleese had any input to the name, but it may have been in the back of his mind when naming the character. Being exposed to British tourists in Spain like this, it is a mystery why Manuel might want to move to the United Kingdom, but his assiduous study of language and frugal lifestyle suggest it was both cultural and economic in intent.

Michael Apter explains Manuel's character as an adult who acts like a child, echoing Sachs' assertion that Manuel views the Fawltys as surrogate parents. John Cleese also notes that children identify strongly with Manuel, and the younger play viewers I spoke to in 2024 said the same. He is endearing, and vulnerable. Manuel is treated like a child, he is subject to orders he cannot deny, he has little agency, he cannot leave but must accept his punishments and ill-treatment in order to stay in his home. Children, particularly teenagers, recognise and empathise with his situation. When he walks like a chimp, bent over and holding the Major's hand after being hit on the head, he becomes the hotel pet, not even human any more. He is the target of most of the slapstick theatrical play in the show – hit on the head, carried about like an object, slumped in a hamper,[63] set on fire. When he gets the chance to inflict it on others – pouring cream in Mr Hutchinson's briefcase – there is an exuberant glee in his eyes, a huge grin on his face.

Andrew Sachs, known to many as Andy, was German by birth.[64] He was a character actor who had worked with Cleese and Booth before, including some work for Video Arts.[65] He'd also worked with John Howard Davies, and had spent some years in Brian Rix's repertory company, where he had worked with actors like Joan Sanderson, Derek Royle, and Elspet Gray, all of whom appeared in *Fawlty Towers*. His wife Melody, a dancer and actress, would also appear in *Basil the Rat*. Sachs would sustain several genuine injuries playing the frequently abused Manuel, including chemical burns from the kitchen fire in *The Germans*. The flames were produced by a chemical reaction, not actual fire, but that did not make the burns less painful: the BBC subsequently paid him £700 compensation.[66] He also suffered a severe headache from being hit with a pan in a different scene but remained cheerful when discussing this and the rest of the show in later years. Cleese always praises Sachs's physical abilities – both actors were good at exaggerated movement, and slapstick – and the whole cast was good at the fast verbal exchanges the scripts demanded.

He was playing the lead in *Habeas Corpus* (an Alan Bennett farcical comedy) on stage when Cleese saw him and decided to cast him. Sachs had suggested that Manuel could be a German, using his own childhood accent, as he was worried about portraying the Spanish accent well, but Cleese turned him down. Germans were seen as competent and efficient – *in Ordnung*, as Sachs put it in his autobiography – so how could the ridiculously inept Manuel be German? And how would the plot of *The Germans* have been possible with a German waiter on staff in the hotel? It wouldn't, as German TV executives would conclude when attempting to make their own version.

JHD and Cleese had seen him on stage in *No Sex Please – We're British*[67] – *"remarkable... wonderful, and so acrobatic"*, and Cleese praises his physical comedy in interviews and commentaries. Sachs himself was 'quiet and thoughtful' but *"put on the moustache and he goes 'ding!'"* and explodes with energy. Sachs suggested Manuel's moustache as a disguise so he would not be noticed in public. He described sitting on the tube opposite a girl discussing an episode with her friend, looking directly at him but not recognising him and Cleese confirmed[68] *"If you meet Andrew you would call him almost retiring, very quiet, almost academic, studiously polite. Then suddenly he clips on his moustache and something else in his personality just slips in."* Sachs remained relatively unknown in the 1970s and 80s while Manuel was known worldwide, to Sachs's relief. He was often asked to appear as Manuel at a wide range of places including business conferences, where he would disrupt procedures and perform skits with CEOs, and he appeared in a number of adverts.

Shortly before his death in 2016 he would become inadvertently embroiled in a tabloid scandal involving his granddaughter Georgina, Russell Brand, and Jonathan Ross, and even then the media referred to him in almost every story as Manuel, '*Fawlty Towers* star'.

Many 'insiders' have thought they recognised Manuel as a version of Terry Jones, as Cleese and Jones fought regularly during the Python years, but Cleese denies it. Manuel is a product of Cleese's fascination with miscommunication – which he might have had with Jones, but does not acknowledge openly.

Polly Sherman is the maid, waitress, interpreter and voice of sanity in the hotel. She acts as go-between for Basil and the unfortunate guests who get on his wrong side, Basil and Sybil, Basil and Manuel, Manuel and various chefs. No one demonstrates significant conflict towards her. She is an art student[69], and can be seen sketching at various points. She speaks German and Spanish.

If she had been written to use Booth's natural accent she would have stood out from the rest of the cast as another foreigner, but an Anglophone one – neither one thing nor the other as far as 1970s xenophobia went – but playing her as an English character allows her to blend into the background at the start of the show. This was something that both writers wanted, as Booth was not a confident actress initially. *"I'm not a comedienne"*.

Maurice Gran:[70] *"At the time I found the character of Polly a bit too straight and I don't know if that was his co-writer's input – if they had the idea that you need one character who was not mad? She could deliver a comic line but I remember thinking at the time she could be a bit funnier, she hasn't got a comic trope, she hasn't got a Thing. If they just said she was absolutely fine except she was claustrophobic, then you could keep locking her in wardrobes. I think they missed a comic beat. I think* [Cleese] *would accept that he's a megalomaniac, so he wasn't that bothered that Polly didn't get the funny lines. It's better on re-watching."*

If Polly has a significant character flaw, it's her passivity: like Fanny Price in *Mansfield Park*, she observes and tacitly condones much more bad behaviour than she calls out, and she colludes with Basil or fails to override him and intervene in a timely manner, when speaking up more confidently might have avoided the impending chaos. But where are the laughs in that? Her interactions with Basil hint at a deeper relationship than that of boss-employee. Comic novelist Jasper Fforde[71] suggests that they may have had a fling, as Polly guesses *"small"* when Basil gestures to his fly – a flippant joke made by a friendly ex-wife in reality, but an extremely odd thing to say to one's boss in a hotel otherwise; Polly is being very bold here.

Polly is not any of the things the other characters demonstrate as their main traits. She is not fussy, vain, snobbish, angry, foreign, or particularly complicated – she is the Marilyn Munster of the ersatz hotel family. She isn't without fault – passivity, sometimes should speak up when she doesn't (or when Basil misunderstands her attempts e.g. *Gourmet Night*), but generally she's the Only Sane Woman. No one is set up to be in opposition to Polly. She exchanges flippant remarks with guests, some of whom she clearly dislikes, but there is no significant conflict or aggression that lasts longer than a couple of sentences. Her behaviour towards the dog in *The Kipper and the Corpse* appears surprisingly aggressive and out of character, as a result, even though it *is* a very annoying dog.

Connie Booth,[72] married[73] to John Cleese for seven years by the time series one started, was a minor actress, mother to a small child, and writer on the show between 1975-9. Since 1979 she has done little acting, and she retrained as a psychotherapist in the 1980s. She began a relationship with writer John Lahr in 1988, married him in 2000, and they live quietly in North London today. She did attend a May 2024 performance of *Fawlty Towers – The Play*, but has given very few interviews since 1980 – the interview she agreed to film in 2009 for *Fawlty Towers Re-Opened* made headlines.[74] She had previously complained – unsuccessfully – to the Press Complaints Commission that unrelated stories about her therapy work would inevitably focus on *Fawlty Towers*. In 1975 she would have been most recognisable to *Fawlty Towers* viewers as the Lumberjack's disappointed girl in the Lumberjack song (*Monty Python's Flying Circus,* s1e9), and as the witch in *Monty Python and the Holy Grail* (1974).

Booth was not a confident actress, later saying that her performance was initially quite stilted as she was not comfortable. Cleese acknowledges that she had no sitcom experience and was uncomfortable with a studio audience, which differs significantly from a theatre audience and the film work she had done previously. He says that they agreed to avoid giving her a major part, not wanting her to have to carry the show as the pressure would be too much. As a result, Booth feels that Polly was the least well-defined of the characters in the main cast, but she still plays a valuable part as a go-between, and the Fawltys are her surrogate parents – just as they are for Manuel. Booth felt that Polly kept the peace between them. Terry Jones agreed:[75] *"Polly is the voice of sanity, the still calm around which the madness happens. And yet she does try to get Basil out of holes. She's got a very good heart."* Scales felt that Polly was a straight guy, not a comic character.

Other regulars: The chefs seen in the show are generic chef characters, comic but broadly unremarkable. The Ladies – Miss Tibbs and Miss Gatsby – are representative of a generation of spinsters (or young widows). These women, whose fertile years spanned 1914-1945, are effectively victims of the two world wars and the associated reduction in British male population, women who were single at the end of their working lives with no close family to support them and no realistic expectation of living comfortably alone until death. Hotel living was a preferred option to nursing homes – the modern assisted living facilities did not yet exist – as you had your food prepared, bed made, and no financial commitments beyond a likely-reduced hotel bill paid from your pension and savings.

The Major is a caricature of retired military men – many likely to be in the same position as the Ladies, in need of a secure home with few external commitments. As his dementia worsens, living in a hotel seems more and more reasonable, as he is not – usually – having an impact on the running of the place. (The stage play's final scene may change that in some ways.) The character was inspired by John Cleese's Latin teacher at prep school,[76] a Captain Lancaster. Roald Dahl also attended the same school, some years before Cleese was born, and used the same man as the basis for Captain Lancaster (no effort there!) in *Danny, Champion of the World* and Captain Hardcastle in *Boy*. Dahl described him harshly: *"Behind the moustache there lived an inflamed and savage face with a deeply corrugated brow that indicated a very limited intelligence.* [He appeared to think that the world was dangerous and] *'...all men are enemies and small boys are insects that will turn and bite you if you don't get them first and squash them hard.'"*

Lancaster reputedly called Cleese *"six foot of chewed string"* but seemed to have mellowed from his angry, shell-shocked 1920s persona by the time Cleese met him in the late 1940s. Cleese thought fondly of him[77] when he became a teacher at the same school aged 18:[78] a boy asked him an English grammar question which Cleese found he could answer based solely on his Latin education. *"My God," I thought as he walked away, "Captain Lancaster did a good job."* In any event, while the Major may have been inspired by a rather angry and frustrated man, the character is rather mild-mannered, and with the exception of one significant flaw, rather lovable. His military service is not detailed in the show but it has been confirmed by knowledgeable viewers that he wears the Royal Artillery Gunner's tie[79] in *Basil the Rat*. The tie pattern features lightning bolts and represents Saint Barbara, the patron saint of artillerymen – quite appropriate for a scene with a shotgun! He also wears an 8th Army tie, which suggests that he was at Normandy in 1944, potentially landing at Arromanches.[80] A clip of Major Gowen celebrating a county cricket win would be used in the 2020s by Hampshire Cricket Club[81] to celebrate new victories, with the hashtag *#eveningmajor*.

There is one more staff member in the hotel, who has no room and no name – the cat, seen in s2e6 *Basil the Rat*. We know very little about this cat: he is black, has been around for a while (Sybil notes that he always has fur-balls in the summer), is reasonably friendly – he allows Polly to pick him up – and he probably *didn't* eat the poisoned veal. (We never *do* discover where that went… but nobody died after eating it – or not on camera, anyway.) The cat does not seem to have been employed primarily as a mouser – there are mousetraps in the kitchen, and they keep rat poison on hand – and it does not find Manuel's "hamster" at any point, although we don't know if the cat and the rat occupy the same spaces very often, of course. While it is implied in that episode that the cat has been there for a long time, for filming purposes he was simply a one-off addition for plot purposes, along with Manuel's rat.

Other more fleeting characters were inspired by specific people, but they will be identified in each episode chapter.

THE HOTEL

Fawlty Towers, the establishment, is a small hotel in a small seaside town – view of the sea possible, between the land and the sky. It is located at 16 Elwood Avenue,[82] Torquay, Devon,[83] and has 26 rooms, twelve with their own bathroom,[84] but no suites.[85] It has spacious leafy grounds and a car park. It offers full meal service[86] in the dining room, room service, and has its own bar/lounge (evening drinks served from 6pm, including Watneys Red Barrel[87] on tap), although it does not seem to have a TV lounge, or TVs in rooms for guests.[88] It may or may not have a *functioning* table tennis table.[89] It is clearly not a failing business, and there are many clues to its continued success, despite the handicap of being co-run by Basil Fawlty. It has at least three regular paid staff[90] as well as the Fawltys, and three long-term residents, as well as a host of international guests. At the start of the show they own a red Austin Mini Countryman; by season two they have a red Austin Maxi; there's also a yellow Ford Cortina which Sybil is seen driving, though this may be Audrey's car. The Fawltys have been married for eleven years[91] – or since 1485,[92] if you ask Sybil – and have run the hotel for twelve[93] years when we first meet them. This means that Basil and Sybil married in 1964 but opened the hotel in 1963 according to their own account – perhaps it was a trial run before marrying, to see how well they got on, or Basil opening the hotel and Sybil backdating her involvement after they married. Terry the chef started in 1978, six months before the events of *Waldorf Salad,* and Manuel arrived at some time between 1973 and 1975. Basil calls it an interesting fifteen years in series two[94] but we can assume there's been some rounding of dates along the way.

While it is not an entirely happy marriage, there are also some clues to the longevity of the relationship on display. In their own way, they both care deeply about the hotel and their guests. Sybil pragmatically wants their existing guests to enjoy their stay, however awkward she and Basil may contrive to make it, but Basil yearns to be more upmarket, appealing to a higher echelon of customer. Both are committed, driven personality types.

The hotel clearly owes a lot to the Gleneagles hotel, as described previously. It also alludes to other stories Cleese and Booth heard during writing. Michael Gwynn, who would play Lord Melbury in *A Touch of Class*, told Cleese about a hotel he had stayed in where a multitude of signs placed around the hotel led to no need for staff at all. Guests should clearly just obey orders at all times, and adherence to that rule would minimise the need for any staff to interact with them. We can see how this idea might appeal to a snob like Basil, for whom most guests are 'simply not good enough' and not worthy to receive more than his fleeting attention. Andrew Leeman, a long-term friend of Cleese and Booth and a Savoy hotel employee, also provided tips and inspiration for the hotel Fawlty Towers, including detailed descriptions of how hotels deal with corpses. In gratitude they would name one[95] after him.

It is a moderately sized seaside hotel of its type. The 'glass' in the hotel windows is obviously not real, pictures on the wall are often askew, and many of the walls wobble – something Cleese does not always ignore. Room 5 is a double (twin beds) with its own bathroom while room 6 is a double (twin) without a bathroom. Room 7 is a single with its own bathroom. Rooms 5-7 are on the same floor as Basil and Sybil's own bedroom. Room 8 is a single which seems to have its own bathroom. There is a hall cupboard on the landing opposite room 6. These rooms are all on the first floor of the hotel but the landing is almost identical to the floor above, where we find rooms 10, 12 and 14 which are all doubles – room 12 apparently overlooks the lawn. Room 16 is "*upstairs, on right*" but is not suitable for gnomes.[96] Rooms 17 and 18 are singles sharing a bathroom in season 1 but by season 2 room 18 has become a double (twin) with a dubiously located bathroom (it may be partially over the stairwell), and it is now on the same floor as room 8.[97] Room 22 is a single with its own bathroom and alleged sea view (the real Gleneagles hotel did not have a sea view either). There is an inexplicable room 58, seen opposite Basil and Sybil's room in series 1. We never learn the room numbers for the Ladies or the Major.

Basil and Sybil's room changes locations between series 1 and 2, and must be located in a section that extends out from the main building: the bedroom door is perpendicular to a window in the hallway, but there is a double wardrobe and other furniture on the other side of the door, in a surprisingly spacious room. Room 9, which is on the same floor as their room in series 2, must have an extremely shallow footprint by contrast, as the passageway directly opposite the Fawltys' bedroom door is a very short distance from room 9's door. This also confirms the room change, as the door to room 58 would be in the side wall of room 9 otherwise.

When we see Miss Tibbs in bed[98] we cannot tell if this is a twin room or a spacious single, but a little later the Ladies offer to take Manuel's hamster[99] to their room, singular. They keep their own stock of toilet paper in their room, and various personal belongings such as an old-fashioned photograph of a man (probably Miss Tibbs' father, rather than a lost loved one, as the man in the picture is older than we'd expect for a boyfriend and the style is older than we'd expect for a brother or other contemporary) and a lilac continental[100] quilt, which is not hotel-standard bedding. We never see the Major's bedroom, although we do learn he has been concealing a shotgun there, to Basil's surprise. We can only assume that Basil has rarely been in the Major's room and Polly has never remarked upon it or even seen it, when cleaning. Manuel lives in an attic bedroom, with a number of personal belongings including a guitar and a 'hamster' cage. Polly is seen once in a small single[101] but it's impossible to tell if she lives there permanently, occasionally, or simply has use of a vacant room from time to time. She and Manuel often leave the hotel in the evenings, and in *The Germans* she says she is not there apart from at mealtimes, but she does not appear to have anywhere else to go. Terry doesn't live in the hotel as far as we can tell.

The interior of the hotel has been mapped occasionally – it's a popular fan activity for most TV shows, and you can even buy Lego[102] sets for some – and if it were not for the quirky stair arrangement we could more easily assume that the room layout actually runs around the entire hotel and that some of the rooms are simply on the other side of the hotel. The up-and-down steps on the upstairs landings were a feature observed in real hotels and put into the set by the designer.[103] They serve as a waiting point for characters appearing in scenes, and offer some opportunities for physical comedy, so getting rid of them would not work. As it is, we only see one wing of the hotel upstairs and the topography simply doesn't work; we can only conclude that either hotel room numbers were reallocated at times, or the hotel is a non-Euclidean construct with TARDIS-like features.

The set was built in the BBC studio, with walls significantly higher than usual to avoid awkward angles caused by John Cleese's height. When he is standing on a dining chair and reaching up as the moose head is put up, in s1e6 *The Germans*, we can see that the top of the walls must be at least 4m high – Basil, who is 6ft5 or just under 2m, cannot reach the top even when standing on a chair. John Howard Davies says that boom shadows and other filming artifacts can be seen in some shots as sometimes it was inevitable because of the unusual constraints of filming. Bob Spiers notes that because of Cleese's height, seated cast members are very low in the shot when Basil is also present, as the camera cannot cut off the top of his head to include them. He adds that the show demanded more of its camera crew than many sitcoms. Shooting around the hotel reception desk was occasionally tricky and so sometimes there would be shaky shots. Hotel bedrooms were very small and so difficult to film in, and the audience would be shown the resulting film on monitors. A pillar that briefly appears on the upstairs landing disappears after s2e1, as it proved difficult to move and film around. Spiers notes in the audio commentary for *The Psychiatrist* that the BBC rehearsal rooms[104] in North Acton occupied a unique space in broadcast television at the time, as a dedicated external space. Other broadcasters had rehearsal spaces in the same location as recording studios, but when BBC Television Centre was built there was no space allocated to rehearse. The benefit of a dedicated space was that the sets could be marked out (with trestle tables for furniture and poles to mark the doors) and left up through the rehearsal period so that actors and crew had a good sense of how the physical elements of filming would go, rather than rehearsing in 'church halls' with no spatial context and no ability to leave things in place for long. *Fawlty Towers*, which relied so much on the farcical properties of doors and physical movement, would not have been the same without it. The facility was closed by the BBC in 2008 and demolished in 2010.

The sets would be assembled in Television Centre for a single day, then removed at the end of filming and transported back to storage. When they were ready to film, the sets would be built for 10am, rehearsed with the cameras in place, then filmed and struck by 6pm if possible. Spiers emphasizes the importance of doors in farce – characters must be able to come in and out of them frequently and on cue – but rehearsal spaces don't have doors, just the poles marking them out, so the camera crew hadn't always seen the space beforehand to get the angles right. Even those who had worked on previous episodes were not at any advantage: as the sets were struck and rebuilt for each recording, any minor discrepancy in the rebuild could make a big difference to a camera angle. There was an awful lot of work going into making sure they could see e.g. the full length of Cleese silhouetted against the door, or Polly over Sybil's shoulder through the dining room door.

The exterior of the hotel was portrayed by the Wooburn Grange Country Club, in Bourne End, Buckinghamshire, and its own arched sign, above the driveway entrance, can be spotted in a number of episodes. This building was badly damaged in a 1991 fire, and eventually a small housing estate was built on the site, despite planning permission for a 39 bedroom hotel.[105] So, like the original Gleneagles hotel which was demolished in November 2015, it can no longer be visited. The Gleneagles was replaced with a block of retirement apartments that have been named Sachs Lodge[106] in memory of Andrew Sachs, who died in 2016 while they were still being constructed. Spiers notes that there was more external filming in series 1 than in 'his' series, series 2 – they had establishing shots of the hotel already and did not need many more.

The show itself was unusual in TV production terms. Prunella Scales described the regime – *"we had a week to work on each episode… I tried to work at home… but with two sons it was distracting. I once moved into a quiet hotel for a few days"*. She would wake up every few hours to learn the lines – the show was structured over a week so that they would get the lengthy[107] script at the weekend, learn the lines completely by Wednesday, reading and blocking Tuesday and Wednesday to get the movements right. Then a day off, and more rehearsing, with a technical rehearsal in the BBC rehearsal rooms on Friday or Saturday, recording in Television Centre on Sunday. The technical rehearsal would throw up issues that would need to be resolved by Sunday morning for what Andrew Sachs described[108] as *"a slow stagger through with cameras"*. The outside shots – car park, grounds, hotel views – had been filmed during the week, or earlier, and were ready for the audience to watch by the dress rehearsal on Sunday afternoon, before the filmed performance on Sunday evening[109]. The cast and crew would then travel home late on Sunday night and begin again at 10am on Tuesday morning. The disruption to BBC technical support that occurred for a week in March 1979 broke this routine, as there was no way to do the technical rehearsal, move the sets, or complete the filming. The cast were almost ready to film *The Anniversary* when the industrial action started on a Thursday, but on the following Tuesday when rehearsals should have begun for *Basil the Rat*, the cast had to reprise *The Anniversary* with a new Roger.

In following this schedule, it mimicked 'rep': repertory theatre, where a static company rotates through multiple shows, rather than the more modern version where a theatre hosts multiple companies and individual performers over the course of a year. Modern TV comedy offers more rehearsal time and is more likely to shoot out of order, on location, than in front of a live audience as if it were a play. Scales and Sachs had previously worked in rep, but John Cleese and Connie Booth had not. Scales wrote[110] *"in rep it was a discipline – forget the truth or the subtext, get the lines learnt by Wednesday, and worry about the rest of it later if you have the time"*. Although she also liked to learn about each character – *"building the inner life"* – she acknowledges the pragmatic approach has advantages. In *Fawlty Towers* actors had the luxury of both approaches – as each episode was much shorter than the average play, there was time to learn the lines and also to ruminate on the deeper meaning of the plot, and the regular cast had time to work on the characterisation over the course of each series. The cast of the *Fawlty Towers* play have had a mixture of both as well – a longer rehearsal time to match a longer on-stage time – and the advantage of testimony from those who came before them in the roles (in the case of Basil, oversight as well). Scales addresses this as well: *"another actor's work can... open doors and stimulate"* one's own characterisation.

Half hour sitcoms are usually like the final two-thirds of a three-act play, because the audience already knows the set-up, the characters and their relationships. This makes it both easier to have running jokes and harder to set up new ones. The characterisation in the show has to be strong and consistent, to carry some jokes from episode to episode. You cannot rely on guest stars. John Cleese has said in a number of interviews that eighty people appeared in *Fawlty Towers* over the twelve episodes. The Internet Movie Database (IMDB) lists 135 actors, although this does include 46 unnamed extras and named characters with uncredited actors, like Lady Morris and Richard Turner. It seems likely that he means eighty people have lines – and most of them were memorable. Only eight characters[111] appeared in more than one episode.

First Broadcast 19 September 1975[1] – A Touch of Class

The sign says: FAWLTY TOWERS, with all letters present and correct, although the S is sideways. This sign is not the same shape as subsequent episodes.

In this episode we meet:
Mr & Mrs Mackenzie (David Simeon,[2] and the uncredited Claire Russell), who have been staying in room 12. They have failed to get their booked alarm call.[3]
The unnamed paperboy (Gary Rich[4]), with one line: *"Newspapers!"*
Mr & Mrs Watson (Lionel Wheeler,[5] Julie Mellon) who will not get any help from Basil.
Mr & Mrs Wareing plus their teenage child (Terence Conoley,[6] Annet Peters,[7] Oscar Peck). This unfortunate family have grapefruit thrown at them, are made to move tables mid-meal, and repeatedly fail to successfully place their drinks order.
Mr Danny Brown (Robin Ellis[8]), apparently a 'wide boy' but later to be revealed as CID, staying in room 7. He annoys Basil from the start by not being deferential enough.
Lord Melbury (Michael Gwynn[9]), who will be staying in room 21. He is the recipient of both kinds of Basil behaviour – ignored and dismissed until Basil hears his title, whereupon he becomes fawning and sycophantic.
Sir Richard and Lady Morris (Martin Wyldeck[10] and the uncredited Pat Symons), who have seen the advertisement in *Country Life*. They will *not* be staying once they realise what kind of hotelier Basil really is.
A number of unnamed police officers.[11]

Not seen: O'Reilly, a local builder, is referred to on the phone but we do not see or hear him until the following episode. We also hear about the fictional Duke of Buckley (made up by Lord Melbury) and Mr Tone (made up by Basil in a vain attempt to avoid renting a room to Mr Brown). An unnamed couple in room 6, whom Basil believes are common, vulgar, horrible, nasty and have *'never sat on chairs before'*. Basil D'Oliveira.[12]

First Broadcast 19 September 1975 – A Touch of Class

Physical comedy: Basil knocks a tray out of Polly's hand, knocks Lord Melbury to the floor, knocks Manuel to the floor, and smashes a painting. Manuel throws a grapefruit.

Sets: hotel lobby, office, dining room, and bar. There are postcards for sale in the lobby.

On the menu: gralefrit, balm carousel, creme pot rouge (grapefruit, lamb casserole, tomato soup – this is meant to be *creme Portuguese*, a tomato-based mixed-vegetable soup).

Not on offer: a gin and orange, a lemon squash, and a Scotch and water *please*!

The episode, and the series, opens with Basil on the phone, asking a guest to confirm a booking by letter. Sybil enters, explaining to Basil that the couple at the front desk need their bill urgently as they have not received their alarm call and need to leave, and then immediately tells him to put up the painting. He diverts from both tasks to tell Manuel off about putting too much butter on the trays, establishing their relationship, Basil's penny-pinching side, and Manuel's language issues as a non-native speaker. Basil asserts that he speaks Spanish, but he struggles for words (e.g. he uses the *Italian* word for butter, *burro*, which means donkey in Spanish. He should have used *mantequilla,* the Spanish word) and Manuel simply does not understand him. *Why was he hired?* We might well ask. The answer is illustrated for us: he's keen to learn, and more crucially for Basil, he's also cheap. Basil learned Classical Spanish, and blames the failure to communicate on not recognising the dialect Manuel speaks, which he implies is not an intelligible one. We are told that Manuel is from Barcelona, where 98% of speakers speak Castilian (classic) Spanish (and 50% also speak Catalan). If the viewer knows this, they are already picking up some clues about Basil.

We meet the Ladies, Miss Gatsby and Miss Tibbs, although we do not yet know their status as long-term residents of the hotel. Sybil asks Basil about the picture again, but he is doing the menu, which he complains is a lengthy task that Sybil doesn't understand. It would obviously be much quicker if he were not interrupted all the time, but neither of them seems capable of articulating this and communicating well with each other. The Mackenzies ask for their bill again, but Sybil then immediately asks Basil about the menu, somewhat inexplicably. The audience are starting to understand the couple's relationship and why they are so exasperated with each other. Basil admits he forgot the couple's alarm call; Sybil agrees that she will take payment from the guests before she goes out. We can see how the power dynamics work in their personal and professional relationship, and why tasks around the hotel get delayed and are ultimately done badly through interruption and frustration, not just incompetence. Sybil would get more out of Basil if she asked him for less – or interfered less often – somewhat paradoxically.

The morning newspapers[13] arrive and we meet the Major, and learn about his reliance on Fawlty and his daily newspaper. We don't yet know much about the hotel itself but we're learning about the characters quite rapidly. Basil is sneering, Sybil is domineering, Manuel is Foreign [and this is clearly shorthand for a personality in 1970s sitcom Britain], and guests are a necessary evil – they are the perpetual thorns in the Fawltys' sides.

The Major and Basil want to talk cricket[14] but more guests arrive, interrupting Basil. We meet Polly very briefly. Basil goes to have morning coffee and toast in his office, adjacent to the hotel's main desk, but is rapidly interrupted by Sybil who has returned from outside – she has seen the advert[15] that Basil placed in Country Life[16] and she is not pleased.

The advertising staff at *Country Life* watch *Fawlty Towers* and love the reference in this episode. They told me:[17]

> "Unfortunately, our records don't go as far back as 1975 to allow us to see exactly what £40 would have bought Basil back then in terms of classified versus display. However, we can certainly help you with what an advert would cost him today."

The 2024 rates to advertise with Country Life vary from a quarter page classified ad at £964+VAT to £3,985+VAT for a full page. We can surmise that had Basil spent the equivalent of six weeks' stay in a Torquay hotel[18] on the ad, he would not have survived to episode two, so the fact that Sybil is merely cross and not homicidal suggests the quarter-page advert is most likely.

Was she reading the magazine while driving, or just sitting in the hotel car park, flicking through it? This is mysterious, even for the enigmatic Sybil. She explains that she does not care about the class of guest as long as their bills are paid – a subtle dig at Basil, as this would be easier if their bills were ready on time. Basil justifies the £40[19] cost of the advert by explaining that Sir Richard Morris and wife are arriving tonight, and he insults some unseen guests in room 6 in the process. The not-apparently-classy Danny Brown arrives to check in and, after an initial sneering glance, Basil decides that Brown is going to lower the tone of the hotel. Brown is not at all deferential, or especially polite, and treats Basil as a social equal – he may be justified in this view, but Basil does not *believe* this to be the case. He attempts to refuse Brown a room but, as ever, Sybil intervenes to thwart his plans. The fictional Mr Tone, Basil's heavy-handed hint to Sybil, is *not* occupying Room 7, and so Basil does not manage to avoid checking Mr Brown into it. Mr Brown turns out to speak Spanish fluently enough[20] that a grateful Manuel can understand him. This further irritates Basil who absolutely detests being upstaged, particularly by someone he regards as being of lower status than him. He feels that Brown should respect him – but it is clear he does not.

Manuel takes Mr Brown upstairs to his room, and Basil resumes work in the office, but Sybil interrupts again almost immediately. He rushes to put up the picture as instructed – and so inevitably she reminds him about the menu again, causing him to abandon the picture again. She dismisses his musical choices – he is a fan of classical music and she is decidedly *not*. And he returns to the typewriter.

In the dining room, a little later, Mr Brown attempts to decipher the menu but has to request help from Polly to translate. He takes it in good spirits and opts for the gralefrit. Basil's efforts with the menu obviously did not include proof-reading. As he has been typing daily menus manually for more than a decade he is surprisingly bad at it. It is moderately unusual for a man in the 1970s to be able to type at all, and Fawlty is clearly not a touch-typist, but practice should make perfect or at least, intelligible.

The scene where Polly explains to Mr Brown that she is a student was re-shot some months after original filming, thanks to the decision to change her study subject from philosophy to art, and so Robin Ellis is wearing a wig in this part of the episode – he had changed his hairstyle for his lead role in *Poldark*, which would debut shortly after this episode – and his black top changes from a high roll neck to a lower round neck and back. His grapefruit is visibly different as well!

While Basil is attending to Mr Brown's wine needs, the bell rings at Reception, and Sybil sends Basil. She can't *possibly* go herself – we realise that she is both efficient at delegating and a little *lazy*. Basil – understandably frustrated with trying to do three things at once – snaps dismissively at the guest. He answers the phone to O'Reilly – from Basil's side of the conversation we gather that O'Reilly is the local Irish builder who has let the Fawltys down on a job around the hotel – and once again ignores the waiting guest. This dismissive behaviour continues until the guest reveals himself to be a Lord. Basil hangs up abruptly, and fawns heavily over Melbury. The audience applauds and laughs loudly – the first really big reaction from them. It's notable that Robin Ellis for one was not used to a TV studio audience,[21] and in other episodes we can see that other cast members aren't entirely comfortable with audience laughter either. It takes them a few episodes to get fully into their stride with responsive audiences, and not all are as responsive as the cast and crew would like.

A nervous fake laugh, dropping into bad French, and a fawning manner – these and some visual tics reveal Basil's absolute desperation to impress Lord Melbury.

Manuel does not appear immediately when summoned, irritating Basil again. He simply wants everything to be perfect for his classy guest but finds himself babbling about wheat instead. Even his own brain lets him down under stress. He picks up Melbury's cases himself, and introduces Sybil to Melbury, who then requests that they keep a briefcase safe for him. Manuel fails to understand the instructions for the suitcases so Basil takes them upstairs himself, dismissing Manuel and comparing him unfavourably to a monkey.

Back in the dining room, Basil rearranges the diners so that the most important guest can have the best table – to the detriment of the Wareing family, who are not at all happy about it as they were in the middle of their meal. Basil offers Melbury dinner as the hotel's guest i.e. at the Fawltys' expense, a bold move given that he has not checked this offer with Sybil. Melbury declines but requests the cashing of a cheque[22] – first £50, then £100, before Basil inadvisedly talks him up to £200 – a large sum. We do see Basil's face after the initial £100 request and it's clear he is somewhat daunted by the request – as he should be. It was clearly a foolish move on Basil's part, but he must not lose face, and he so desperately wants to impress Melbury that he cannot back down either.

£200 in 1975 was a little over one month's average salary for a UK worker (if he was male; the gender pay gap was much bigger than it is today, as the 1970 Equal Pay Act would only come into force from 29 December 1975, and women earned nearer £150 a month on average). The equivalent in 2025, by cost of living and inflation calculators, is around £2100, just under a month's average salary. We know that the cost of the magazine advert at £40 was enough to shock and anger Sybil – what is a sum five times that going to do to Basil? We also learn later[23] that the cost of a single room for one night is around £8 including VAT – so Basil is about to lose a month's worth of room income to this one guest. The audience may or may not have realised Melbury's deception by this point, but even those who believe he is genuine will be horrified at the risk Basil is taking. The Fawltys don't have that kind of money on hand in the hotel and so Basil has to send Polly to the bank in the town. Polly goes into town[24], but is waylaid by Mr Brown and his friends who are sitting in a car[25] in the High Street, watching for Melbury. During this scene Michael Gwynn appears from the bank without his moustache – but blink and you've missed him. JHD says that this was intended to be clearer, to indicate his fraudulent activities earlier in the episode.

Basil shows a little physical affection to an ungrateful and dismissive Sybil – *"well, don't"* – and deliberately fails to tell her about the cheque cashing request. He already knows she would not approve. She tells him off for moving the Wareings and apparently attacking Lord Melbury with a chair. Basil praises Melbury's demeanour, fawning over his perceived upper-class nature, and defends the state of his suitcases – "only the rich would have such tatty cases" goes the logic. Melbury isn't *nouveau riche*, the kind of man who buys his own furniture,[26] he's old money. Basil still hasn't put the picture up.

The phone rings and no one but Basil responds – he dissuades Manuel from answering, but then Sybil interrupts. Polly returns, confirming that she has been to the bank for the money, and attempts to speak to Basil about it – but he dismisses her. In the lounge, Basil serves the Major with his usual drink, and Mr Wareing attempts to order drinks. He snipes at Basil about seating arrangements in the lounge, after the family's experience in the dining room. Basil fails to act on this request at all, as Melbury arrives and requests a drink too – which of course he receives, on a silver tray with Basil in fawning attendance at his elbow while he drinks it.

Melbury advises Basil to get his coin collection valued. He claims to be dining that evening with the Duke of Buckley – a Sotheby's[27] expert – and suggests he gets the coins valued at the same time. Mr Wareing is still trying to get his drinks, and Polly is still desperately trying to tell Basil her important news. She disillusions Basil finally: she's been told by Mr Brown, who turns out to be a detective from the local CID,[28] that Melbury is a con man. Naturally Basil wants to believe in the seemingly classy Melbury and not the apparently classless Brown, so attempts to argue with her. Sybil intervenes again and opens Melbury's briefcase, despite Basil's repeated forbidding. The case is full of bricks and not precious items, confirming Brown's story and exposing Melbury's lies. Basil loses his temper. Sybil offers to call the police, and Polly explains that they are already here, in the person of Brown and his colleagues.

Basil dismisses Sir Richard and Lady Morris – the *Country Life* guests – until they identify themselves, and even then he is accidentally rude to them as he is distracted by the reappearance of Lord Melbury. Basil, barely managing to suppress his fury, tears up the cheque and inadvertently lets Melbury know that the game is up. Melbury runs, pursued by the police. Basil yells at him, and joins in the chase, managing to kick Melbury. Sir Richard and Lady Morris are distressed by this behaviour and leave,[29] ruining Basil's hopes for higher class clientele. He yells after them *"you snobs! You stupid stuck-up toffee-nosed half-witted upper-class piles of pus!"*[30] Hypocrite, thy name is Basil.

The police leave, preventing Basil from having a pop at 'Melbury', and Brown apologises to him and offers him a drink, which Basil declines. He starts to put up the painting and everyone is apologetic and sympathetic – until Mr Wareing reappears, still in search of his drinks order. Basil snaps, and smashes the painting. Over the credits we see him manhandle Mr Wareing into the bar, where he gives him bottles of Scotch and gin. The music obscures his words slightly but it is clear he is telling Wareing to serve himself.

This episode has directly and indirectly affected a range of TV comedies such as *The Black Adder,* series 1 of the *Blackadder* franchise, which has no opening, establishing episode. Richard Curtis, co-writer, attributes this[31] to John Howard Davies, who recommended that they do without it because *Fawlty Towers* had similarly omitted it. Both shows open *in media res,*[32] establishing the characters and relationships off-screen and expecting the audience to simply pick up the situation and follow it from the start. *"There'd be no justification for Basil hiring Manuel – he just wouldn't do it – or marrying Sybil. Starting with them all in there, you can be funny from the beginning."*

Cleese says[33] that the outright snobbery shown by Basil Fawlty in this episode is the key to understanding his character. The fear that Melbury will look down on him is his key motivation. In the *Fawlty Towers: Re-opened* documentary, filmed in 2009, he adds that it is not obvious to him why they chose this as the first episode. While it does establish Basil's snobbery well, that was not the overall aim of the series. It is unclear what he thinks would have been a better episode, however – *The Builders* must follow this one, because of the continuation of the O'Reilly storyline, and the layout of the set follows *The Builders* for the rest of the show. Plotwise, many of the s1 episodes build on what we learn about Basil in this one. Cleese often says, in many interviews including a pre-broadcast *Radio Times* article, that there is a lot of his father in the characterisation in this episode, demonstrating Cleese senior's obsession with class and aspiration.

In the *Re-opened* documentary we can see JHD looking at the BBC's written archives, which are held in storage at Caversham, near Reading. He notes that the programme cost £20K in 1975. of which he thinks that John Cleese probably only got about £400. We can estimate the equivalent filming cost of this episode at £210,000 in 2024 – very cheap for a filmed sitcom – and Cleese's payment as £4200. (We do not know whether Booth got the same money or if that payment was shared.) The scenery was wobbly because there simply wasn't enough in the budget to structure it properly. He also looks at a drawing of the original set design, which is instantly recognisable as the lobby we see on screen. The same design, minus a wall or two, will be used for the 2024 stage play – it is not exactly timeless, being very 1970s, but as close as sitcoms set in the real world can get.

Former TV technical staff member[34] and writer John J Hoare writes at length about the pilot script and the differences between that and the finished episode on his Dirty Feed[35] site. There are a number of interesting changes including some to the physical comedy, with stage directions originally instructing Manuel to throw the grapefruit out of the window rather than onto the Wareings' table, for instance. Hoare particularly loves this original stage direction: *"INSTEAD OF MURDERING [Manuel], BASIL TAKES HIM BY THE ARM AND LEADS HIM BACK INTO THE KITCHEN."* We can tell immediately that the relationship between Basil and Manuel includes a *lot* of "instead of murdering him" behaviour. Hoare adds: *"That instantly became one of my favourite* Fawlty Towers *jokes, despite merely being a stage direction. Funny writers don't stop being funny just because they're not writing dialogue"* and he calls for the publication of the original production scripts in addition to the already published transcripts,[36] which have minimal stage directions. He also writes at length about the re-shooting of scenes, including those between Robin Ellis and Connie Booth.

Ronnie Barker did refer to his previous hotel show, *His Lordship Entertains*, as *Fawlty Towers – Mark One,* but did not appear to bear the show any grudges. His sequel to *Porridge, Going Straight,*[37] featuring the permanently disgruntled ex-con Norman Stanley Fletcher, alludes to *Fawlty Towers* in episode 5 – a conman Fletcher knows of puts worthless valuables into the safes of small hotels, including one in Torquay.

First Broadcast
26 September 1975[1] – The Builders

The sign says: FAW L TY TOWER – the S has gone and the L is wonky. The sign is now a new shape and the letters are smaller.

In this episode we meet:
A delivery man (George Lee[2]), with a garden gnome.
Mr O'Reilly (David Kelly[3]), an incompetent Irish builder.
The Orrelly workmen (Lurphy – Michael Cronin,[4] Jones – Michael Halsey, Kerr – Barney Dorman) who are also incompetent.
Mr Stubbs (James Appleby[5]), a more expensive but competent English builder.
There are no guests in the hotel this weekend – deliberately so, to allow for the building work.
We briefly see a friend of Sybil's in the car outside: the actress[6] is not credited and is not the same person who plays Audrey in *The Anniversary* – but it is not unreasonable to assume this is intended to be Audrey's first appearance.

Not seen: Hadrian. The *Emperor* Hadrian. Never mind.[7] Denis Compton.[8]

Physical comedy: Manuel is punched by the "*Hideous Horangutan*", the bearded workman Lurphy. Basil smacks himself on the bottom and forehead when punishing himself for hiring O'Reilly; he folds in on himself in despair; Polly slaps him several times. Basil attempts to strangle the garden gnome. Manuel is smacked into the wall where the dining room door was. Basil fakes leg pain in an attempt to stop Sybil calling Stubbs. Sybil smacks Basil, throws the cash box at him, and kicks him several times before she uses an umbrella to hit Basil and beat up O'Reilly.

Sets: hotel lobby, Polly's bedroom, the office.

On the menu: Beef, veal, or sausages – "bangers" – for breakfast if Manuel can a) pronounce them and b) find the external kitchen door. A cup of tea and a biscuit, offered to O'Reilly. He takes the tea but is denied the biscuit.

First Broadcast 26 September 1975 – The Builders

Not on offer: Saturday evening dinner for the Major and the Ladies, who have been sent elsewhere.

At the start of the episode, a guest leaves and Polly answers the phone and gives the hotel address – 16 Elwood Avenue.[9] Basil and Sybil are preparing to leave for a short holiday, going golfing and presumably staying overnight in a local hotel themselves. Audrey has recently had a hysterectomy, according to Sybil. Breakfast tomorrow will only be served for the Major and the Ladies (Miss Ursula Gatsby and Miss Agatha Tibbs, seen in the previous episode but not credited until this one) so it will be a quiet weekend. The Fawltys trust that Polly and Manuel can cope.

Manuel is practising his English and irritating Basil at the same time. He requests that Manuel cleans the windows. The ladies discuss the break: the builders will be in the hotel for the evening, specifically in the kitchen. The Fawltys will be going to Paignton, a few miles away, while the ladies and the Major will be going to the Hotel Gleneagles for dinner that evening. This is the same name as the hotel that inspired *Fawlty Towers* and it *was* still in existence in 1975, although it's unclear if it was intended to mean the real one or simply a fourth wall jab to antagonise Donald Sinclair further. We don't know exactly how the Major and the Ladies will get there, as long-term residents of the hotel who do not appear to run cars, but it may be within walking distance. Basil finds a picture of himself drawn by Polly but does not recognise it as a portrait: *"it's a junkyard, isn't it? Why's it got a collar and tie under it?"* It's telling that other viewers of the picture recognise it instantly as Basil.

Polly complains of a lack of sleep. O'Reilly phones, and Sybil answers but hands the phone straight to Basil as she has previously asked him to deal with this builder, of whom she disapproves. Basil waits for her to be out of earshot before confirming with O'Reilly that he will be doing the requested work after all. O'Reilly still hasn't finished their garden wall – which we can assume is the unfinished work mentioned in the previous episode – resulting in a large pile of bricks they need to remove from the grounds. "We've been waiting four months." Sybil is very dismissive. Stubbs is *her* preferred builder, and she lets Basil know this in no uncertain terms. Audrey arrives and Sybil leaves. Basil confirms with Polly that the builders will be creating one door and blocking off another, and that it will be O'Reilly's men after all. Polly objects, but Basil will not listen. Polly clearly knows that Sybil will be very unhappy when she finds out – and the rules of farce demand that she *will* find out.

Polly draws Manuel – this may be the sketch she sells to the chef in a later episode. She wants to go for a nap, and somewhat foolishly leaves Manuel in charge. She instructs him to wake her when O'Reilly's men arrive, and he claims to understand her, although he has demonstrated that he does not understand her previous comments very well. Manuel pretends to run the hotel *Manuel Towers* and orders himself around in the guise of Basil. The caller from the start of the episode delivers a garden gnome with a very large nose, but Manuel, not paying attention, attempts to rent him a room rather than simply accepting the delivery. The delivery man tries to make Manuel understand, but eventually gives up and leaves, depositing the gnome in the lobby anyway. Basil rings, but Manuel says *"he not here"* and hangs up. We can infer that Basil has said something like *"it's Mr Fawlty"* and Manuel has failed to understand or to recognise his master's voice.

The *"Orrelly men"* arrive and confirm their identity to Manuel after a moment of confusion. Basil rings again and Manuel hangs up. Manuel tries to wake Polly but she won't wake so he leaves her to sleep. Manuel hangs up on Basil a third time. The builders start work without confirming the details with a very distracted Manuel. Basil rings again and Manuel insults him before realising to his horror that it's Basil. Basil makes Manuel insult one of the builders and the builder punches Manuel. We hear Basil's smug satisfaction with this outcome.

The next morning, Basil arrives home ahead of Sybil and is horrified to see the result of the building work – there is no kitchen door as requested, the drawing room door is still in existence, but there is a new door at the bottom of the stairs and the dining room door has gone, leaving no interior route to the kitchen. He calls Polly downstairs, demanding to know what she has done to the hotel, and he physically and verbally attacks her in his rage. She blames Manuel briefly for not waking her but then takes the blame when she realises Basil will punish Manuel. Polly argues with Basil that it is his fault for hiring O'Reilly, and he sarcastically accepts and spanks himself. Sybil will return at lunchtime, and Basil has a very loud panic attack at the thought. The volume in this scene is very high.

Basil vows to call O'Reilly and sends Polly to check on breakfast, though she pauses to sketch Basil first. O'Reilly is obviously polite enough to Basil on the phone, so they have a reasonable conversation for a moment or two. Manuel appears and Basil pauses the conversation to have a row with Manuel about the missing door. The Major arrives for breakfast, calm and unfazed by the missing door: *"These things happen you know. I wonder where it's got to. Don't worry, it's bound to turn up."* He lives in a world where it is not alarming when pieces of the building disappear – a hint at his dementia. Manuel and the Major go to the dining room via the kitchen's external door, though the Major has to lead Manuel (who is walking like a chimpanzee,[10] thanks to having his head bounced hard off the new wall by Basil) and not the other way around. Basil returns to the phone to argue with O'Reilly about the doors, and eventually instructs him to return.

O'Reilly appears and explains that his men will not work on a Sunday so it's just him. He wants to stop for a cuppa and a biscuit, provided by Polly, but Basil

First Broadcast 26 September 1975 – The Builders

will not let him do so. O'Reilly warns him that he worries too much and will die of a stroke before he's 50. Basil confirms that that would suit him just fine. O'Reilly isn't worried about the building work, dismissing everything as merely in need of a lick of paint and a bit of dismantling. He believes they have plenty of time and is relaxed but Basil is *not*, as Sybil will be back in four hours. O'Reilly's sanguine *"There's always someone worse off than yourself."* is countered with Basil's cynicism and callousness: *"Is there? I'd like to meet him. I could do with a good laugh."*

Sybil returns early with a friend[11] – from context this *should* be Audrey. They have not yet started playing golf for some reason and Sybil is fetching more clubs. Basil first attempts to distract her then embraces the problem and blames the door error on Stubbs. Sybil is cynical and asks where O'Reilly is. Basil asks why she thinks he has anything to do with it – but his van is parked outside, a clear giveaway. Basil passes that off as inviting O'Reilly over to fix Stubbs's mess, but Sybil points out that Stubbs should be the one to fix it, and for free. She wants to call Stubbs at home, but Basil claims to have done that already, creating a convoluted timeline crammed full of lies – his usual method of 'fixing' an issue.[12] The phone rings and Basil claims it's Stubbs. Sybil speaks to him but hands the phone to Basil and goes through to the office where it becomes obvious that it's Polly on the phone instead. Sybil loses her temper and shouts, daring Basil to lie to her again. She knows it was O'Reilly and should have stopped Basil from doing it, after they have used him three times in the last year. He stopped their running water for three weeks by changing a washer, the garden wall hasn't been finished, etc. She shouts about how dreadful O'Reilly is and then he appears, just after she's called him a thick Irish joke. She will not be mollified by his calm manner and reassuring words. His deeds speak against him. She assaults him, physically and verbally, and throws him out of the hotel.

Sybil calls Stubbs, who will come round the next day to fix the problem. Sybil goes to Audrey's for the night, but not before instructing Basil to move the garden gnome … then she changes her mind and leaves the gnome in charge: *"I'm sure he's cheap and he's probably better at it than you are."* O'Reilly moves to leave but Basil stops him: he is going to fix all the doors, since they now have the whole of Sunday to complete the work without further interruption.

Sybil returns the next morning, when Reception has been restored to its apparent former state – under Basil's instructions, the second lounge/bar door has gone as well as the stairs door, and the dining room and kitchen doors are now in the right place. The Major is very pleased to see the dining room door has been found. Sybil is not. Stubbs arrives, and Sybil has to apologise for calling him out unnecessarily – until Stubbs points out that the work is sub-par. There has been no RSJ[13] put in, for the lintel, and on a supporting wall this spells impending doom.

Stubbs alerts Sybil to the danger and goes to get his workmen. Basil has taken the garden gnome and is going to see Mr O'Reilly… the threat is implied but the audience is quite sure about where the gnome will be put.

⁂

BBC shows recorded at this time all had live studio audiences so there is no canned laughter, it is all recorded at the time of filming. For filmed sequences, however, there were monitors for the audience to watch, and John Howard Davies explains in the audio commentary for the episode that there might be unexpected silence after a joke because the audience was now looking in the wrong place i.e. they were looking at the monitor and not back at the stage in the studio. This meant that they might move a laugh (using recorded audio) from one bit of the soundtrack to another, for maximum effect.

In TV, actors don't have to wait for the audience to quieten down after a laugh the same way a theatre cast does. The acoustics in the television studio – smaller than most theatres – make it easier to hear lines, and the soundtrack is recorded on boom mics so the pace of the action can continue despite a big laugh. There is no need to wait or to slow down the show until a laugh dies down. The cast could ignore the audience, therefore, in order to play the show fast and simply *trust* that it could be understood.

Unfortunately, this meant complete silence in much of the recording on this occasion. Cleese claims frequently that 70 members of this particular studio audience were Icelandic visitors and had not really understood anything they had heard or seen. It must have been particularly baffling for them as the show had not yet aired, so they had absolutely no context for anything they saw. David Kelly, in a 2007 interview,[14] claims the same thing, and added that there was also a party of Young Conservative farmers from Wiltshire who were not *"a barrel of fun"* either. John Howard Davies calls the Iceland story apocryphal in the DVD commentary, but it's still clear that this episode created a different pattern of laughter to other shows, and the episode needed more editing than usual as a result. It is often ranked least favourite of the episodes in polls and this may be why. Human nature means we laugh more when other people laugh, and the lack of audience response does affect how we see the show as well as how the cast performed it. John J Hoare found a quote from the *Sunday Sun* that may explain the issue more accurately: *"The tension can affect everybody: one actor, says John, suddenly changed his performance at the filming stage. "I was tired and started fluffing… and, oh, the whole show was less good than it should have been."*[15] Although Cleese is specifically referring to a different actor and a different episode here (and it's unclear exactly who he means, as he never clarified), the quote could also apply to Cleese himself in this episode. The episode isn't unfunny, but it lacks a certain something – the *zing!* is missing.

John Cleese has said in interviews that the builder, Stubbs, was named after Imogen Stubbs's father, and this claim has been repeated in a number of books and in the audio release introduction. However, as he also says that the Mr Stubbs in question was a builder who advised them on various terms in this episode (such as the RSJ), it seems unlikely to have been the father of the then 14-year-old Imogen Stubbs, who was a naval officer. Moreover, Cleese says he was introduced to him through Nicky Henson, who was recently divorced from *Una* Stubbs. It seems much more likely that it was Una Stubbs's father, who had worked in factories and was a practical man, who had provided the advice and got the namecheck as a result.

Cleese is not fond of the episode – *"there would be better ones... it was the least good of the twelve shows"* – and blames the unresponsive audience for the poor reaction. It is also the episode with the most surprising outburst of anger – Sybil, not Basil, losing her temper with O'Reilly and abusing him with xenophobic language, adding to the abusive language used earlier in the episode (e.g. the delivery man calls Manuel a dago twit; dago is one of the racist words used on more than one occasion in the script). She also hits him with an umbrella, and the production team padded it to avoid hurting David Kelly in real life, ironically making it *"twice the weight so [I] really felt it. He likes a woman with spirit, and by God, Sybil had spirit!"*[16] He told Robert Sellers in 2007 that a builder named O'Reilly in Wales had tried to sue the BBC, thinking they were targeting him with this episode. It did not get anywhere. He also said *"I knew it was pure gold, and I was a great fan of John Cleese... we got on like a dream. I've had something like seventy-eight repeats of that episode. It made me very big in Malawi."*

First Broadcast 3 October 1975[1] – The Wedding Party

The sign says: FAW TY TO W ERS – the L has gone, the W is wonky – but the S has reappeared.

In this episode we meet:
Mrs Peignoir (Yvonne Gilan[2]), the incongruously surnamed French antique dealer. She is strangely interested in Basil.
Richard Turner (Mark Allington[3]), a romantic interest for Polly.
Alan Bruce (Trevor Adams[4]), who will be staying in room 12 with Jean Wilson (April Walker[5]), despite Basil's clear disapproval. Jean is a dressmaker and old school friend of Polly's.
Mr Philip Lloyd (Conrad Phillips[6]) and Mrs Rachel Lloyd (Diana King[7]), who will be staying in room 14. Rachel is Jean's mother, Philip her stepfather.

Not seen: Mrs Lloyd telephones an Ann, of whom we know nothing more.

Physical comedy: Manuel attacks Basil when drunk; Basil tries to strangle him. Manuel collapses while hungover; Basil falls when lifting him, then performs a fireman's lift. Basil feigns injury to distract Mrs Lloyd. Manuel hides in a laundry hamper in the kitchen. Basil and Mr Lloyd grapple in a doorway. Manuel is hit on the head by a non-padded pan.[8]

Sets: hotel lobby, bar, kitchen, office, upstairs landing, Basil and Sybil's bedroom (which is apparently opposite room 58), room 14, room 12, room 10 which Basil shows to Mrs Lloyd; Mrs Peignoir's bedroom, number unknown.

On the menu: Sandwiches for Mr Lloyd, and coffee.

Not on offer: condoms or batteries. *Disgusting.*

First Broadcast 3 October 1975 – The Wedding Party

The episode opens with a group of well-dressed guests in reception – we hear Sybil's signature laugh/inhale (based on Connie Booth's own[9]). The somewhat oddly-named[10] Mrs Peignoir,[11] a French antique dealer, is introduced to the Major as a woman *"searching for antiquated relics"*, which certainly describes the Major. Basil doesn't know what Ricard[12] is so she settles for a sherry. Sybil is socialising, and delegating all the work to Basil; it is Manuel's birthday so Basil will be doing all the work for the evening. Basil recommends '*How to Murder Your Wife*'[13] – *"very funny. I saw it 6 times"* – the implication is that he was drawing inspiration from it. The old ladies think it's very hot, and they are right: 1975 was a hot dry summer with an official drought declared, right up to the time of filming. They also inexplicably think that Basil is somehow getting *taller*.[14] Polly is kissing Richard Turner, a male friend of hers, in Reception. He looks down her top and kisses her again, which sets the prudish Basil off.[15] He accuses her of running a massage parlour then criticises a sketch she has left there and tells her to put on more clothes, before answering the phone with the Freudian *"Fawlty Titties"*. It is Audrey, whose husband George has left her again.

A couple arrive and request a room. She has the giggles and is being goosed by her confident young companion, Mr Bruce.[16] She enquires about a double bed, but that would significantly inconvenience Basil. The request for a breeze baffles him. Then she identifies herself as Jean *Wilson*, not Mrs Bruce, and his level of offence rises to a point where he cannot contain it. He cannot bring himself to give them a double room and alleges that only two singles are available on different floors as *'the law of England'* forbids him to give them a double. The couple don't argue with him, having correctly surmised that it will not be worthwhile to do so, but they do request two singles next to each other. Luckily for them, Sybil arrives and overrules Basil's prudish strategy, putting them into a double room. The Fawltys have a territorial battle over the guests. Basil mentions his Korean War[17] history, claiming to have killed four men. Sybil counters that he poisoned them.

Manuel appears in his day clothes – JHD notes that he wears a coloured shirt here, considered exotic and 'continental' at the time – although Basil thought he'd already gone out for the evening. It is his birthday. He wants to thank Basil for his kindness since coming here from Spain *"leaving my mother… leaving my five brothers and one sister"*. Basil refuses to hear Manuel's entire speech, but it appears heartfelt and genuine.

Polly and Jean greet each other, and they discuss the wedding they will all be attending. We learn that Jean has made Polly a dress, which she will try on shortly. Alan needs batteries for his razor so Polly suggests a nearby chemist might still be open, given the time of night. Richard and Polly will meet Jean and Alan later for a drink. Basil reacts badly to Alan's enquiry about a chemist, as he assumes the couple want condoms.[18] When Alan requests *'a couple'* from Basil he is disgusted, and the clarification that Alan wants batteries does not help: Basil is presumably now thinking about sex toys! Even after Alan explains that he wants batteries for his electric razor[19] Basil is not mollified – he is now clearly embarrassed at his mistake but cannot back down. He feigns disgust at the unshaven beard instead.

The Fawltys are seen in their separate beds – normal for a 1970s sitcom of course, but also quite indicative of their relationship after 11 years of marriage – and Sybil is smoking and laughing at a magazine while Basil is reading *Jaws*.[20] Audrey rings, and Sybil sympathises with her husband troubles. The two women clearly complain to each other about men on a regular basis. The hotel doorbell rings and Basil resignedly goes to answer it, while complaining about the couple again – Sybil's responses to Audrey intersperse with his lines to make it sound like a conversation.

It is not Alan and Jean – it is Mrs Peignoir, who is drunk. He switches from angry to apologetic and obliging instantly, the same way that he suddenly fawns over Lord Melbury in the first episode. He claims that she has not put him out – because she is attractive and flirty and that serves to undo all perceived insult for him, replacing his distaste for the unmarried couple with flattery. She falls on him and at that compromising moment Alan and Jean arrive. Basil becomes very loud, and hurriedly laughs everything off as of course there's no problem because again he is very embarrassed. He claims to Alan and Jean that he thought it was a quarter past 10 but he has already told Mrs Peignoir that it is a quarter past 11. He speaks faster and faster[21] in his panic. How *dare* this couple catch Basil in any kind of compromising position when he has just accused *them* of impropriety?

Basil returns to Sybil, but Mrs Peignoir calls goodnight to him, wishing him a good sleep and using his name, which embarrasses him, and then she appears to knock on the door. He blusters again (*"some key who forgot to get the guest for their door"*) then goes to look. A drunken Manuel accosts him and they both fall to the floor. Alan passes by – although it is not obvious how this passageway is on the way to his allocated room – and sees Manuel declaring his love for Basil on the floor. He says nothing, but the viewer can guess what he's thinking. Unusually for a seasoned TV actor, he looks directly into the camera at the end of this scene. It has to be intentional.

Basil speaks French – badly, but reasonably confidently – at breakfast, still flirting with Mrs Peignoir. Manuel is *'overhung'* – clearly suffering very badly from his previous evening's activities. Jean and Alan observe his interaction with Basil, and pointedly call his behaviour disgusting, alluding to Basil's previous verbal attack on them. Jean's mother Rachel and stepfather Phillip Lloyd have arrived: he wants sandwiches sent up to the room as they won't be able to have lunch, she wants to use the phone first, and her conversation echoes Sybil's *I know!* verbal tic. Jean and Alan greet her, and Jean runs upstairs to see Mr Lloyd.

First Broadcast 3 October 1975 – The Wedding Party

Jean is hugging Mr Lloyd enthusiastically in his bedroom – the audience know he's her stepfather but Basil does not.[22] Basil attempts to stall Mrs Lloyd to prevent her seeing this – this is actually quite thoughtful of him, given that he is clearly still quite prudish. He feigns pain (his 'Korean war wound' is playing up, though we know he was only in the catering corps) then diverts her to the kitchen, via an ad libbed line when the door sticks. Here we can see that Manuel is still suffering – he is in the hamper. Polly takes sandwiches to Mr Lloyd and also hugs him – Basil also sees this and clearly panics. He again attempts to divert Mrs Lloyd, taking her into a different room to apologise for something, but fails to think of anything convincing. He cannot bring himself to tell her about the young women hugging her husband, so he distracts her with a discussion about the "*nicer*"[23] bedroom and whether or not she would wish to change rooms. She is confused. Polly leaves and Basil shows Mrs Lloyd to the correct room – which is exactly the same.

Polly visits Alan and Jean to try on her new dress, while Alan gets a back massage from Jean – which of course Basil can hear from the landing. He thinks it is sexual noise and is horrified when Polly leaves the room, still doing up her clothes. He is genuinely speechless for a moment then orders Polly to leave the hotel.

Alan and Jean are discussing Basil's 'scandalous' behaviour with her parents, when Basil arrives and threatens to throw them out for having a very good time – *"not here you don't"*. This is not the kind of hotel in which one should be having any kind of fun. Sybil intervenes again in an attempt to be the voice of reason and find out what Basil has told Polly and the guests. She explains the family relationships to Basil, who is again speechless. He actually repents – *"what have I done?! I've told them to leave"* – but makes it Sybil's problem: *"why didn't you tell me?"*. He 'generously' says he will clear up her mess and reacts badly to being told that he should just own up to making a mistake. He tells Polly to stay and tells the Lloyds that his *wife* has made the mistake. They agree that she has, clearly meaning her relationship with Basil.

The Major and Basil discuss Audrey and George; Basil admits to not liking Audrey. The Major admires Sybil, but also agrees with Basil when he says she is not a fine woman after all. Mrs Peignoir appears and compliments Basil's choice of music (Chopin). She flirts with him again and Basil is flattered and amused. He has not yet fixed her bedroom window[24], however, and he must now do so. She is grateful and compliments his strength and charm, then tells him she will sleep in the nude but it is *"not so much fun on your own"*. Nudge nudge, wink wink.[25] He feigns the war wound again – he is a loyal man, even if he doesn't much like his wife. As comedian and writer Steve Punt points out:[26] *"Basil is actually a prude – confronted with any actual opportunity, you know Basil is not going to be unfaithful to Sybil. He's absolutely* petrified *when a woman is tapping on his door in the night. You just know Sybil has it wrong."*

Mrs Peignoir requests a 7am morning call. She accuses Basil of leaving his tape recorder in her room on purpose so he could come back to collect it. Basil takes it from her and locks the door to prevent her returning. He is scared of her or the repercussions of her actions.

Sybil has returned to the hotel and can hear groaning, which she investigates. She knocks on her own bedroom door, after finding it locked. Basil mistakes her for the over-amorous Mrs Peignoir, and tells her, loyally, to go away. Cleese points out that when Sybil uses Basil's name he *should* have realised it was her, several lines before he actually does. He tells 'Mrs Peignoir' to go away in no uncertain terms – *'my wife will hear us'*. His expression when Sybil says "*this* is *your wife*" is priceless. "*Oh what a terrible dream.*"[27] He unlocks the door and lets her in. Sybil tells him there is a burglar downstairs – but of course it is really Manuel who is still very hungover and unwell. Basil assaults him, hitting him with a frying pan,[28] and the guests arrive to see Basil in a compromising position on top of Manuel. *Disgusting.*

John Cleese talks often about taboo, relating to this episode. Anxiety and embarrassment make audiences laugh, although few sexual jokes are actually funny in themselves. He thinks that Basil and Sybil may not have had sex since the Second Punic War[29] and so Basil is repressed, frustrated, and worked up. The phrase *"I'm not a prude but-"*, like other similar statements, always means *"I am a prude and-"* especially when we see other tropes at play at the same time. Mrs Peignoir represents a coquettish flirtation which makes Basil uncomfortable but is just about acceptable. The overtly sexual behaviours in the episode – Polly flirting with her friend, Jean and Alan's behaviour before checking in, and the scenarios Basil accidentally creates in his mind – are all more than his prudish mind can cope with.

In 2024 Cleese, discussing yet another potential reboot of the series, suggested that Basil had a casual fling with a guest at some point, producing a child who will help him run the hotel in his old age. This is at total odds with this presentation of Basil. It *is* plausible if such an encounter happened a long time before this episode, so his prudish behaviour is a learned response to adultery and Sybil's inevitable wrath (since Basil is not good at covering his own tracks); alternatively, it might happen long *after* series 2, when his prudish behaviour has mellowed and his fear of Sybil is finally dwarfed by his desire for some kind of non-combative personal connection. As Cleese has proposed writing with his younger daughter Camilla (b.1983), and the fictional daughter is likely to be younger than her for TV casting reasons, we can expect the latter scenario if that version of the show is ever made.

First Broadcast 10 October 1975[1] – The Hotel Inspectors

The sign says: FAW TY TO W ER – the second W is wonky, the S has disappeared again.

In this episode we meet:
Mr Hutchinson[2] (Bernard Cribbins[3]), who travels in spoons and is extremely pernickety.
Mr Walt (James Cossins[4]), who travels in outboard motors and is extremely patient.
Three hotel inspectors (John – Geoffrey Morris, Brian – Peter Brett and the uncredited Chris – Lewis Alexander).

Not seen: Bill Morton, a mutual friend of Audrey and the Fawltys: named after the show's tireless vision mixer.[5] Henry Kissinger.[6] Squawking Bird,[7] unless Mr Hutchinson gets access to a TV in time.

Physical comedy: Mr Hutchinson is choked, punched, carried out of the dining room, flanned, and chased out of the hotel. Basil and Mr Hutchinson have a fist fight.

Sets: Hotel lobby, dining room.

On the menu: Spanish omelette with frozen peas, prawn cocktail, pate, lamb casserole, cheese salad, ginger beer, water (cold or tepid).

Not on offer: Fresh peas.

The episode opens with Sybil on the phone to Audrey, demonstrating her terrible laugh. Both Fawltys smoke, though Basil never does get his cigarette lit. Sybil calls Basil to the hotel front desk to deal with a guest even though she is there, because her personal call is more important than their guests. Basil greets the guest, Mr Hutchinson,[8] who turns out to have a pretentious manner of speaking and pompous air. He cannot use one word where fourteen will do (and Cleese praised Cribbins' ability to never miss a beat when speaking, as this part is very demanding). He would like a taxi at 2pm, but wants Basil to call it for him, as he does not like to make his own telephone calls. He requests that Basil draws him a map so he can find the Post Office later that day, as the printed map *"has curry on it"* – an odd detail as *Fawlty Towers* does not seem to offer anything so 'exotic' on its menu. Sybil deals with another guest, Mr Walt.[9] There is a confusion over a pot of Pens labelled Bens, as it's implied Sybil's P looks like a B. *"Well, when Ben comes you can give it to him."* Mr Hutchinson thinks that Basil has written Boff on the map, not P Off (for Post Office), implying that Basil's P *also*[10] looks like a B. Basil accidentally tells Mr Walt to P Off[11] when explaining. Manuel takes Mr Walt to his room.

Mr Hutchinson asks about lunch then says if anyone wants him he'll be in the lounge. Basil enquires as to who might want him – *Henry Kissinger*? Sybil has been networking with Audrey and has information that might prove useful: there are hotel inspectors in town. Basil takes this seriously, despite previously mocking and having a general lack of respect for Sybil and Audrey's gossip. There are three men in town, discussing hotels they've stayed in in Exeter the previous night. He suggests he calls their mutual friend Bill Morton to hear more. The Major arrives and is sent away. Mr Hutchinson interrupts Basil's attempt to call by pinging the bell multiple times until he is heard: he wants to reserve BBC2[12] in order to watch a programme that evening. He suggests that Basil look into renting TVs to guests as he has a wide experience of hotels: *"in my professional activities I am in constant contact with them"*. Basil jumps rapidly to conclusions – Mr Hutchinson who travels a lot for business and has a wide range of experience with hotels must be one of the inspectors… but unfortunately for Basil, on this occasion 2+2=5.

Basil confirms that there is a table-tennis table in the hotel – in the south wing, overlooking the car park. Mr Hutchinson tells Polly off for spilling his grapefruit juice at breakfast, and Basil gets her to seat him in the hotel dining room for lunch, even though it is not yet lunchtime. Sybil queries this and Basil hints that he has overridden the usual procedure for a good reason – but doesn't tell her why. Polly is sarcastic to Mr Hutchinson but he does not notice her tone. Mr Hutchinson wants a Spanish omelette and interrogates Basil about the freshness of the hotel vegetables – frozen is not fresh. He opts for a cheese salad and ginger beer instead, with a glass of fresh water. He receives a telephone call at the hotel reception, and leaves the dining room, as do Basil and Sybil.

Manuel confuses Mr Walt, the guest from room 7, by incorrectly implementing the hotel's complicated dining room arrangements[13] *"for I am not one to know it easily"*, and then Basil makes it worse by moving him back, attempting to give Mr Hutchinson the best table despite the rota. (Manuel didn't even choose the right table according to the rota, Basil suggests.) Mr Walt is upset and tense. He asks for the wine list and an ashtray, and orders a drink – Basil corrects his pronunciation of the wine. Basil attempts to open the bottle but the cork is stuck in it. The scene is ad libbed from this point, until he finally gets it to pour – and it splashes the table. The wine is corked but Basil does not understand this term – *"I just uncorked it, didn't you see?"* and given the physical business with the cork this gains them an extra laugh from the audience – and attempts to correct him again.

Sybil explains to Basil that Mr Hutchinson is a spoon salesman, not a hotel inspector. Basil is sarcastic to Mr Hutchinson in his irritation. Mr Hutchinson is still upset about his orders as he gets the wrong food, thanks to the table changes, and is then cross with Polly for bringing him the wrong dish. Basil and Polly squabble and Sybil intervenes again.

Basil asks Manuel about the wine and it is implied that Manuel took the bottle away to the kitchen – but he did not. Basil brings Mr Walt a second bottle of wine, not realising Manuel has already opened the replacement bottle and put it on Mr Walt's table. Mr Hutchinson gets a second wrong dish and Polly attempts to cover for Manuel. Mr Hutchinson cancels his meal in disgust. He loses his temper and shouts at Basil – directly accusing Basil of being rude. Polly attempts to cover again – *"he told me to shut up"*. Basil and Polly attempt to bamboozle Mr Hutchinson by pretending to be talking to each other while looking at Mr Hutchinson and *vice versa*. Manuel steals the 'wrong' plate from Mr Walt in an attempt to rectify the confusion about meals. Basil uses the cliched *"he's from Barcelona"* line to Mr Walt.

Basil tries to impress Mr Walt by talking about wine but gets it wrong – a Bordeaux *is* a claret – and only manages to insult him further. Basil realises that Mr Walt is, by his own account, here with two colleagues and therefore deduces that *he* must be the hotel inspector, since he now knows that Mr Hutchinson is not. Mr Hutchinson starts to complain again as Manuel attempts to give him an omelette despite his protests. Basil destroys the omelette and places the plate on the table behind him – where the Major gleefully grabs it and tucks in, a nice visual gag for those paying close attention. He has also gained the extra bottles of wine as neither Manuel or Basil is paying attention.

Basil antagonises him further, and the obstreperous Mr Hutchinson gives as good as he gets. The Misses Gatsby and Tibbs, at the table behind them, are unmoved – they have become inured to such behaviour during mealtimes. Basil attempts to strangle Mr Hutchinson in exasperation and eventually punches him, dropping him face down into his omelette as he passes out. Basil and Manuel carry him into the bar and Sybil orders Basil to call a doctor – but Mr Walt comes out to interrupt him before he can do so. Mr Hutchinson revives off-screen and comes back to shout at Basil, and punches him, felling him briefly. Mr Hutchinson repeatedly punches Basil in the stomach. His *"I'm not a violent man, Mr Fawlty"* is responded to faintly, from the floor: *"yes you are."*[14] He hits him a final time and stalks off, announcing that he will not be expecting a bill for his stay after this behaviour. Sybil spots Basil on the floor and asks sarcastically *"You've handled that then, have you Basil?"* Basil attempts to cover himself with Mr Walt, explaining that the fighting is not real. He offers him dinner as a bribe, then £50 and £60 not to mention it, nor to write about it, as he still thinks Mr Walt is a hotel inspector. Mr Walt, however, is simply another travelling salesman.

Basil has a cringing, fearful reaction before relief kicks in. Inspiration strikes, and he and Manuel hurry to the kitchen.

The real inspectors arrive at the end of the episode, suggesting one eats there and the other two try the Clairmont. Basil appears and 'pies' Mr Hutchinson in the crotch and face while Manuel pours cream into his briefcase, before the salesman can leave the hotel. Basil kisses Manuel on the head for helping him and triumphantly returns to the hotel front desk to greet the newcomers: *"And what can I do for you three gentlemen…?"* [15] He screams in pure agony as reality dawns.

To modern British audiences, Bernard Cribbins[16] is one of the show's best-known guests. By October 1975 he'd narrated classic children's series *The Wombles*[17] (an episode of which was shown earlier the same evening), read 23 stories on *Jackanory,*[18] voiced the road safety squirrel Tufty, had two hit[19] singles, appeared in the 1966 Doctor Who film *Daleks: Invasion Earth 2150 AD*, 1970's *The Railway Children*, two Carry On[20] films, and a Bond film[21] among other work. To Generation X viewers he is a warm comfortable presence. To subsequent generations he was also the voice of Buzby,[22] a regular on BBC Children's programmes, a regular in BBC Radio adaptations such as *Neverwhere* and *The Silver Chair,* and Wilfred Mott, a regular character in *Doctor Who* 2007-2010, with a repeat appearance in the 2023 anniversary specials, filmed shortly before his death in 2022. He is one of the UK's most loved actors – so his extremely irritating little man in this episode comes as a huge surprise to some. Cleese describes Cribbins as one of the two best comedy actors in England at the time of filming Jimmy Cossins (Mr Walt) is the other.

Cribbins wrote about the episode in his autobiography.[23] He had been working for Cleese in a Video Arts film called *How Not to Exhibit Yourself,* a training video about manning an exhibition stand at Olympia. He and Cleese were required to shout at each other during this film, and Cribbins felt this *"could have been a training video for appearing in* [Fawlty Towers]". Cleese contacted him in 1975 to ask him if he would be in the show, and *"getting word from some friends in the industry that it was destined for great things"* Cribbins agreed. On 17 August 1975 – though he *wrote* 27, that was a Wednesday – he arrived at Studio TC8, BBC Television Centre, to record the show. He called it *"pure farce"* with a *"devilishly clever"* script, and credited Cleese with a *"barnstorming performance"*. He writes at length about the fight scene and the ending. During the dining room scene, where Basil attempts to throttle Mr Hutchinson, Cleese *"being about 8 feet 6 inches in bare feet...was a very strong young man"* and during the rehearsal he was rather too enthusiastic for Cribbins's comfort. *"You don't die in television, John!"* Cleese eased off and Cribbins survived. He also gave JHD camera tips for the punch up – *"when I knee him in the cobblers, then you shoot from the side!"* While JHD was an undoubted veteran of the scene and not in need of advice, it's likely he did listen to Bernard Cribbins on that one. Cribbins praises the four main cast members, an amazing team of actors. He was honoured to be in 'their gang' for the episode of what he regarded as one of the best sitcoms ever. It is clear he loved every minute of it.

Cribbins had previously appeared in a number of Brian Rix farces, some with Andrew Sachs. Cleese had only worked for Rix on TV but had seen many farces on stage in the 1960s and early 1970s. This episode is a classic farce of mistaken identity and snobbery, and hinges – as do two of the three previous episodes – on Basil's inability to avoid jumping to conclusions and fawning up to the wrong people as a result. The plot is worthy of a Feydeau or Whitehall farce. The rules of farce,[24] according to Ray Cooney,[25] include *"truthful and recognisable"* characters – *"ordinary people in a predicament ... they are unable to contain"*. Mr Hutchinson might have been expressly designed to irritate Basil Fawlty, being the finicky guest counterpart to Basil's controlling and overbearing hotelier. Farce requires *"teamwork. You can't have selfish actors... [they] need each other."* Put the two quirky men together and things become chaotic; add the supporting cast and it rapidly escalates.

Mr Hutchinson's idiosyncratic manner of speaking is somewhere between Miss Anne Elk (based on Graham Chapman's partner, David Sherlock, who had an unusual style of speech), and Mr McGough who 'caught poetry', from the *Monty Python's Flying Circus Off Licence* sketches.[26] In the second sketch, John Cleese plays the shopkeeper who tells the splendiloquent Mr McGough to *"just shut up!"* and we can only assume that it must have been at least in the back of his mind when writing Mr Hutchinson. The Northern accent was Cribbins' own choice – not his natural accent, but he and Cleese both felt it was appropriate for a man who travels 'in spoons'[27] to be from somewhere at least in the vicinity of Sheffield, home of British cutlery.

This episode, although it is well-respected, is not often named as people's favourite, nor is it quite as quotable as other episodes. But it does live on where others have slipped slightly from memory: it forms a major part of the plot of *Snavely,* the first episode of *Amanda's,* and of *Fawlty Towers: the stage play.* It is a very significant episode in terms of legacy.

First Broadcast 17 October 1975[1] – Gourmet Night

The sign says: WARTY TOWELS, our first anagram although it is missing the F.

In this episode we meet:
Mrs & Mrs Heath (Jeffrey Segal[2], Elizabeth Benson[3]) and their son Ronald (Tony Page[4]). Ronald does not like his food. Mrs Heath's name is Yolande.[5]
André (André Maranne[6]), a French restaurateur.
Kurt (Steve Plytas[7]), a Greek chef introduced to the Fawltys by André.
Colonel and Mrs Hall (Allan Cuthbertson,[8] Ann Way[9]), both Justices of the Peace in Torquay. Colonel Hall has a facial tic, Mrs Hall is rather small. Both of these facts will cause Basil discomfort. Her name is Petal.
Mrs and Mrs Twitchen[10] (Richard Caldicot[11], Betty Huntley-Wright[12]). Mr Twitchen is Treasurer of the local Rotarians. His name is Lionel or Leslie.[13]

Not seen: the Housters, four guests who fail to arrive (based on real friends of John Cleese and Connie Booth).

Physical comedy: Kurt becomes rather difficult to handle when drunk. There is some classic farcical food and seat swapping. Basil headbutts a desk, and hops around being a duck. Ronald is cuffed by an irritated Basil.

Sets: hotel lobby, dining room, bar, kitchen, André's restaurant kitchen.

On the menu: Trifle, chips, mayonnaise, bread, paella, bread and cheese, salmon mousse, mullet with mustard sauce – raw *and* cooked, eventually.

Not on offer: ketchup or salad cream. Lobster thermidor, Tournedos de Medici. Duck, with orange, cherries, or anything else. Tomato juice – seen briefly on Sybil's tray before mysteriously disappearing, thanks to a cut scene.

Basil is trying to get his car to start and is working on the engine himself, as many 1970s car owners would have done. It is a red Austin Mini Countryman,[14] which we saw parked in the hotel car park in the previous episode. Manuel denies all knowledge of Sybil – *"she not here"* – leading to the oft-quoted *"This Basil's wife. This Basil. This smack on head"* when Basil slaps Manuel, who resignedly nods and leaves without a word. Sybil tells Basil off for attempting to fix the car himself, and orders him to take it to the garage.

Polly arrives, happy that she has sold a sketch and offering wine to everyone. Kurt, the new chef recommended by André, declines saying that he likes it *"too much"*. He has provided food samples for the Fawltys to try. We learn that he bought the sketch from Polly for 50p, and is a fan of her work. It is a portrait of Manuel, of whom Kurt is implicitly rather fond. Sybil suggests she could buy a sketch of Manuel to put on Basil's bedside table, implicitly to torment Basil. Kurt compliments Manuel, who makes a good artist's model. Basil returns to the car engine, hoping Sybil will not notice.

Some time later, Sybil, Basil, and André, a local restaurateur, have Sunday dinner, cooked by Kurt. They compliment the meal. Sybil and Basil want to ask André about hosting a gourmet night. The Major is not happy with his soup. Ronald Heath, a child eating in the dining room with his parents, does not like his chips – they are the wrong shape and are *"awful"*. His over-indulgent mother calls him 'highly strung' (*"Yes, he should be"* mutters Basil malevolently). Basil responds to a request for salad cream by offering mayonnaise, but it is rejected. *"That's puke, that is."* *"Well at least it's* fresh *puke."* Basil is proud that his chef cooks fresh food and insulted on his behalf by the child's demand for salad cream, which Basil regards as rather vulgar. Basil sarcastically talks[15] about the chef's skill with a jar and a tin opener, though this rant about tin openers will be undermined by his approach to the Waldorf salad in series two.

André confirms that a gourmet night will be a good idea and suggests Thursdays. Sybil and Basil squabble over advertising the night, and Basil makes it clear that he wants to avoid any 'riff-raff'[16] attending. André, Manuel and Kurt speak in the kitchen. Manuel promises to make them both paella (an offer revisited in *The Anniversary*).

We cut to Thursday night. Some guests have cancelled,[17] so the gourmet night is now down to four diners. Polly asks Basil if he likes the menu, which has been specially printed for the occasion. The Ladies are sent upstairs for dinner – they have been banished from the dining room. The Halls arrive. Colonel and Mrs Hall, both local Justices of the Peace, are implied to be well known in the community – the Misses have heard of them, and Basil has met Colonel Hall before. Basil sucks up to the Colonel, as we know by now this is his typical fawning behaviour. The Colonel does not remember him, but worse, Basil does not remember that the

Halls' daughter is deceased and puts his foot in it, embarrassing himself painfully. He fails to remember his own name in his confusion.

Basil towers over Mrs Hall, and simply cannot avoid making short jokes. He misunderstands the Colonel, thinking *"two small, short and dry"*[18] refers to Mrs Hall, who is from Basil's perspective certainly too small. The Twitchens (Mr Twitchen is Treasurer of the local Rotarians) arrive – and of course their name sounds like Twitching, which Colonel Hall does. We can guess what is going to happen here, if we've paid any attention to sitcoms before. The building blocks of farce are in play.

Polly devises a number of ways to explain that Kurt, the new chef, is drunk – *he's potted (the shrimps), he's soused (the herring), he's pickled (the onions) and he's smashed (the eggs) in his cups, under the table*. Basil still doesn't understand, despite a mime or two as well. Although the British have many terms for drunk, Basil doesn't seem to drink much and probably hasn't used many of them himself. He attempts to introduce the Halls to the Twitchens but cannot bring himself to say Twitchen to a man who is twitching – Colonel Hall's tic is mesmerising and paralysing Basil. He fakes fainting to get out of the situation. Polly returns to tell Basil outright that Kurt is drunk, almost unconscious. Basil drops a bottle of wine in shock.

Polly explains that Kurt loves Manuel but Manuel does not love him back, and while he has clearly made mild physical advances to Manuel, Manuel will not reciprocate and the response to this is problematic for modern viewers. *"You only had to be nice to him."* Basil – and possibly the audience – entirely blames Manuel for the outcome of this encounter. It's worth noting here that Kurt's sexuality is not the focus of the joke, however, and he is not being mocked for having feelings – only Manuel's responses are being laughed at. Basil has not even noticed the chef's sexuality and has to have it explained to him. The live audience don't react to one of the jokes here: when Basil says *"I should never have hired a Frenchman"* Polly corrects him: *"He's Greek, Mr Fawlty."* Basil throws out *"they invented it"*, a jab at cliches of homosexuality in Ancient Greece, but the joke simply misses and they continue into the kitchen in silence. It's unclear whether Basil meant Kurt or André with the French remark, but Polly means Kurt.

They attempt to revive Kurt, and Michael Apter draws particular attention to the way they go about this: initially, Basil taps him gently on the cheek and shakes him, although Polly has already told him that Kurt is drunk. Basil initially seems mildly perplexed by the idea that Kurt has only drunk half a bottle – which is in his hand – as if he is confused about how this could have affected him so much. Polly draws his attention to multiple empty bottles she has found. Seamlessly, he transitions to smacking Kurt rather hard. He changes from kindly to aggressive without a break, demonstrating Apter's theory of opposite qualities again. *"What *appeared to be compassionate sympathy is disclosed to be fury"*, a line which sums up almost every situation Basil finds himself in. Cleese told Apter that he finds it essential to transition smoothly between these opposing actions to get a laugh from the audience – it is no use stopping and signalling the change to the audience, the laugh comes from their noticing the change for themselves. A break destroys the link between the two opposite behaviours.

Polly suggests that André could provide a substitute dish, as Kurt cannot provide one. Sybil checks on the diners, and then finds Basil on the phone to André. Basil starts to type a new menu as Sybil attempts to find out what is going on, screeching *why?* repeatedly at him. Basil attempts to leave, to fetch a replacement dish of duck from André, but has to take the menu to the dining room first – Sybil or Polly could do it but ... they don't. He does a fairly decent duck impression before explaining the new menu to the diners, who are not terribly impressed with the change. The Colonel attempts to order from the original menu but Basil gives him the new menu – it's all duck. *"Duck with orange, duck with cherries, duck surprise."* The surprise is that it has no orange or cherries, a classic sketch comedy punchline, in the manner of the *Two Ronnies*.[19] *"If you don't like duck you're rather stuck."* Sybil and Polly attempt to prep starters and vegetables for the duck, while Basil passes on the starter orders. There is some excellent silent slapstick comedy with the plates and chairs for Colonel and Mrs Hall – their plates are swapped seven times, so the final time they simply swap chairs instead. The guests want to place drink orders too. The three salmon mousse starters are surprisingly not too bad, according to Mr Twitchen – but the mullet is still raw. Basil had plated it up in the kitchen while the others prepared the salmon, and he failed to notice it wasn't cooked. The chef is sick on it[20] before the mistake can be rectified. Polly takes the wine order and is informed that there is a hair in the Colonel's mousse. *"Well don't talk too loud, everybody will want one."* Manuel serves the Colonel's wine, and he twitches after sipping it, making Manuel think the wine is bad.

Basil finally gets to André's restaurant[21] and collects the sauces, and a covered duck. He returns to Fawlty Towers, where the trolley is already prepared for the main course. Manuel goes to fetch it. In the best farcical tradition, Basil drops the duck as the dining room door fails to move when he leans on it, the resistance knocking it out of his hands. We can see part of a crew member wearing beige trousers behind the door, crouching to move the door on cue. Polly thinks they might be able to salvage the duck but before they can rescue it, Manuel enters – at this point we see the bearded face of the crew member too – and he steps on it, wedging it onto his shoe. Basil retrieves it but it is clear it cannot be saved. Basil throws it at Kurt, although it misses his head and catches him in the chest instead. Sybil goes to the lobby to call André for another duck while Manuel and Polly stall the guests with their own brand of 'entertainment' – singing (*'I Cain't Say*

No" from *Oklahoma!,* hammed up in an over-the-top American accent that doesn't reflect Booth's own) and very bad guitar playing. Sybil then tells them a funny story – we don't hear most of it, just her laughter at the end.

The second duck is prepared, but naturally at André's restaurant things go wrong again. While André and Basil aren't looking, a waiter replaces the serving dish so Basil picks up the wrong one. His car – always unreliable – has broken down, and he loses his temper with it, beating it with a tree branch. This iconic scene of a man punishing his car – *"I'm going to give you a damned good thrashing"* – is often cited as a top ten comedy scene. Cleese notes that the most awkward part of the scene was obtaining a suitable branch – it took three attempts. He is a man on the edge of a breakdown, and for a change, quite understandably so. Nothing that has happened so far has been *his* fault – Kurt drinking, the door knocking the duck out of his hand, even picking up the wrong dish is an accident he simply couldn't have foreseen. Working on the car himself instead of taking it to a mechanic is the only part of this scenario that is genuinely Basil's fault.

He rushes the food to the hotel on foot, without opening the covered dish – and it's a dessert. He searches the trifle for the duck, as if by some incomprehensible means it has got inside the dish, but it is not there. The guests are not amused. *"What about the duck, Fawlty?" "Duck's off, sorry."*[22]

Gourmet Night owes a good deal to classic theatrical farce, and a keen eye will be able to spot all the signs of the eventual punchline long before we reach it. The dining room scene with the repeatedly swapped plates and chairs is almost magical in its sleight-of-hand. John Cleese says in interviews that *Gourmet Night* and *The Germans* are the two most-liked episodes, but he doesn't like them as much as other episodes as they contain 'laboured' scenes that don't work as well as he would have liked and could be considered overkill. They are certainly the two with the most problematic scenes, but also some of the most-loved farcical elements.

Cleese says in commentary for this episode that he doesn't know when the decision was made to change to anagrams for the hotel sign in the opening credits. The perception among the viewing public is that every episode had one, and it's not the case at all – only seven of twelve episodes, and only one true anagram. He notes that all the exterior filming for series one was done in a week – barring the opening shot for the pilot – and this episode is probably the *most* reliant on exterior film, including extensive use of a second location. *A Touch of Class* uses Cookham High Street in place of Torquay, this episode uses several roads in Harrow, and *The Germans* features Northwick Park Hospital, also in Harrow.

Teenager Tony Page appeared as Ronald in his first TV speaking part, and was paid £90 for the role, more than his weekly wage as a Naval recruit in 1977. He told the *Daily Mail* in 2015: "*John was supposed to cuff me round the head, but my reflexes were so fast, every time he went to hit me, I ducked. In the end he had to knock me with his elbow so I wasn't expecting it. I sometimes get* [the show] *out and watch it to cheer myself up.*"

"*I hope it's nothing trivial*", said of the absent Housters, is a quote from the American author Irvin S Cobb: in full, "*I've just heard about his illness. I hope it's nothing trivial.*"

There are lines cut from this episode that do appear in the first script book, published in 1977. John J Hoare deals with them in detail on his Dirty Feed site.[23] Basil's dialogue with Ronald and his mother about the chips is longer and includes the line "*he* likes *cooking. That's why he became a chef*", a nice contrast to series 2's "*chef* has *just opened the tin*", although of course series 2's chef is *Terry*, who is not obviously a 'tortured genius' style of chef. Hoare points out that we see tomato juice on Sybil's tray in one shot before it disappears in the next, reflecting filmed-but-cut dialogue, and – unappetisingly – that Kurt's vomit is *slightly* visible in one shot. Additionally, the famous car rant loses a scripted curse – the now-mild 'son of a bitch' – and the absurdly funny "*I've never liked you*". Basil's attitude to the car in the broadcast version is one of warning and repercussion – "*you've tried it on just once too often*" – but the unbroadcast version is more personal, a story of mutual dislike between man and machine. Hoare additionally notes that a publicity shot of the episode, taken during the dress rehearsal on the afternoon of recording, shows Kurt in the final chaotic scene although this does not appear in the script or the stage directions (which were edited for the script book). He hopes that this means the original script did end with Kurt reappearing from the kitchen to add to the chaos. It would be understandable, however, the chef was written out of this scene before the final performance, as it could be considered 'one joke too many'.

First Broadcast 24 October 1975[1] – The Germans

The sign says: Northwick Park Hospital, no hotel exterior or sign.

In this episode we meet:
Sister (Brenda Cowling[2]). She is brusque but firm and efficient, and will not take any nonsense from Basil no matter how sarcastic and rude he is to her.
Doctor Finn (Louis Mahoney[3]). He is polite to Basil despite Basil's visible double-take on meeting him.
Mr & Mrs Sharp (John Lawrence, Iris Fry).
Mrs Wilson (Claire Davenport), a pompous woman.
Various unnamed German guests. Willy Bowman,[4] Nick Kane, Lisa Bergmayr,[5] Dan Gillan,[6] Barbara Bermel[7] (uncredited).
A regular TV extra, Derek Suthern,[8] appears in the fire drill scene with a pipe, and is often mistaken for Graham Chapman.

Not seen: Goebbels, Hitler, Himmler, Eva Braun, von Ribbentrop.[9]

Physical comedy: Basil is hit on the head by a moose, falls over Manuel, has a vase of flowers knocked onto his head, is hit on the head by the moose a second time, is sprayed in the face by the fire extinguisher, is hit on the head by a frying pan, has exaggerated facial expressions when in hospital, goose steps while doing Hitler impressions, is hit on the head by the moose a third time, is sat on by the Major. Manuel has Basil trip over him, is set on fire,[10] is shoved back into a burning room by Basil, is hit on the head by Basil's fist, has the moose head fall on him after it bounces off Basil. The moose is quite battered by the end of the episode, but it's better off than Basil or Manuel.

Sets: Northwick Park hospital rooms and corridor, hotel lobby, kitchen, office, dining room.

On the menu: prawn cocktail, egg mayonnaise, grilled plaice, veal chop with rosemary, cold meat salad, pickled herring.

Not on the menu: the mould that Sybil failed to scrape off the cheddar. Eva Prawn, Prawn Goebbels, Hermann Goering, four Colditz salads.

The episode begins at the Northwick Park hospital – unusually, not the hotel opening. Sybil is preparing for an operation, while instructing Basil to fetch and carry for her, perform the hotel fire drill the next day, and collect various items she will need. Unappealingly, she also needs someone to *"scrape the mould off the cheddar"*. And, crucially for the plot, a moose head that Basil has inexplicably bought from a local antiques shop needs to be put up on the wall.

The Germans – always referred to *en masse* – will arrive the following day as well. They are weighing on Basil's mind throughout the whole episode.

Sybil's operation is very minor indeed, it turns out – an ingrowing toenail on her right foot. Basil feels rather sorry for it. A brusque nurse chivvies Basil out to the corridor where he is surprised by a doctor. Sybil's hospital doctor is a black man, and we see Basil's visible surprise when he first appears on screen. Basil does treat him politely and his main reaction to the conversation is a childish glee at the thought of the pain Sybil will be in after her treatment, but his initial recoiling and facial expressions – Cleese's mastery of physical comedy demonstrating much more than any lines could say – do not sit comfortably with audiences today. It is not conceivable that Fawlty, a hotelier who has been overseas, has not met a black man before 1975, but many of the audience may not have done.[11]

The Major asks after Sybil's health but is clearly having a very confused day – this episode showcases his dementia much more than most episodes and is the most problematic as a result. He remembers a member of staff named Elsie, who pre-dated Polly. He reminisces about his past: *"strange creatures, women. I knew one once"*. He recalls a day at the cricket[12] with a girl who used offensive epithets to describe the cricketers. This scene has been edited for broadcast in the UK since 2013 (commercial channels) and 2020 (BBC iPlayer), though it remains unexpurgated on home media. Basil doesn't pull him up on any of the language, but rather agrees with him about women in general. The Major is clearly approaching senility by this point, but that is no excuse for the language. This is not a kind portrayal of a declining man who forgets his manners, but a portrayal of encroaching dementia in a racist old man.

Polly arrives looking for her German book (a phrasebook or simple language textbook, not a book in German as she is not fluent), as there are German guests arriving the following day. The Major has no love for Germans, though as he has got rather confused in the previous conversation he continues to talk about women

First Broadcast 24 October 1975 – The Germans

and Germans interchangeably for a while. The Major wants Basil to open the bar for a drink as it's nearly dinner time – not quite 6pm.

The phone rings but no one is around to answer it so Basil has to do it himself. It is Sybil, distracting him from the job he was trying to do, which is of course the job she is calling him to check on, reminiscent of the menu task in the first episode. Manuel appears, but is much too late to be of help. Basil asks him for a hammer, but Manuel first thinks he wants a ham sandwich, then a hamster. The moose head is now on the reception desk. Manuel is practising his English, in a very posh voice, when the Major reappears and thinks the moose is talking directly to him. *"I speak English well. I learn it from a book."* The Major compliments the moose head, then discusses it with a bemused Basil – it is clear he thinks it is computerised in some way, as he thinks it might be Japanese. He is surprised to hear it is Canadian. Polly brings in fresh flowers and Basil complains about the smell.

Sybil rings again and Polly answers. Basil yells that he's doing it now. Polly confirms that the moose head is up before it falls off the wall in the next beat – *"it's down again"*. The moose has hit Basil on the head. He staggers forward to speak to Sybil, but falls over Manuel who is on the floor, and then Manuel knocks the flowers onto his head as well.

The following morning Basil and Manuel put the moose head up again. Basil warns some guests that the fire drill will shortly be happening, at 12 o'clock. Polly reminds him and he correctly notes that he is already preparing – she is interfering in exactly the same way that Sybil does. She raises the reasonable point that as she is only in the hotel at meal times she won't be available to help in the event of a real fire occurring outside those times. Sybil calls again, and Basil agrees that he is going to do the fire drill. We can infer from the conversation that Sybil has moved the fire alarm key and Basil was not aware – are we surprised? No, we are not. He opens the safe to obtain the key, and triggers the burglar alarm. The guests appear, thinking the fire bell is ringing. They argue with Basil that this is the fire drill, but he disagrees. The Major, interestingly, insists that it *is* the burglar alarm – presumably he has heard both bells before, but how can he tell the difference without hearing both in quick succession? Does he have perfect pitch? Basil insists that the fire alarm makes a different sound, and that the drill will be at 12 o'clock – but of course now it *is* 12 o'clock, as they've been arguing for a few minutes. He demonstrates the difference between the two bells to the assembled guests, and they are indeed a semitone apart. When he triggers the fire alarm the guests start to leave, and Manuel and Polly start to evacuate the hotel correctly. This means Basil has to recall them, as it is now not a realistic evacuation scenario.

Basil sends Manuel into the kitchen to start the chips for dinner, after convincing him that there is not in fact a fire – drill, or otherwise. The phone rings and Basil shouts *"I'm doing it"* at Sybil. He shoos the guests from the lobby in a tone between despair and anger: *"because obviously if there was a fire you'd all be standing down here like this in the lobby. I don't know why we bother. We should let you all burn."* Manuel, meanwhile, has set fire to the kitchen in the process of cooking the chips.[13] He sheds his burning gloves and emerges into the lobby, covered in scorch marks and clutching a frying pan, with which he is smacking out the remaining embers on his jacket. He screams *fire*, but Basil tells him *No* and sends him back into the kitchen, despite his protests. Basil turns off the alarm and yells at Manuel, banging on the kitchen door, to shut up.

Sybil has phoned again, and Polly explains that they've had the fire drill. Basil goes to quiet Manuel and discovers the truth about the fire. Basil calmly calls everyone to the lobby: *"can I put it this way?* [in a strangled voice] *Fire? Fffff-fire."* He sets the alarm off again, after futilely looking for the key a second time[14] – after a moment or two he simply gives up and smashes the glass with the telephone receiver after it rings again. He wrestles with a large fire extinguisher, managing to spray himself in the face before Polly takes it into the kitchen to use correctly. While Basil is bending over, trying to wipe his eyes, Manuel stands next to him holding the heavy pan above his head – apparently attempting to help somehow, but we can see what is about to happen. Basil straightens up into the pan, dealing himself a blow to the head. He draws his fist back to punch Manuel before passing out. This scene could be a training video for what not to do in the event of a fire.

Basil wakes up in a hospital bed with a bandaged head and a sarcastic Sybil thanking him for 'coming to see her', as if he is merely visiting. He has a look of utter terror on his face. He is clearly concussed and is not sure what is happening. When the nurse appears, ready to tell him off, he insults her – the concussion has removed his barely functional politeness filter, and he now tells the unvarnished truth. He is not afraid to speak his mind.

Basil prepares to leave the hospital against medical advice, although he appears to acquiesce when the doctor appears, even getting back into bed obediently. Basil respects authority, even when concussed. But as soon as the doctor and Sybil have left the room, he escapes.

Basil returns to the hotel, still bandaged, and assures the Ladies that he is fine – though only after mistaking Manuel for Sybil. He is confused by one of the German guests who has been conversing in German with Polly in the previous scene. He claims to 'get by' in German but clearly does not understand anything they say to him. *"I see, you're volunteering to go out to get meat. No need."* They had actually asked about hiring a car. He mimes hunting meat, which is more than usually confusing for the guests. Polly sends him to have a lie down, but he calls her Elsie, the previous hotel employee mentioned by the Major in the first half of the episode. He is accosted by the Ladies again and tells them that a blow on the head is worth two in a bush. He attempts to speak to the Germans without mentioning the war but his tongue gets away from him and he simply can't avoid his internal monologue coming out.

Polly, concerned, calls the hospital. Basil admits to not having voted to enter the Common Market in 1973. He attempts to take the guests' order but can't avoid mentioning the *"old differences"*. *"When you said prawn I thought you said war."* The women are visibly upset and the men are trying to stay calm. *"Will you stop talking about the war?"* Basil counters *"Me? You started it!" "We did not start it." "Yes you did, you invaded Poland."* That small part of the British psyche that *still*, even in 2025, chants "two world wars and one world cup" at football matches, has emerged from Basil's subconscious and he can no longer stifle it. He starts to do Hitler impersonations, and then – in a clear sop to the studio audience who remember *Monty Python* – says *"I'll do the silly walk" and* begins to goose step in an attempt to rally the crying German women. The men tell him off: this is not funny, not for the women, not for any German people. They're right, and the audience knows it. Basil retorts *"Who won the bloody war anyway?"*, at which point Dr Finn and a white-jacketed orderly appear, armed with a large hypodermic needle and intending to sedate Basil and take him away. He runs from them: through the kitchen into the lobby, briefly hiding behind the office door (which has a glass panel he fails to notice) before sneaking out through the office's second door while gesturing to Manuel to be quiet. He then somewhat inexplicably hits Manuel on the head, making a noise, and claps his hands together loudly, at which point the moose head falls on him again. He is knocked flat, on top of Manuel, and the Major then sits on *him*, drink in hand – mainly to tell off the moose (which he still believes to be either sentient or automated).

The Germans get the last line: staring at the scene in disbelief, they shake their heads. *"However did they win?"*

Andrew Davidson writes that some people who were around John Cleese during the filming of this series say he compared Basil Fawlty to Adolf Hitler. He quotes JHD: *"He said he was a failed Hitler,*[15] *no power... a kind of madman, unwilling to accept the facts. I think there is a bit of Basil in* [many men]. *It's that impotent rage against the world and females."*

In *Fawlty Towers: Fully Booked*[16] John Cleese is quoted as saying that one of his fondest memories is from a visit to Hamburg: *"A German voice shouted to me 'Hey, Mr Cleese, don't mention zee war'. I thought that was terrific. It's taken a little time but I felt really good about that."* He repeats this line, with variations, in many interviews and so it's debatable if it happened *exactly* that way. The viewing figures for *Fawlty Towers* were good in Germany, however, so the details don't matter much. They even attempted a remake, although it did not get terribly far. The events of the episode do not reflect badly on Germany or the Germans, who are the most sympathetic characters in it. One of the German guests shouts at Basil, but understandably and only after his wife has been reduced to tears by Basil's insensitive behaviour. Their demeanour throughout is otherwise calm and dignified, unlike Basil's.

Basil is stuck in the past while the German guests are, like the rest of Europe, moving on.

Unlike other guests that have upset Basil in some way, however, his behaviour towards them is not a defensive response or a natural consequence of events, but stems from an internal and possibly ingrained prejudice that he cannot successfully suppress. When he first encounters them he genuinely is attempting to be polite, but the head injury he sustained has removed a filter from his barely-functional social skills and he rapidly starts to say exactly what he thinks. He starts with a linguicist (see chapter 2) stance, judging their use of their own language as *"something wrong"*, although we can charitably attribute this to his fear that there's something wrong *with him* after his head injury. The relief is visible when he realises they are speaking not gibberish but German. He then starts to break down – not abusing them directly, but raising the spectre of Nazi Germany conversationally, something that was often seen as taboo at that time. Indeed, it is illegal in Germany[17] today to use or discuss many elements of Nazism, including 'forms of greeting' that include the *sieg heil*.[18] British TV was comfortable addressing the Second World War generally – *Dad's Army*[19] and *It Ain't Half Hot, Mum*[20] were big comedy hits at this time (and *Dad's Army* is still popular to this day), and shows like *Colditz*[21] and *Secret Army*[22] addressed the historical drama side – but there was still a mild sense of unease among viewers when Germans or Germany were shown. Gore-Langton describes the episode as the greatest of the show and feels that the episode is not anti-German *per se*: *"more a satire on a particularly buffoonish side to the British character."* However, the viewing public tended to think it *was*. *"They laughed all the harder as Basil stamped like a bison over the guests' feelings in one of the most politically incorrect moments in modern comedy. As usual there was an intellectual justification to the scene."*

John Cleese justifies the behaviour when pressed and believes that the audience wouldn't associate the characters with the war. In 2009, he told[23] *The Guardian* about watching the show with German TV executives in 2000: *"They started off by watching the Germans episode with me and they thought it was hilarious. They do not identify with the Nazis any more than we identify with Nelson. It's long enough gone now. Their fathers were not Nazis so they can laugh at it."* And on the DVD commentary, recorded in 2009: *"If you looked at the Germans, all the people he was interacting with* [in the episode] *are much too young to have had anything to do with the Second World War."* However, Nick Kane and Lisa Bergmayr, playing the older German couple who attempt to rent a car, were both over 60 at the time of filming so their characters would have been in their late 20s during the Second World War. Kane's character – none of the Germans were given names in the script – would have been an active participant, and his wife might have been. Willy Bowman, the older German in the dining room, was also 60 at the time of filming. The younger Germans would have been children old enough to remember 1945, at least. Cleese is disingenuous at best when he claims the characters in the scene had *nothing* to do with the war. Middle-aged and older Germans could be forgiven for thinking the behaviour and the mindset *was* directed at them; middle-aged and older Britons may well have agreed with Basil.

Steve Punt: *"'Who won the bloody war anyway?' That was the attitude of a whole generation. In Britain – ultimately leading to Brexit – there was a whole generation who didn't understand how Germany lost but were then successful. It released a deep-seated national resentment against Germany's recovery – they had the best currency, best cars. We had strikes and inflation and we didn't understand it. I visited Germany with school and found it nothing like the cliches – so polite, so beautiful. I cannot remember any sitcom episode ever that had that cultural impact – it nailed something no one wanted to talk about: resentment."*

Children in playgrounds throughout the 1970s and 80s – the younger half of Generation X – did Hitler impressions by mimicking *Basil Fawlty*, not Hitler himself – finger under the nose, silly walk, *"don't mention the war"*. Yet most of us would have been too young to have watched the show ourselves: we absorbed it from our parents or older siblings, or from impressionists, experiencing this episode as impressions of impressions. Punt notes that the physicality of the goose step is inherently funny and harks back to the Ministry of Silly Walks in *Monty Python's Flying Circus*. The physical fear that the angular and awkward Cleese invokes in reviewers and fans alike when he moves is exacerbated to breaking point when he goose steps, making a movement with frightening connotations completely terrifying.

But for all that it is a very funny episode. Punt's favourite part is *"the fire drill, which gets forgotten about because of the Germans. It has the most brilliant scene with the set up for the fire drill, but the alarm goes off too early. Fawlty is trying to get them to go back. You can tell it's all in real time because it's capped by this superb joke – he demonstrates the two alarms, then there's a two second pause and the phone rings, and he smashes it to pieces. It builds and builds. It's a highlight moment, the result of setting it up slowly and carefully."*

Andrew Sachs wrote[24] that after the show was bought by German TV, the company contacted him to ask if he would play Manuel as a German in their adaptation. They told him that they would not be doing *The Germans*, but he noted that they did show the original episode in Germany: *"which allows me to assert that the Germans are now sufficiently mature psychologically"*.

Between the Wars

The first episode of *Fawlty Towers* was promoted reasonably well in the *Radio Times* – in the 1970s this was the best way to get BBC TV listings, as there was no Ceefax,[1] no on-screen TV guide, no internet. The *TV Times* was no competitor, being only able to provide ITV listings (and later Channel 4) at this time: the BBC had the monopoly on BBC listings. Daily newspapers could provide the evening's listings, and the following day, and weekend papers could cover the whole weekend, but if you wanted to plan your *"televisual feast"* viewing further ahead you bought the *Radio Times*. *Fawlty Towers* did not merit a coveted cover photo – that honour went to *The Explorers*, a David Attenborough series – but it did get a two-page spread with colour photos of John and Connie, a 'pick' on page 3, a review from a regular columnist, and a photo montage on the day's listing. (It would get a front page in February 1979 for the second series, reflecting the increased interest in the show.)

The first series completed filming and was broadcast in autumn 1975 and then almost immediately repeated in January 1976. The Cleeses were repeatedly asked about a second series as their writing partnership clearly worked very well. Their marriage was, however, already shaky during the recording of series 1. April Walker, Jean in *The Wedding Party*, told the *Radio Times* in 2021:[2] *"I didn't realise at the beginning of rehearsals that actually John and Connie were going through a very difficult period in their marriage...* [Cleese would ask Booth] *'Did you enjoy the show you saw last night?' and I thought, 'This sounds very odd to me.'* [Then] *I twigged that they were about to break up."* Andrew Pixley[3] claims that Cleese was already living in another house by that time, and in May 1976 Booth called an end to the marriage. News of their effective separation broke in June 1976.[4] Michael Palin wrote in his diary on 2 June: *disappointingly accurate account of J and C's new living arrangements, whereby they share the house, but not the bed.* He declined to give John Cleese's phone number to a journalist when he was called for information. Sachs, on the other hand, claimed to only notice difficulties between them when rehearsal began for series 2, and thought they were still together: *"Despite what we later learned about their fraying marriage, John and Connie would often make up and even have a cuddle"*. Cleese confirmed that it took two years for the 'doubts' in the marriage to become a formal split, and that he moved in and out and in again before the end. Scales called them "*a happy unit"*, even when they had split.

Cleese does not like blaming the show[5] for the split: '*We bust up for personal reasons, but there was a lot in that relationship that was very positive, and we used the positive parts when we were working together'*. He and Booth are still very complimentary about each other and the show in interviews, even today. Cleese has sometimes said "*all relationships have a clock attached to them*" and he felt that his had simply ended in good time. The couple were so amicable during this period that many of the cast claimed they only realised the couple had split up in 1979 when they arrived at series 2 rehearsals separately – months after their divorce had been finalised. They *were* happy to continue working together, and eventually series 2 would emerge… but not quickly.

A number of other projects would engage both Cleese and Booth in the meantime. In 1976 Cleese started the Amnesty International Benefit concerts, and his work with Video Arts [6]continued – less entertaining than his TV comedy, but infinitely more lucrative.[7] Cleese had been adding fictional films to his CV via the International Film and TV Year Book – *The Bonar Law*[8] *Story, Abbott and Costello meet Sir Michael Swann,*[9] *The Young Anthony Barber,* and *Confessions of a Programme Planner.* He had hoped[10] that someone would notice but apparently gave up after four years and no comment. Booth meanwhile was acting on stage, including a tour of Tennessee Williams's *The Glass Menagerie* in 1977. Both Booth and Cleese starred in *The Strange Case of the End of Civilization as We Know It:* a Sherlock Holmes-inspired comedy, also in 1977.

Palin records in March 1977 that Cleese planned to spend the tax year 1978-79 outside the UK and would be completing the Python film then in pre-production (*Monty Python's Life of Brian*) and "*a series of seven* Fawlty Towers" before that date. We know he did not in fact do so, and this claim may be one source of the 13th episode rumours.[11] The filming of *Life of Brian* did eventually take place that year, after writing had been completed in a 14-month period between December 1976 and January 1978. Booth joined Cleese, while he was filming in Tunisia, to complete the series 2 scripts after their divorce was finalised in September 1978. *Life of Brian* premiered two weeks after the final episode of *Fawlty Towers – Basil the Rat –* was broadcast, and caused consternation among church leaders and commentators who had missed the start of the film (or the *point* of the start of the film), and who were upset at the apparent blasphemy. Cleese would spend quite a lot of December 1979 defending the film.

Gore-Langton describes the second series as "*a killer*". Cleese totted up the time invested in the second series' 3 hours of broadcast material: six weeks of writing for each episode, one week of location filming, and one week in the studio for each episode – a total of 43 weeks, for which he was paid £9000. *"We found the second series so demanding... it was a huge effort to get those scripts as good as I think they finally were."* One of the fears was that the audience would get the jokes too early, as they now knew the Fawltys and staff fairly well. If the show became *too* predictable, it would no longer be fun. The expectation was considered to be unreasonably high, because the audience was remembering all the highlights of series 1, and expecting the scripts for series 2 to match those highlights – which is why they ended up taking so much longer to perfect. The show was formally commissioned and booked in October 1978 and all the scripts – enhanced by a stay in 'the worst hotel in the world' in Tunisia – were submitted to the BBC by Christmas 1978.

During 1977-78 the first series was sold to 45 TV stations in 17 countries, including Germany, where it was very popular – as was *Monty Python* before it – and Spain, where Manuel's nationality was changed to Italian.

On the technical side, Bob Spiers took over the production of series 2, as John Howard Davies had become Head of Light Entertainment. JHD asked Spiers, a relatively new director, to name a show he would like to direct, so he asked for *Fawlty Towers* – and JHD handed it over, to Spiers's amazement. Selected episodes were also released on vinyl so fans could replay them at will – it was still unlikely that the average home would have a video recorder, and video tapes of TV shows were rare items, not commonplace retail items. The show would not be released on VHS tape until 1984. JHD was told the vinyl records wouldn't sell well but he persuaded BBC Enterprises to release them anyway. Veteran radio comedy producer John Lloyd produced them and made £100,000,[12] so JHD asked if he could have a little of that as it had been his idea. He was eventually given a cheque for £25,[13] after writing the sleeve notes as a formal role for which they could pay him. He never cashed the cheque. The first record included *Communication Problems* (as *Mrs Richards*) and *The Hotel Inspectors*; the second *Basil the Rat* and *The Builders* in 1981. The third was *The Kipper and the Corpse* (as *Death*) and *The Germans* (as *Fire Drill*), in 1982. All 12 episodes were released on cassette (and are now available on CD and as an audio book) but no more were made available on vinyl. Andrew Sachs recorded short audio descriptions to link the scenes and explain visual gags to the listener.

An illustrated book of scripts was published in 1977 to satisfy the fans' clamour for more material, although it only featured three of the scripts including arguably one of the weakest episodes, *The Builders*. Book 2, with the other three scripts from series 1, would not be published until 1979. The scripts from series 2 would not appear until the *Complete Fawlty Towers* was published in 1988.

The rumblings of series 3 continued for a while. Sachs wrote:[14] *"'We'll forget about it for a year',* John told us, *'and then decide if there's any juice left in it or whether we ought to try something different'"*. Nicky Henson:[15] *"They offered John everything to do another series, and he said no. There were two series of six and if you do a third series, and it's not as good as the other two, you devalue the currency."* There was nothing left – all the situations had been explored. Booth: *"We felt we'd done it."*

Editors listening to Cleese discuss the show at the 2024 press launch of the West End play must have relished the opportunity to contrast his words: *"We felt after 12 shows that we'd done the best we could possibly do. If we did another series people would say "well it was very funny, but it wasn't as good as the first two series". In which case why do it if you're not desperate for the money?'"* with his deeds: *"As well as the stage show, Cleese is planning a TV sequel*[16] *to* Fawlty Towers *written with his daughter Camilla and set in a luxury Caribbean resort, run by Basil's daughter."*

First Broadcast 19 February 1979[1] – Communication Problems

The sign says: Fawlty Tower – no S. This is the same opening shot from *The Builders* s1e2.

In this episode we meet:
A large number of guests, including:
Mr Yardley (Melvyn Pascoe).
Mr Firkin (Johnny Shannon[2]), a regular visitor who has a hot tip for a filly running at Exeter.
Mr Thurston (Robert Lankesheer[3]) who doesn't mind being interrupted but would like to go to Glendower Street.
Mrs Alice Richards (Joan Sanderson[4]), an elderly woman from Brighton who doesn't like to over-use her hearing aid. She will be staying in room 22.
Mr Mackintosh (Bill Bradley[5]), who disputes a mysterious extra charge on his bill.
A delivery man, Mr Kerr (George Lee), who may be the twin of s1e2's delivery man.

Not seen: On the phone we hear of Mr Hawkins, a supplier who may not be able to deliver something on time but eventually acquiesces; Mrs Richards' sister Stephanie, who is obviously dealing with her estate agent in her absence.
    Frank Sinatra, Winifred Atwell,[6] the fictional Marjorie Atwell (who looks like Winnie apart from not being black), Winston Churchill.

Physical comedy: Mrs Richards bangs her head on the office shelf when Basil mimes speaking to her then shouts at her. Basil mimes the horse's name to Polly. Basil drops the vase.

Sets: hotel lobby, office, dining room, room 22, kitchen.

On the menu: Unusually, while we do see Terry at work in the kitchen and Manuel laying tables in the dining room, no food is mentioned or served in this episode. Basil does ask Terry if he likes *Cavalleria Rusticana*,[7] but Terry has never tried it.

First Broadcast 19 February 1979 – Communication Problems

The hotel is extremely busy. Manuel is carrying a trunk downstairs for a couple, who are leaving, while Sybil gives a receipt to another leaving guest. A third guest asks Polly for the key to no 17 and she confirms she's booked a taxi for him. Brenda the new chambermaid can't start until Monday so Polly agrees to do the rooms until then. Sybil answers the phone to a Mr Hawkins who eventually agrees to deliver an order at 5pm. A fourth guest asks if the hotel accepts cheques (they do, with a bankers – cheque guarantee – card[8]). Mr Thurston, a fifth guest, approaches the desk but Mrs Richards – number six! – interrupts to ask for change for her taxi. Polly asks if Mr Thurston minds being interrupted – he doesn't – so Mrs Richards gets her change and gives it to the driver. Polly returns to Mr Thurston, who wants directions to Glendower St, but Mrs Richards interrupts to insist that she has not yet completed her interaction. Polly diverts her to Manuel, knowing full well that they will not entirely understand each other. A ridiculous conversation of misunderstandings ensues... and Polly finally gets to use the *'he's from Barcelona'* line herself.

Mr Firkin will be checking out as well, and as a parting gesture gives Basil a tip on a horse at Exeter[9] – 3pm, Dragonfly. Polly does not hear this as she moves away, and Basil cuts the conversation short as Sybil appears as well.

Sybil asks pointed questions about the horse. The Major appears and says it is St George's Day (23 April 1979) which would make it a Monday – nearing the end of the spring season for racing at Exeter, a National Hunt[10] course, but not implausible. Basil then says it is actually 8 May, which would be a Tuesday and too late in the year for most races at Exeter. It seems most likely that this is the real date of the episode but that neither of the Fawltys wants to correct the Major, as they've come to realise it would be futile. Although no one in the show would have been able to predict the date during filming, this means that the action of this episode happens in the week after Margaret Thatcher becomes Prime Minister, something Basil would certainly have had an opinion about.

Manuel rushes down to say that Mrs Richards has a problem with her room. The Major is confused about St George and the dragon and the Fawltys' marriage. Eventually he concludes that St George didn't need to marry the dragon, he could have just not turned up at the church... Basil, wisely, doesn't pursue that too far.

Mrs Richards wants to speak to the manager but when Basil identifies himself as the owner she insists on the manager, who – thanks to her earlier conversation with Manuel – she thinks is a Mr CK Watt (*Si! Que? What?*). They confirm that he's the same person. Her room costs £7.20+VAT per night.[11] She wants a bath – Basil demonstrates that her bathroom does indeed have a very 1970s avocado-coloured bath, but it's not considered big enough for her – or, she claims, a mouse. She complains about the view as it's not interesting. Suburban Torquay is not simply good enough. Basil becomes quite sarcastic. What did she expect to see from a Torquay hotel? *"Sydney Opera House? The Hanging Gardens of Babylon? Herds of wildebeest sweeping majestically...?"*

She wants a reduction in her bill to Basil's scorn: *"why, because Krakatoa's not erupting at the moment?"* The room is cold, the bath is too small, the view is invisible, and the radio doesn't work. The radio does work (*"you don't"*), as Basil demonstrates. She can't hear it, so Basil asks if she has a hearing aid. Aha! She does. It's not in need of repair but she doesn't put it on, as it wears the battery out. Basil quietly offers her a 60% discount if she turns the hearing aid on... but she does not hear him. He suggests she speaks to Sybil, passing the buck.

Basil asks Manuel to put the bet on for him – at a time where betting is only legally possible at the racecourse or in licensed betting shops ("turf accountants") his options are very limited, and he cannot go himself or Sybil will guess why he's gone out. We might ask here: Why doesn't he ask Polly? He may already know that Manuel understands betting shops, as betting was seen as a masculine activity. He doesn't know for sure that Polly does, and she may not have agreed to do it.

Sybil is on the phone to her hairdresser discussing her latest wig, which is the wrong colour. *"Cosmopolitan, page 42 – you see Burt Reynolds?"* The audience thinks she means him for a beat, but she goes on to explain that she means a woman in the photograph behind Reynolds, talking to James Caan. Sybil goes to attend to the laundry and Manuel gives Polly Basil's winnings of £75.[12] Polly counts it in the office and Sybil sees her. The Ladies return from an outing and meet Mrs Richards who complains to them about a lack of toilet paper. They offer her some of their personal stock, but she doesn't hear them. Mrs Richards asks Polly for paper – but does not specify further so Polly assumes she means writing paper and asks her what she wants it for and how many sheets she will need, and explains that they keep it in the lounge. Mrs Richards calls for the manager, who she still thinks is Mr Watt. Basil gives up after a brief attempt to explain, and calls Manuel to take toilet paper to her room. He tells Mrs Richards to turn her hearing aid on, but she cannot hear him. He writes her a note but she cannot read it without her glasses. They are on her head but she cannot hear them explaining where her glasses are, and she misunderstands Basil pointing to her head to mean that he is indicating the dining room. Once she leaves Polly takes the opportunity to give Basil the money from Manuel, in the office.

Mrs Richards returns and shouts at Polly for not spotting that her glasses were on her head – *"didn't God give you eyes?"* *"Yes"*, says Polly, *"but I don't use them 'cause it wears the batteries out"*, using Mrs Richards' own argument against her. Manuel has been sent to take toilet paper to room 22 but misunderstands and comes past with arms full – he has brought (at least) 22 rolls.

Basil is very cheerful, celebrating his win in the kitchen with Terry while making himself a snack – presumably some afternoon tea before the dinner rush, as he won't get his own dinner until after 9pm. He sings and dances to *"Camptown Races"* rather tunelessly – director Bob Spiers notes that John Cleese is tone deaf and would have someone sing the song to him before takes. Sybil is suspicious of his good mood – it's unusual for Basil to be happy. He assures her that he is not and that he'll let her know if it happens. *"Just my way of getting through the day, dear. The Samaritans were engaged."* If Basil couldn't entertain himself with such little joys, he implies, he would be suicidal.

Manuel greets him and congratulates him but Basil hushes him with a confusing instruction: *"Manuel, you know nothing."* Manuel is offended – he has been making an effort with his language and is proud of his progress. Basil explains: he means that Manuel should say that he knows nothing about any horse, and calls him *"nitwit"*. Manuel remembers the horse, but also that it was called Dragonfly, not Nitwit. Basil takes pains to clarify with Manuel *"before one of us dies"* that Manuel should forget absolutely everything about the horse. Manuel proudly proclaims that he will forget *"eventually"* – he is proud of his language skills, which have improved considerably since series 1. Tom Salinsky[13] calls this a superfluous scene, but feels is also justified for the jokes alone: *"The scene contains not a scrap of new plot information but is stuffed with brilliant one-liners to ensure not just that we remember it, but that we also don't realise why we have to remember it."* This comes back to bite Basil at the end of the episode – a spectacular brick joke.[14]

Sybil informs Basil that Mrs Richards has had money stolen from her room – £85 (£406 today), taken from a bag which she had hidden under the mattress. Mrs Richards, who has clearly already irritated Sybil, is very cross. She asks Basil what he has to say for himself and he mouths his replies, making her think that her hearing aid is malfunctioning. She adjusts it, at which point he shouts into it, startling her and causing her to bang her head on the shelf behind her. Sybil elbows him out of the way. Basil picks up a crumb from the floor – *"is this a piece of your brain?"* – then threatens to *"visit [her] in the small hours and put a bat up [her] nightdress"*. He reminisces cheerfully with Sybil about their relationship – *"Nice to share a moment like that, isn't it dear? ... Do you remember when we were first manacled together? We used to laugh quite a lot"*. Sybil agrees: *"but not at the same time, Basil"*. He reflects mournfully on how his life is passing him by. We might feel some sympathy for him at this point, if he had not been so cruel to Mrs Richards in the previous scene – however much she deserved it. Sybil asks him what they should do – *"give it another fifteen years?"* he asks with a note of optimism in his voice – but she means the money.

Sybil remembers that Polly was counting money earlier, and Basil tries hard to divert her from thinking about it. Sybil asks Polly about it, after Basil has had a chance to warn her but too soon for them to get their story straight. Polly claims the money is her winnings and that she had put a bet on earlier, when she heard that Basil had been given a good tip. Basil explains that had he been allowed to bet he'd have won £75 on a £5 stake, 14-1. Sybil is suspicious that he knows the exact odds and realises that she may be in the middle of an elaborate ruse. She asks Polly the name, and Basil mimes the horse name to Polly who fails to get it initially... Birdbrain, Fishwife, Fly (after guessing Small when Basil gestures to his trouser fly), Flying Tart,[15] Dragonfly. Jasper Fforde thinks this hints at a previous relationship between Polly and Basil: among his peers, at the time, he says it was widely assumed that Polly and Fawlty had had an affair as Polly says 'small' when Basil points to his crotch. That might be a Booth-Cleese in-joke (which would seem funnier if we didn't know they'd just divorced), or it might be hinting at a previous affair between the characters. As Cleese claims in 2024 that Basil had a child with a guest, Fforde's theory now seems more plausible than in previous years. Certainly it does not seem that Basil's sexual needs are met within his marriage, and while he's too terrified of Sybil to sleep with paying guests – the flirting of Mrs Peignoir and Raylene notwithstanding – there'd be more opportunity with Polly. Sexual exploitation of employees dominates the 1970s, in retrospect.

Sybil threatens Basil: *"you know what I'll do, Basil."* Basil retorts *"You'll have to sew 'em back on first."* Sybil has emasculated him, almost literally. Coupled with the above point about sexual activity, the next episode's claim about the Fawltys' marriage and active sex life seems even less likely to be true.

Basil and the Major are in the bar – the Major claims that he is going to a memorial service (it seems more likely that he has just been to it, as the time is 6pm) and is wearing a loud tie. *"I didn't like the chap."*[16] For an almost inexplicable reason – the plot device is much stronger than the internal logic – Basil gives his winnings to the Major to look after. The Major naturally misunderstands Basil, but eventually leaves with the money. Basil promises to retrieve it from him in the morning and celebrates with a drink. The audience applauds Cleese's ability to throw and catch an ice cube.

The following morning Basil is greeted cheerfully by the Ladies. Mrs Richards interrupts him while he is trying to answer the phone, to ask if he has called the police about her money yet. The phone call is from her sister Stephanie, but Mrs Richards cannot hear her – her hearing aid is not on, so Basil has to intervene and relay the message. Mrs Richards has had an offer of £87K (£415K) for her house in Brighton. She takes the phone to refuse the offer – the price is £92.5K (£442K) and not a penny less. This is more than 4 times the average house price in 1979, and equivalent to around £1.2M in the Brighton housing market today. Basil hears this and decides to remove a disputed 32p from another guest's bill. *"Let's enjoy ourselves."*

The Major has completely forgotten about the money and the remembrance service – *"I don't remember that, old boy"* – to Basil's distress. The Major thinks

First Broadcast 19 February 1979 – Communication Problems

he went to the theatre with a woman who wasn't Winifred Atwell (or Winston Churchill). He eventually remembers and produces the money just as Sybil appears from searching for it, and she claims it for Mrs Richards. Mrs Richards announces that it is £10 short – she had lost £85 and the winnings were £75. Basil has an over-exaggerated response and attempts to raid the charity box to raise the money for her. Sybil continues looking for the missing £10, leaving the lobby to look in the Major's room as he claims it was in his pocket.

Mrs Richards interrogates the Major. Basil tries to explain that this is in fact his money and – another lie – that he's been saving it to buy a present for his wife which of course explains why he can't simply *tell* Sybil about it, in clichéd sitcom fashion. He asks the Major to confirm his story, but the Major fails to remember anything about the previous day, including his own movements, and cannot corroborate anything for him. Manuel appears, so Basil turns to him. Manuel, on cue, remembers that he was told to deny everything. He declaims this dramatically to the group – *"I know nothing, I am from Barcelona."* Basil is distraught.

Mrs Richards leaves Reception to finish her breakfast. Sybil returns and instructs Basil to give her £10 from the till. He headbutts the till then starts to disrobe – *"I'm going to give her the shirt off my back too."* Manuel appears, grinning – he is very proud of himself for doing exactly what he was told to do. Basil is not impressed. *"I'm going to send you to a vivisectionist."* As he is howling quietly into the reception desk, a delivery man appears with a vase for Mrs Richards. Basil feigns fainting, falling backwards through the open office door. It turns out that she bought the vase yesterday and left some money behind in the shop. The cleaner found some money hidden in a dropped glove, and almost threw it away. They have brought it back for her – but it is actually £95, not £85. Basil agrees to give it back. He kisses the sky in triumph and gloats to Polly. *"I'm £10 up on the deal! For the first time in my life, I'm ahead, I'm winning!"* Mrs Richards appears and he gleefully questions her – *"the money that you have there, is it yours or mine?"* She confirms it is hers and that she is still short, so Basil hands over a £10 note. Sybil reappears and asks what is going on and why Basil is holding money. Polly confirms 'her' winnings, and Basil says he was going to put them in the safe for her. All's well… until the Major appears. He has remembered after all, Basil *did* give him the money. *"You won it on that horse!"* Basil, who was handing Mrs Richards her vase, drops it in shock as Sybil snatches the money from his hands. *"That cost £75."* Sybil takes the £85 from Basil and starts to count it out to her…

At the end of the day of course, *someone* is £10 up, as Mrs Richards thought she'd lost £85 but it was in fact £95; from the £85 that Basil was holding at the moment the vase breaks, Sybil will repay her £75. We will never find out whether Sybil puts the £10 in the till or gives it back to Mrs Richards to placate her. It would be more than the cost of her room for the night, if so. Ultimately Basil has lost his original £5 (£23.89) stake despite winning.

Steve Punt loves this episode. *"Basil's speech to Mrs Richards has come to embody sarcasm. So many people can quote it.* "I wish you were a mouse." *Mrs Richards gives as good as she gets, and this is farce. These are not stereotypes, they are stock characters, going back five centuries or more, to Ben Jonson,*[17] *Shakespeare.*[18] *We don't have time to have an intimate background. Mrs Richards is a hard of hearing old lady, tetchy, and exploits her deafness. That is the* dodgy *part – implying that she exploits it."* While it's clear she does manipulate her situation, she is not explicitly exploiting her disability to manipulate people, just to make life easier for herself. Cleese acknowledges that she does exploit it but it's only a minor part of her character.

The most-quoted – and misquoted – line from *Fawlty Towers* may well be from Basil's bedroom rant. *"Hordes of wildebeest sweeping majestically* [across the plain]." He actually trails off before the sentence ends, though most people do not believe this until they re-watch the episode.

Jasper Fforde believes that while the show *"punches down continually"* – poking fun at the old, deaf, demented – *"crucially, it was always still really funny"*. There's *"a little sense of wickedness about it, subversiveness"* which also occurs in other 1970s sitcoms like The Fall and Rise of Reginald Perrin[19] or *"anything with Ronnie Barker and his stutter."*[20] In a similar vein, Top Gear *"on the BBC was funny, despite punching down ... [James May and Richard Hammond] were the acolytes of the funny boy at school"*, a bullying culture but successfully played for laughs. Fforde feels that the show lost the comedy when it left the BBC, something he thinks is crucial when assessing shows like this. *"Being 'cruel' on the BBC is perceived as funnier and less mean than it would otherwise be, because the BBC is a bastion of tradition and authority"*. The comedy lessens the impact of material that might otherwise be quite nasty. Jasper Fforde had what he calls *"a dementia adventure"* with his late mother, in the years before she died in 2023, and he continues to raise money for Alzheimer's UK – but he still confirms Mrs Richards to be *"one of the funniest characters ever written"*. Punching down, or attacking characters weaker than the aggressor or the audience, can still be funny if it is written with heart and not malice.

First Broadcast
26 February 1979[1] – The Psychiatrist

The sign says: WATERY FOWLS. We see the paperboy rearranging the letters.

In this episode we meet:
Mr Johnson (Nicky Henson[2]) who will be staying in room 6, which has a bathroom, and his unnamed extra guest (Imogen Bickford-Smith[3]) who will mainly be staying in room 6's bathroom without Basil's approval.
Dr and Dr Abbott (Basil Henson[4], Elspet Gray[5]) who will be staying in room 5, a twin room which does not have a bathroom. She is a paediatrician – that's children, not feet, despite Basil's belief to the contrary – and he is a psychiatrist.
Raylene Miles (Luan Peters[6]), an Australian who will be staying in room 7, which does have a bathroom.
Mrs Johnson (Aimee Delamain[7]), Mr Johnson's 77-year-old mother.

Not seen: Mr Johnson wants to speak to a John Lawson on the phone. Gladstone,[8] Earl Haig,[9] and Baden-Powell,[10] who are inexplicably not sex symbols. The unknown guest who will be staying an extra night in room 16, meaning that Mrs Johnson cannot have her own room as the hotel is completely full. The Speaking Clock, as Basil cannot get through to it. Audrey, who is having a moan to Sybil after an altercation with her husband.

Physical comedy: Basil listens at the wall of room 5; gropes Raylene in room 7; attempts to shoulder-charge room 6; drops a glass and throws the champagne and bucket at Manuel. He also falls off a ladder [11]outside room 5; turns Manuel upside-down; falls through the door of room 5; accidentally threatens the Abbotts with a broom; grabs Raylene with a hand full of black goop – leaving a handprint on her breast; hides in the wardrobe of room 7, and curls up and hops like a frog. A busy episode for Basil.

Sets: hotel lobby, office, kitchen, dining room, rooms 5, 6, and 7, the Fawltys' bedroom, a cupboard on the upstairs landing, and the upstairs landing itself, which plays a significant role in the farce.

On the menu: Cognac, port, coffee. Grapefruit. Beef. Sandwiches, which Raylene declines. Champagne (one glass per registered guest).

Not on offer: French food – they do offer it in France, where they seem to like it. Sybil sends Mr Johnson to a restaurant in Orchard Street[12] instead. An ice cream cone, which Manuel puts into a plant. Welsh cuisine. Game pie, not actually on the landing wall, despite Basil's assertions.

Basil phones the operator to complain that he cannot get through to the Speaking Clock[13], which appears to be engaged. Sybil is on the phone to Audrey who appears to have sustained an injury caused by her husband George – *"I don't know why she stays with him"* combined with *"call me back when you've staunched it"* suggesting a nosebleed.

Mr Johnson checks in, and tells Sybil the now-clichéd '*pretentious? Moi?*' joke. Sybil flirts with him. Basil thinks he looks like a monkey and makes various pointed remarks about him. Sybil defends attractive men and suggests that Basil would prefer her to think about Gladstone and Earl Haig. Basil does ape impressions, while Sybil deals with the next guests to arrive, the Abbotts.

Basil's tendency to snobbery and fawning behaviour resurfaces when he realises the Abbotts are doctors, although he thinks that Mr Abbott is somehow two doctors – *"did you take the exam twice?"* – as it does not occur to him that Mrs Abbott could be a doctor. He escorts them obsequiously to the stairs.

Mr Johnson explains to Sybil that his mother will be arriving the next day. They've had no luck finding her a room in this or any nearby hotels, so she'll be sharing with him. *"Lucky mum!"* Sybil enthuses over elderly people with *"a good life force"*, then reveals that her own mother has *"more of a death force"*. She recites a long list of her mother's morbid fears: Vans, rats, doorknobs, birds, heights, open spaces, confined spaces, footballs, bicycles, cows, *"and she's always on about men following her, I don't know what she thinks they're going to do to her"*. And death. Sybil does not seem terribly sympathetic to her mother's worries, or to her guest's desire to make his telephone call without interruption.

The Abbotts want to go out before dinner (7.30-9pm tonight), and they borrow a guidebook for Torquay from Mr Johnson. Mr Johnson wants to go out for dinner himself. Basil is nothing but scathing in response to his request so Sybil sends him to a local French restaurant, the Pomme D'Or. There is presumably a good reason for not sending him to André's.

First Broadcast 26 February 1979 – The Psychiatrist

In the dining room Basil offers the doctors post-dinner drinks on the house, in another demonstration of his fawning behaviour. He makes small talk and discovers that Mr Abbott is a psychiatrist, which sends him into a spiral of paranoia and secrecy. Sybil and Terry try to calm him in the kitchen – with some quite affectionate behaviour and phrasing; in the next kitchen scene Sybil even calls him *darling* but this only makes him more worked up. He doesn't *"want some total stranger nosing about in my private parts"*. Off-screen, Cleese had been in therapy for a long time by this point, and would marry a psychotherapist as his third wife. Connie Booth would go on to train as a psychotherapist in the 1980s as well.

Basil claims that everything psychiatrists do is about sex – *"everything's connected with sex. What a load of cobblers"* – inadvertently proving their point. The Abbotts speculate on how the Fawltys can arrange a holiday without closing the hotel (we know that they can, from *The Builders*, although there will be a contradictory claim in *Waldorf Salad*) but Basil misses the context and thinks that they are talking about sex, leading him to claim defensively that the Fawltys 'manage it' two or three times a week, which he considers normal. The Abbotts are perplexed, still thinking Basil is talking about holidays. *"My wife didn't see how you could manage it at all."* Basil is offended, despite his own prudishness, as he believes Dr Abbott is calling his manhood into question. (The audience is justifiably perplexed at the idea of Basil and Sybil having sex multiple times a week; see *Communication Problems* for more evidence regarding this implausibility.) Basil returns to the kitchen and tells Sybil what he thought just happened. She sets him straight. He is absolutely horrified, realising what he has just said to them, and runs after them as they are leaving the lobby for a walk, in an attempt to set the record straight. He shouldn't make so much effort, as they are now even more convinced he's quite mad.

Raylene Miles[14] arrives to check in. She has a lot of cleavage on show and a St Christopher medal above it, which draws Basil's attention. He's not looking at her breasts, *honest*. He compliments her pendant and she thanks him, although she's clearly not offended at the thought that he might also be complimenting her cleavage. Mr Johnson arrives back from dinner, sneaking a girl in behind him and sending her up the stairs while he gets his room key. Basil escorts Raylene to her room instead of Manuel, but she has left a bag behind in Reception and Sybil picks it up. It has taken Raylene 7 hours to arrive at the hotel by coach – presumably from London. As the chef has left for the night and she does not fancy sandwiches, Basil directs her to Leek House,[15] a Welsh restaurant five minutes walk from the hotel. Basil shows her around the room but the light is not working in her bathroom, so he attempts to fix it for her. He gropes around the door frame for the light switch but Raylene is standing there, stretching, and he accidentally gropes her left breast just as Sybil brings in her bag. Despite Basil trying to explain the genuine mistake,

Sybil tells him off in no uncertain terms *"if you're going to grope a girl, have the gallantry to stay in the room with her while you're doing it"*. Basil of course resents this as he *wasn't* trying to grope her – it was accidental.

Basil leaves her room and encounters Mr Johnson leaving his own bedroom – Bob Spiers noting that Nicky Henson couldn't see Basil from behind the door in the set, and so needed a cue from the crew to make his entrance on time. Basil reminds him that he cannot have a guest in his room, and Mr Johnson brazens it out. He asks Basil for champagne and agrees that he will only have one glass, which is all Basil will allow him – one glass per guest. Johnson invites Basil to join him, knowing he will refuse.

The Ladies are concerned that the psychiatrist has *"come for the Major"* – implicitly, to take him away to a psychiatric institution. They are obviously aware that he is declining, and are very relieved to hear that he has not been targeted. Basil enters the Abbotts' room in an attempt to listen to the activity he imagines in Mr Johnson's room. They catch him, and so he claims to be checking the walls. The female Dr Abbott then finds him *"checking the door"* of room 6. He directs her to a communal bathroom at her request. Manuel brings up the champagne, but Basil drops it while attempting to force the door open. He berates Manuel *"you continental cretin! …dago birdbrain, God knows how they ever got an Armada[16] together"*, blaming Manuel for his own clumsiness. The Major warns Basil that there is a psychiatrist in the hotel as well. He is concerned that the psychiatrist is *"dressed up as a guest"* – the Ladies appear to have warned him and they are all suspicious.

Manuel brings a second tray of champagne to replace the dropped one, giving it to Basil[17] who personally delivers Mr Johnson's champagne and single glass, and fails to spot any sign of the 'dolly bird' he believes to be in the room with him (she is hiding in the *en suite* bathroom). He empties the ashtray into his open hand and, outside the room, checks the butts for lipstick. While he is doing this, the male Dr Abbott appears, also wanting directions to the bathroom. Basil sneaks into Raylene's room to *"check the walls"*, thinking she has gone out, and Dr Abbott comes in when he hears her shriek. Basil has been trying to listen at the wall to Mr Johnson's bedroom, although he would in fact be listening at the bathroom wall and not the adjoining bedroom wall. The geography of the hotel is rather flexible and TARDIS-like, at this point, as there is not quite enough space between the room doors to account for both bedrooms and a bathroom. Sybil and Mr Johnson both try to find out what is happening, and Raylene comes out of her room to explain to Sybil as well. She seems very understanding, under the circumstances.

Basil calls Manuel to help him with a ladder, as he intends to look in at the window of room 5 to see Mr Johnson with his girl. Unfortunately he gets the wrong window, and accidentally spies on the Abbotts preparing for bed.

First Broadcast 26 February 1979 – The Psychiatrist

He pretends to be checking the windows in the same manner as the walls. The window is clearly plexiglass, as it wobbles. Manuel lets go of the ladder so Basil falls off. Manuel rushes to get Sybil to help Basil: *"he try to see girl, she drive him crazy"*. Sybil thinks he means Raylene again. Outside the hotel, she slaps Basil. Back inside, she storms upstairs and, slapping him again, locks him out of their bedroom when he tries to explain about the girl. Her earlier good mood and affectionate manner have completely vanished. Manuel explains that he had told Sybil about Basil and the girl, thinking he is helping, so Basil silently picks him up and shakes him. Dr Abbott appears from the bathroom in her dressing gown in time to witness this. Basil pretends that he is merely training Manuel in the art of hotel management, and manages to fall through the Abbotts' open doorway in the process.

Basil isn't sure where he can sleep – there are no empty rooms and he cannot get into his own, so he sleeps in the landing cupboard. Polly arrives with breakfast trays and sees him crouching on the landing. He attempts to make peace with Sybil, with her breakfast tray, but she won't have it. He persuades her to open the door by asking for his razor and tries again to tell her the truth. She agrees to hear him out and he explains that Mr Johnson has smuggled a girl in and that is the source of his agitation, not the Australian guest.

There is a knock on Mr Johnson's door and his girlfriend hides in the bathroom again – but it is only Dr Abbott returning his guidebook. Basil pounces, broom in hand, as she emerges from the room – but of course Mr Johnson has not had Dr Abbott staying in his room overnight! He pretends that there is something on the wall and sweeps above his head. The Abbotts despair as they walk away: *"there's enough material there for an entire conference"*. Basil accidentally touches something disgusting and dirty in the cupboard before bursting out to grab the strange woman he hears on the landing – but it's Raylene. He has managed to grope her breasts again, and leaves a black handprint on her top. Sybil emerges to see this altercation, and he gropes Raylene a third time in his confusion. Basil goes into Raylene's room but realises she is changing clothes and unaware of his presence, so when there is a knock on her door he hides in her wardrobe in panic. Sybil comes to apologise to Raylene, who has been in her bathroom. Raylene is still willing to give Basil the benefit of the doubt until they both spot Basil in the wardrobe. *"Do you imagine, even in your wildest dreams, that a girl like this could possibly be interested in an ageing Brilliantined stick-insect like you?"* Basil's hair has Brilliantine[18] in it, a hair cream that makes it sleek and shiny. He explains that he's been checking the wardrobe doors and hinges... but finally understanding that this story doesn't work, he comes clean: he came to apologise and he's been trying to see the girl in room 6. They argue for some time on the landing, with Sybil accusing him of wanting to grope the guests, a jibe too far for prudish Basil.

"Shut up!" "Oh, you've done it now." Sybil's tone is quiet and calm, but deadly. Basil loses his temper and tells her what he really thinks. *"I'm fed up with you, you rancorous coiffured old sow. Why don't you syringe the doughnuts out of your ears?"*

Basil attempts again to reveal Johnson's guest – opening the door of his room to accost him while Sybil waits. Mr Johnson agrees with him when he asks: Mrs Johnson *is* in the room. Basil thinks he has him now – *"I thought you told my wife that you were single... so who's this Mrs Johnson?" "She's my mother." "This bit of crumpet's your old mummy, is she?"* He taunts her to come out – and she emerges. It *is* Mr Johnson's mother. Basil cringes and offers her some champagne.

The Ladies and the Major are behind Sybil at the top of the stairs, all watching. They all leave, and the Abbotts come up the stairs after them. Basil has folded his hands over his head in despair, and is hopping up and down on the landing like a frog, just in time for the Abbotts to see him doing it. *"I'm on holiday"* says Dr Abbott.

This episode attracts surprisingly little criticism, even though it features behaviour that could be considered voyeurism and sexual assault – crucially, Basil really does not mean to do it. Where most claims made in this vein are dubious when examined, we can see for ourselves that he is focused on the *other* young woman staying in the hotel, the one he wants to prevent from being sexually active with a guest. He wants his prudish side to win, not his voyeuristic side.

We are told that the hotel is fully booked, so for plausibility we have to accept the conceit that Raylene is the only attractive single woman staying – at least, officially. Despite Basil's claims to be in a sexually active marriage, he is really quite neutral, even *neutered*[19], in demeanour, so Raylene is not obviously made uncomfortable by his behaviour, despite the groping, right up until he hides in her wardrobe near the end of the episode. She accepts his truthful explanation that the groping was accidental on both occasions, and also overlooks the attention her cleavage gets at the start of the episode. Even Sybil gives him the benefit of the doubt initially. Basil is not a sex pest in anyone's view, and he is not particularly prone to flirting, despite Sybil's watchful eye and occasional remarks. She is more of an open flirt than he is, and clearly finds Mr Johnson attractive, just as she does Mr Brown, Mr Libson, and a number of other single male guests. Bob Spiers notes that Prunella Scales was very good at flirting. Spiers also records that Cleese told him just before filming that his own psychiatrist was in the audience, which must have been alarming.

Right: Blue plaque on Sachs Lodge, Ashelden Road, Torquay. *Copyright Rob Hurley 2024*

Below: BBC studio recording ticket for The Builders, 3 August 1975. *Wikimedia Commons*

BBC tv LIGHT ENTERTAINMENT presents

JOHN CLEESE
starring in
"FAWLTY TOWERS"
by John Cleese and Connie Booth
with
PRUNELLA SCALES
ANDREW SACHS
and
CONNIE BOOTH

BBC tv
Television Centre

Sunday
3rd August, 1975

Doors open 7.30 p.m.
Doors close 7.45 p.m.

Complimentary Ticket
Not for Sale

Children under 14
Not Admitted

Basil as Roger Mellie and Manuel as Sid the Sexist, Viz issue 337 cover, August 2024. *Copyright Simon Thorp. Reproduced by kind permission of Viz magazine*

Unused version of Viz cover image, August 2024. *Copyright Simon Thorp. Reproduced by kind permission of Viz magazine*

Above left: Basil, as portrayed by Adam Jackson-Smith, July 2024. *Author's own photograph*

Above right: Mrs Richards, as portrayed by Rachel Izen, July 2024. *Author's own photograph*

Left: Polly, played by Victoria Fox, July 2024. *Author's own photograph*

Above left: Manuel, played by Hemi Yeroham, July 2024. *Author's own photograph*

Above right: Mr Thurston et al, as portrayed by Greg Haiste, July 2024. *Author's own photograph*

Right: The Apollo Theatre, Shaftesbury Avenue, London, July 2024. *Author's own photograph*

Above left: Andrew Sachs as Manuel.
© *MovieStillsDB*

Above right: Connie Booth as Polly.
© *MovieStillsDB*

Left: John Cleese as Basil.
© *MovieStillsDB*

Prunella Scales as Sybil, John Cleese as Basil.
© *MovieStillsDB*

Basil frantically retyping the menu for Gourmet Night.
© *MovieStillsDB*

Basil explaining how many donkeys should be on the trays. Manuel is confused.
© *MovieStillsDB*

Basil attempting to impress the Doctors Abbott. © *MovieStillsDB*

Basil, Polly, and Manuel looking as professional as possible. © *MovieStillsDB*

First Broadcast 26 February 1979 – The Psychiatrist

This episode was full of technical challenges for the filming crew, as it includes a large number of sets and a lot of cast movement in and out of doors. This is very difficult to film without cues for the actors, as they cannot see when Basil is outside the relevant door, so crew members would be hiding in the set to cue some entrances. The effort pays off, as 'door acting' is a key element of theatrical farce. Spiers notes that timing is crucial for farce, especially as set doors *"notoriously don't open"* first time, and that the audience will not laugh as much if they see a big physical joke for a second time – for example, Basil dropping the tray and Manuel catching the champagne. The technical constraints also worried him when filming certain scenes: the staining of Raylene's top meant that if they had to reshoot they would have to clean John Cleese's hand thoroughly and change her top, and they could not then edit in any previous shots as the hand print would move. He calls this an *exhausting* episode, and it is.

First Broadcast
5 March 1979[1] – Waldorf Salad

The sign says: FLAY OTTERS.

In this episode we meet:
Mr and Mrs Johnston (Terence Conoley again, June Ellis[2]) whose prawns may not be entirely edible.
Miss Doris Hare and Miss Gurke (Dorothy Frere,[3] Beatrice Shaw[4]), whose food is not particularly nice either.
Mr and Mrs Arrad (Norman Bird,[5] Stella Tanner[6]), who wanted the cold meat salad but got the wrong dish, after waiting half an hour.
Mr Libson (Anthony Dawes[7]), who is listening to Sybil's travel monologue and is still waiting for his radiator to be fixed (he has only asked three times).
Mr and Mrs Harry Hamilton (Bruce Boa,[8] a Canadian, and Claire Nielson[9]) – he's an Ugly American who apparently dislikes England, she's an Englishwoman now living in California. They will be staying in room 12.

Not seen: Burt Lancaster, who may or may not have a palm tree. Marcel Proust.

Physical comedy: Basil berates an invisible chef. *"I just smashed his backside about it."* Basil removes the salad from Mr Hamilton's hands. Clearly Sybil hits him off screen. Kitchen starts smoking during steak cooking though no evidence of it once Mr Hamilton goes in. Mr Hamilton threatens to punch him.

Sets: Hotel dining room, lobby, kitchen.

On the menu: Prawn salad, plaice with sugar, plaice without sugar, lamb, fruit salad (*"chef's just opened the tin"*[10]), paté, grapefruit with a cherry. Vodka and bottled orange juice (forget the screwdrivers). Scotch. Lettuce and tomato, green salad. Rare steaks. Waldorf salad once Sybil takes charge.

First Broadcast 5 March 1979 – Waldorf Salad

Not on offer: Cold meat salad. Salt in the salt cellar. Screwdrivers. Waldorfs. Ritz salad (apples, grapefruit, and potatoes in mayonnaise – this sounds revolting, but clearly Basil is panicking). Freshly *squeezed* orange juice.

Unlike most other episodes, this takes place almost entirely in real time – the evening of the Hamiltons' arrival.

Sybil is talking at guests rather than helping to serve dinner – she talks about how hectic life can be while Basil *runs* around the dining room doing all the actual work. Basil speaks to Mrs Johnston, who says her prawns are off. He argues with her, pointing out that she has eaten half of them. When Mr Johnston asks Basil to deduct them from the bill and Basil argues, the compromise suggested is that they deduct half now and the rest if she brings up the other half later. Manuel silently brings a water jug into the dining room, looks bemusedly around him, fails to see Mr Arrad proffering his glass, and deposits the jug on another table. That table's guests, Miss Hare and Miss Gurke, complain to each other about the meat – *"it's all gristle"* – but in true English fashion assure Basil everything is fine when he asks them about it. Manuel brings the wrong food to Mr and Mrs Arrad, who attempt to complain to Basil but find that he complains to them about Manuel, to their bewilderment. Manuel inspects Mr Arrad's dish closely before Basil puts it back while Manuel attempts to mime that he believes there's a problem. We don't find out what Manuel thinks has happened to this dish but from the mime and the close inspection Basil and Manuel give the dish, it may be a bug of some kind; meanwhile Mrs Arrad has managed to put sugar on her plaice as there is, inexplicably, sugar in the salt cellar. Terry the chef has already clocked off but does agree to replace the ruined plaice.

Sybil continues to monopolise solo diner Mr Libson, ignoring the other guests and the bell at reception; Mr Libson does not appear to be enjoying the conversation. Basil snipes at Sybil then takes the Johnston's mains – two lambs – to reception with him. Mr Johnston comes to collect them, sarcastically recommending the "self-service" restaurant to Mrs Hamilton.

The Hamiltons are at reception. She is perky and well-dressed, in a long fur coat, so Basil is nice to her. Mr Hamilton, who arrives slightly later, is unhappy about the weather and the distance from London, the M5 motorway[11] (*"a little backstreet"*), and generally grumpy. Basil is openly rude to him until he realises the couple are together, and once again we see his demeanour change from hostile and aggressive to fawning. Mr Hamilton asks about dinner although it is past 9pm and Basil is apologetic, suggesting they go straight in to make things easier, but Mr Hamilton is insistent that he wants to freshen up first.

Mr Hamilton insists that he wants dinner, and is unhappy that the chef stops at 9 – *"has he got something terminal?"* This is interesting as the stereotype of

Americans is that they eat dinner much earlier than the British generally do. They have driven 5 hours from London to get there, and could have stopped on the way.[12] Hamilton complains that in *"this country you cannot get a drink after 3"* – for younger viewers, the time before all day drinking was possible is now hard to imagine. Hamilton is referring to the hours dictated by law in England and Wales at the time – pubs could only open 11am-3pm and 6pm-11pm, with an early closing time on Sunday nights. The Major's habit of appearing at the bar on the dot of 6pm is another reference to this (hotel bar hours were permitted to be more flexible for residents though, usually choosing to stay open a little later). Scotland relaxed its restrictions in 1977, allowing local authorities to set their own hours, but England and Wales – and therefore Torquay – had to wait until 1988.

Mr Hamilton offers £20[13] (the equivalent of three nights' stay in 1979, or around £125 in 2024) to keep the chef on for 30 mins. Basil goes to speak to Terry, who is just finishing up in the kitchen. He claims he has a karate class to go to, and Polly calls him. Terry negotiates with Basil – two hours overtime and he'll stay for 30 mins and be late for his class. Basil settles on 1.5hrs overtime, cash, and Terry leaves at 9.30. Polly gives the game away however – Terry doesn't have a karate class to go to, he has a date with a hot Finnish girl. Basil retracts the offer and the money, and dismisses Terry for the night. Polly and Manuel also leave, so it's just Basil and Sybil left to deal with the Hamiltons. Basil shows them to a table, and Sybil, who is just finishing a starter, asks about their room then goes to the kitchen. Basil brings them a menu and offers them a drink – Mr Hamilton requests a Scotch and water, and a screwdriver.[14] Basil is flummoxed, having never heard of this drink. He thinks that something is wrong with their room and that they plan a little DIY. Mrs Hamilton eventually takes pity on Basil and explains to him what a screwdriver is.

Sybil sits down with her main course and chats to the Hamiltons. Mrs Hamilton explains that she has lived in California for 10 years now, praising the climate there. Mr Hamilton hates the climate in England, finding it too gloomy – and he is rather a gloomy person himself. Basil tries to defend England – particularly the English Riviera[15] – but Sybil gives away his lie, explaining that he complained at length about the weather earlier the same day. The Hamiltons dislike the screwdrivers Basil has brought, as he used bottled orange juice instead of fresh – this was very common in the 1970s,[16] and of course the Hamiltons, living in California with fresh orange juice freely available, can tell the difference.

Sybil is reading a Harold Robbins[17] novel – the Hamiltons like him but Basil lays into the 'awful rubbish' before realising this. He covers by explaining that he's talking about Harold Robinson, whom he has made up on the spot.

Mr Hamilton asks for a Waldorf salad and Basil doesn't understand what this is either. He questions them a couple of times, attempting to offer paté or

First Broadcast 5 March 1979 – Waldorf Salad

grapefruit instead, and speaks to an imaginary chef. Sybil hears about the £20 when Mr Hamilton complains about the salad, and she interrogates Basil. She takes charge – in the time it takes for her to get the truth about the £20 and for Basil to complain to her she has found the apples, and she assures him she will look for the celery and other ingredients. Basil invents a substitute 'Ritz salad', then when that offer is rejected he tells Mr Hamilton a long shaggy dog story about a delivery driver who may have fractured his arm, in order to explain the possible absence of celery. Mr Hamilton loses his temper. *"Is this a hotel or isn't it?"* Basil responds, somewhat enigmatically: *"well, within reason."* Hamilton squares up to Fawlty – he is nearly as tall and possibly angrier – and tells him to bust the chef's ass, an instruction that Basil is also bewildered by. He is intimidated by Hamilton, repeating back all the instructions to him meekly or shouting them angrily at the imaginary chef in the kitchen. He just about manages to prevent Hamilton bursting into the kitchen himself, which would expose the lie.

Sybil brings the green salad and Waldorf salad, which she has had no trouble assembling, and then goes to reception briefly before returning to her own dinner. Basil meanwhile has a loud conversation with himself off-screen, as 'the chef', then appears with two more green salads, explaining why he can't bring the Waldorf salad and claiming to have *"smashed his backside"* about it. Sybil assures him that there wasn't a problem, but Basil removes Mr Hamilton's salad to the kitchen where he continues to pretend to have a conversation with 'chef', apparently hitting him off-screen. Sybil brings back the salad and asks Basil to bring the wine – when he appears through the doors it is clear that Sybil hit him. She reminds 'chef' to put the steaks on.

Sybil tells the Hamiltons that the Fawltys haven't had a proper holiday for 8 years, contradicting the claims made in *The Psychiatrist*, and ignoring the short breaks they do regularly manage, as seen in *The Builders*. She has a long list of things she does to relax – it is noticeable that all of them are solo or 'girls night' activities. Basil, wearing a hat dipped over one eye to cover a mark from being hit, brings the wine and proffers an apology letter from the chef. He is very insistent that the Hamiltons read it, and when they refuse he reads it to them. Naturally the letter exonerates Basil. Smoke starts to appear from the kitchen, where the steaks are burning. Basil slumps in despair, then rushes back there and yells at the invisible chef again, unaware that Mr Hamilton has appeared from the dining room and can see that no one else is there. He attempts to cover his lies by claiming that the chef was there a moment ago, but Mr Hamilton does not believe him and suggests to his wife that they leave. Basil can't leave it alone and continues trying to excuse himself. Mr Hamilton loses his temper again.

A crowd gathers as guests appear from the bar and down the stairs, drawn by the yelling. He calls it the crummiest, shoddiest, worst-run hotel in Western

Europe. The Major angrily defends the hotel – or not. *"No! No, I won't have that! There's a place in Eastbourne..."*

All the guests are polled as to whether or not they are happy, and the regular residents confirm that they are quite content really. Basil defends the hotel, channelling Winston Churchill in a surprisingly calm inspirational speech, which sounds like it is working until a little voice – Mr Johnston – says he is not satisfied, and neither is his wife. All the guests start to speak up – re-airing their complaints about 'off' prawns, broken radiators, the half-hour wait for food, and so on. Mr Hamilton threatens to bust Basil's ass – as Basil says, *"everything's bottoms with you"* – before tightening his tie comically tight. Basil finally snaps and yells at the guests. *"This is typical, absolutely typical. The kind of arse I have to put up with from you people. You ponce in here expecting to be waited on hand and foot. Well I'm trying to run a hotel here... this is exactly how Nazi Germany started. A lot of layabouts with nothing better to do except cause trouble. Pack your bags and get out".* Mr Hamilton offers to pay for 10 taxis,[18] for all the guests assembled. Basil breaks into German again to shoo them out – *"Raus! Raus!"*[19] – perhaps he has learned some key phrases since *The Germans*. Sybil intervenes and Basil challenges her with a threat – either they go or he does. Her unblinking gaze gives him the answer and so he tells them all to stay – he'll leave. Basil bids farewell to the hotel and Sybil – *"have fun helping to run a hotel"* is a particularly barbed jibe, given how little he feels she does – and walks out into the pouring rain. Mr Hamilton calls the taxis. When Basil returns, soaking wet, he asks Sybil for a room – noting that room 12 is now free – and reels off a list of demands including eggs, bacon, tomato and Waldorf salad for breakfast, washed down with a hot screwdriver. The Hamiltons leave quietly behind him, while the Major raises a glass cheerfully. He isn't going anywhere.

~

Mr Hamilton, while as grumpy and picky as Mr Hutchinson (*The Hotel Inspectors*) is possibly the only guest who is even angrier than Basil Fawlty. While Basil is mildly unreasonable – and actively lies to him – Hamilton is very unreasonable himself, and has anger management issues. The viewer's sympathy lies mostly with Basil as Hamilton is rude from the outset and doesn't seem to understand that the UK isn't the USA and that some things will need explaining or adapting. He was also wrong about a Waldorf salad, which didn't typically include grapes in 1979,[20] although it now does as a result of the character's insistence.

This episode divides viewers: while many take the episode at face value and understand the tension raised by cultural differences, you can also find reviews from younger British viewers who are baffled by the confusion in the episode as globalisation has smoothed out many regional and cultural differences; Americans who cringe in embarrassment at the portrayal of the Ugly American; some who don't understand why Basil fails to understand Hamilton's seemingly straightforward requests; and even some who don't realise Boa was meant to *be* American,[21] which suggests a severe lack of attention to the episode's dialogue!

The history of the relationship between the USA and the UK in the 20th century alone would fill a whole book, but a contextual point that younger viewers may miss is a particular British attitude, held over from the Second World War (compare with *The Germans*), that Americans were obnoxiously '*overpaid, oversexed, and over here*', and not really welcome. A resentment of their relationships with British women, their apparent abundance of money to spend, and their unwanted physical presence in British spaces still persisted, nearly 40 years after American forces arrived in the UK. Americans were – and sometimes still are – perceived to be looking down their noses at the British, and Hamilton's remarks about the motorway, opening hours, and the weather all serve to irritate the audience, even before he and Basil butt[22] heads. The jibes about British cuisine, famously sneered at by American GIs in the 1940s[23] and other tourists in this period, do not improve matters. The provision of bottled orange juice doesn't help the UK's case, but Mrs Hamilton is correct: this *was* the norm at the time and her husband *does* have to accept that there will be some problems with his demands.

As an additional complication, British holidaymakers were legally limited in their ability to travel overseas with any significant amount of money, so there is a significant degree of envy stirred in those watching Mr Hamilton throw large amounts of money at Basil to keep the chef on, and hearing the fur-wearing Mrs Hamilton talk about her luxurious-sounding life in America. To more modern eyes there is nothing particularly offensive or controversial here, of course, as we can now take travel and fresh orange juice for granted.

The most obvious US-UK relationship at play is of course that of the writers, who had divorced – amicably – by the time this episode was written and filmed, and it is tempting to think that some aspects of the script reflect the Cleese-Booth relationship and any unresolved tensions therein. However, Connie Booth remained in the UK – her daughter was of school age when the couple divorced – and lives in London with her second husband to this day. Cleese, meanwhile, married two more American wives and has lived all over the world, including in the USA – although his fourth wife is British. Any international tension we see in this episode is a result of the characters' own neuroses and the audience's projection.

Spiers discusses the intensity of the farce and timing in the opening scene and is extremely impressed that the cast managed to pull this episode together with a mere five days of rehearsal. The choreography is amazing, a ballet of silent moves and dialogue, which the sound department captured perfectly – we hear only a very small amount of noise from other diners, which is plausible. The scene requires a lot of props and intense concentration from the cast. He talks about how he sees the flaws in the filming, more than 25 years later – a camera zoom that should have been edited out, the reflection of a studio light, a boom shadow – but that they dwell more in his mind than they do for the viewer. Most people would not notice these flaws, or would rationalise them away – the reflected lamp could be a hotel feature, for example. The show was *"going out two weeks ahead of us"* – a claim that is true of most of this series but not this particular episode which was filmed six weeks before broadcast, as the order was changed. The problem for the cast was that the newspaper critics and reviewers were giving feedback on the start of the series, *Communication Problems* (then also known as *Mrs Richards*, as episode titles were not finalised even at broadcast), while the cast were still filming later episodes. Spiers notes that audiences were inevitably comparing the two series, and so there was a pressure to be as funny as the first series, especially after the long gap between them. *"There was a feeling…* [that it] *just wasn't as good as the first."* But time has proved that it was as strong. *"Now they are interchangeable – nobody really knows which was the first series and which was the second series."* An original shooting script of this episode would sell for £12,000[24] in 2023.

Spiers describes the final scene of the episode as one of the *"nightmare scenes"* that appeared in the scripts from time to time – a large ensemble of actors, technically difficult to block and film, and a long rant from Basil. He points out that Cleese would wreck his voice doing this week after week, so there had to be a bit of space between such rants.

First Broadcast
12 March 1979[1] – The Kipper and the Corpse

The sign says: FATTY OWLS

In this episode we meet:
Mrs Chase (Mavis Pugh[2]) and her dog Prince, a Shih-tzu, who likes walnuts and cheese footballs.
Mr and Mrs White (Richard Davies[3], Elizabeth Benson – a repeat performance as a different character), staying in room 18.
Mr Andrew Leeman (Derek Royle[4]), staying in room 8. He's not feeling too good, even before he checks in.
Dr Price (Geoffrey Palmer[5]), who is quite hungry.
A couple in room 12, a small elderly gentleman (Len Marten[6]) and a tall redhead (the uncredited Julie La Rousse[7]). From Sybil's phone conversation we gather this may not be his wife.
Mr Leeman's friends Mr Xerxes, Mr Zebedee and Miss Young (Robert McBain, Raymond Mason, Pamela Buchner[8]) who drop him off and come back for him the next day.
Mr Ingrams (Charles McKeown[9]), also assigned to room 8, who puts his pyjamas on shortly after checking in at 8am, and has a blow-up sex doll. McKeown was a frequent *Python* collaborator.

Not seen: Sybil and Audrey are discussing some regular guests on the phone. *"No, that wasn't him, that was a new one."* Polly calls Mr Simkins, the local undertaker; his men arrive near the end of the episode.

Physical comedy: There's a kipper in Basil's jumper. The staff carry a body out of a bedroom disguised as laundry, and Miss Tibbs folds sheets on top of the corpse. Polly slaps Miss Tibbs when she has a panic attack. Basil hides the corpse in a wardrobe but also locks Miss Tibbs in by mistake. Mr Leeman's arm falls out of the wardrobe door. Miss Tibbs faints when she finds Mr Leeman in the office. They take him outside when attempting to hide him, just in time for other guests to see the corpse and crash their car. Then he visits the kitchen, going into the laundry hamper. Dr Price refuses to let him stay there so back to the lobby they go. Manuel & Dr Price mimic a bullfight when trying to get food. Manuel gets poked in the eye. The laundry firm takes the hamper – but Basil is hiding in it.

Sets: hotel lobby, bar, kitchen, dining room, room 8, room 18, Miss Tibbs' room. She has a photo by her bed and a lilac continental quilt (duvet) on her bed, unlike the bedding we see in other rooms – this is her own personal bedding, as she lives there permanently.

On the menu: Scotch. Sandwiches – ham, cheese, tomato (Dr Price opts for ham). A saucer of warm milk, a bowl of tepid milk. Continental or full breakfast – eggs, bacon, sausage, tomato, fried bread. Kippers, which should have been eaten by the 6th of the month. Orange juice. Toast, butter, marmalade, tea and coffee.

Not on offer: sausages (chef will have locked them away in the evening; Dr Price has to cook them himself in the morning – but they are even more out of date than the kippers, being dated 3rd of the month). Cheese footballs, reindeer.

The Major talks to Mrs Chase about her dog but does not understand the breed name – Shih-tzu – and mishears "Lap dog" as "Lapp dog" – he doesn't think they could catch a reindeer. Dr Price asks for sandwiches and Sybil goes to organise those. The phone rings in the background. Basil speaks to the couple in the bar while Sybil speaks on the phone. The couple go to bed, and Mr Leeman's friends drop him off, establishing in their parting conversation that he's not feeling terribly well. He asks for breakfast in bed, which Basil is sarcastic about, but Sybil obliges, offering him a choice. He opts initially for continental – looking rather bilious at her description of the full fried breakfast – but then agrees to kippers.

Basil, still in full sarcastic flow, suggests that Mr Leeman sleeps with his mouth open so that Basil can drop in pieces of kipper to avoid effort. He looks around for Sybil, fully expecting to be told off for this impertinence, but she is not there so he slaps his own hand and imitates her.

At breakfast the next morning Dr Price wants sausages and coffee; Mrs Chase orders eggs for herself and a bowl of tepid milk and a plate of sausages for her dog, as well as another cushion. Basil discovers that the kippers[10] are out of date but everyone assures him they will be fine.

Manuel gets confused when positioning the dog, the cushion, and his milk, as Mrs Chase berates him constantly – *"on the table, on the table... now put that under him!"* – and the dog bites him. She tells Manuel off and appears to think he is from Calcutta. Polly brings the eggs and sausages and gets involved in preparing food for the dog at the table. When she attempts to help Manuel, she is bitten too.

Basil worries about the kippers, but Sybil makes him take the breakfast up to Mr Leeman – it's after 8am. The laundry men are coming and Sybil must deal with that instead – *"My god, the woman's work is never delegated".*[11] Polly spices up the sausages intended for the horrible dog, using Tabasco sauce – a surprisingly vindictive move on her part. The dog is quite unhappy about this, and Mrs Chase becomes distraught.

Basil rants at Mr Leeman, failing to notice that he is not responding. He thinks Mr Leeman is being rude, just as he perceived him to be the previous night. Basil got up at 5.30 this morning and feels disgruntled at the lack of response to his effort. He leaves the room muttering about the rudeness displayed. He gets very little response from Sybil, Terry, or Manuel either. Polly takes up some milk, which Basil had forgotten to add to the tray. Basil complains to Sybil that Mr Leeman did not speak to him, after she eventually acknowledges his presence. Terry cooks Dr Price's sausages. Polly announces Mr Leeman's death and Manuel, distracted from filling a salt cellar, covers the doctor's sausages in salt, rendering them inedible. Basil panics about the kippers and rushes upstairs to remove them from Mr Leeman's tray. Polly calms him down and Basil realises that Mr Leeman is cold and has been dead for hours – a huge relief as it means that the hotel is not responsible for the death after all.

Sybil brings Dr Price to examine the body, interrupting his breakfast, and Basil opens a window while still clutching the kippers. Dr Price asks who found him, and Polly says she brought up the milk – but not the tray, Basil had brought that. Dr Price is incredulous and doesn't believe the sequence of events as explained to him – Basil spoke to the dead man but Polly then brought up the milk? This doesn't make sense to him. Dr Price announces that Mr Leeman has been dead for about 10 hours[12] and wonders why Basil didn't notice. Basil rants about not assuming guests are going to die in the night. Basil repeats that he has been up since 5.30am and is very tired. Dr Price is also baffled by the kipper sticking out of Basil's jumper. *"I've been looking for that!"* says Basil as Sybil ushers him out of the room. When they get downstairs and she tells him to get rid of it, he throws it into the kitchen.

Sybil hurriedly makes up a bill to leave in Mr Leeman's wallet, although she does refrain from charging him for breakfast. Polly calls the undertaker, although when Miss Gatsby appears in reception she talks instead about 'somebody, anybody', attempting to cover up the death and avoid upsetting Miss Gatsby. Miss Tibbs sees Manuel and Basil moving the body along the upstairs landing, and attempts to help before realising that they are carrying a corpse. Polly arrives and slaps her before she can become completely hysterical but she faints. Manuel and Basil carry both bodies, living and dead, into room 18, as it is the closest. That room's occupants appear on the stairs at just that moment, as the unwritten rules of farce demand. It would be far too simple if Manuel and Basil simply got away with their plan.

Polly delays the guests, and warns Basil that Mr & Mrs White want to come into their room. Not unreasonably, they just want their things, but Basil locks the bedroom door to keep them out. Mr White is increasingly cross about this. We see Basil and Manuel put Mr Leeman in the room's wardrobe and shut the door, before the guests are let in. We hear moaning from their wardrobe – the audience haven't seen before now that Miss Tibbs is also in the wardrobe so this is a surprise. She has regained consciousness and, finding herself staring at a corpse, is very distressed. Manuel sings to cover her moans, before she knocks on the wardrobe door. Basil claims to have lost the key but Manuel helpfully reminds him that it is in his pocket and retrieves it, to Basil's obvious irritation. Manuel rescues Miss Tibbs from the wardrobe and Polly consoles her. Basil pretends to the Whites that the old lady often hides in cupboards, and tells her off. Polly attempts to signal to Basil that Mr Leeman's arm has also come out of the wardrobe door, but it takes him a while to get the hint. He distracts the guests by jumping up and down in the corner by the bedroom door while Polly puts the arm back, and Manuel starts dancing in imitation of Basil.

Sybil reassures Miss Tibbs, in her bedroom, that Mr Leeman would not have done her any harm – *"he was dead, dear"*. Miss Tibbs is not convinced that this makes any difference to his behaviour – *"a man is a man!"* Miss Tibbs claims that they are the hotel's oldest residents, and plans to complain to Basil about the experience. Manuel and Basil take the corpse to the office, where the Major appears. He is looking for the morning newspaper, which is already tucked under his arm. He thinks Mr Leeman doesn't look well and cautions Basil against keeping the corpse in the office. Dr Price is still waiting for breakfast so Basil goes to cook the sausages.

Shrieking is heard from the direction of the office. Miss Tibbs has found Mr Leeman's corpse and, after a good deal of screaming, faints again. Basil and Manuel take the corpse to the kitchen but have to divert to the exterior of the hotel, where the Whites are just leaving – they have apparently given up on their stay in the hotel. Polly takes the laundry to the kitchen and Mrs Chase requests that they call a vet for her 'seriously ill' dog who is suffering from the spiced-up sausages Polly gave him earlier. The sausages Basil put on for Dr Price have burned, and he comes into the smoky room, rebuking Basil for keeping a corpse in the kitchen, an obvious health hazard. Basil feebly protests but acquiesces. They put him into the laundry hamper and move him to the lobby. Sybil cannot come to help as she is trying to assist Miss Tibbs, who has a thousand-yard-stare and is very traumatized by the morning's events. Manuel attempts to clear the dining room but Dr Price is firm – he has not had breakfast and he is going to have his sausages, come hell or high water. The Whites somewhat inexplicably reappear and go back upstairs – they have not in fact checked out so still have their key. Manuel takes the tablecloth from Dr Price's table after some argument, and they briefly mimic matador and bull before Basil appears and "explains" the situation to Manuel by poking him in the eye. Basil puts the tablecloth back on the table and assures Dr Price that he *can* have his breakfast: the sausages will be ready shortly.

Mr Ingrams checks in, and Sybil gives him the key to number 8 – which is Mr Leeman's room. They have already stripped the bed, but this does seem unnecessarily quick for a room turnaround. Mr Leeman's friends come to collect him but Basil mistakes them for the undertakers. He explains that Mr Leeman is in the laundry basket, which Basil has been sitting on, but when he attempts to show them the body, they realise the laundry has been collected already. The audience already knows this, but Basil does not.

Dr Price is waiting rather impatiently in the dining room, and smoke is appearing from the kitchen doors. Polly, Basil and Manuel bring the right basket back to the lobby from outside. The visitors explain that Mr Leeman is going to a meeting. Everyone realises that these three people are not the undertakers. Polly helps cover for Basil, explaining that they misheard 'linen' as 'Leeman'. Manuel is slumped over the basket but helps Basil carry it upstairs when prodded. They remove the body from the hamper – the Major, passing by, asks if this is another one but Basil reassures him that it's the same one – and take him back into room 8. Mr Ingrams – who is in his pyjamas already, despite it still being not long after 8am – is seen inflating a sex doll. Mr Ingrams was named after Richard Ingrams of *The Spectator,* who gave the first series of *Fawlty Towers* a terrible review – clearly some grudges have been held.

They make a rapid exit and put Mr Leeman in one of the beds in room 18 – but Mrs White is lying down on the other. They hastily remove the corpse and take him downstairs again. Manuel climbs into the hamper himself, in some distress. He quits on the spot: "*I stay here* [in the hamper], *is nice!*". Unfortunately, one of Mr Leeman's friends wants the hat he had previously put on the lobby hat stand… and we now see that Basil has balanced Mr Leeman on the hat stand behind him. He cannot move or let anyone pass without allowing the body to fall to the floor, and so he attempts to talk the visitor into simply leaving without his hat. Manuel is called to fetch the hat – but he is still hiding in the hamper. When Polly extricates him, he positions himself to hide the corpse, and so Polly has to fetch the hat. Miss Tibbs, finally back to her normal self, comes to complain to Basil. The

Whites reappear to ask what is going on, and everyone is assembled in the lobby when Mrs Chase complains that they poisoned her "baby" – the dog – and claims that Basil was going to call a vet but has not done so. Dr Price emerges with his self-cooked sausages and complains that they are off. Basil, now free to move away from the corpse as Manuel is propping it up, agrees that everyone deserves an explanation and promises that Sybil will give it. They all move to the hotel reception desk while Basil climbs into the basket and the laundry men return to carry it away. Miss Tibbs discovers the corpse again and shrieks, as the Major asks Mr Leeman what is going on. Sybil yells repeatedly for Basil, who is being driven away in the laundry van. For once he doesn't have to face the music immediately, and Sybil will need to deal with everyone. We can only imagine what happens when he returns!

―――

There is visible snow on the ground as the laundry van drives away. The start of 1979 had seen a lot of snowfall in southern England and these remnants are left over from heavy snow in February 1979. We know from the autobiography of 'professional extra' Harry Fielder[13] that this was a day's shooting completed two weeks before the studio recording. We also know from the programme schedules that filming for the episode took place on Sunday 4 March and so the exterior shooting must have been around 15-16 February, two very cold [for southern England] days in the middle of an unusually cold month, with temperatures between −9C and 0C. Fielder wrote that he worked with another regular extra, Joe Santos, on this shoot *"loading a huge basket into the back of a van and driving off. A fortnight later in the studio we enter and pick up the basket which contains a dead body. (But we don't know that.)"* His website[14] is still live and shows a picture from the episode. Fielder was a regular bit part player, appearing in *Doctor Who* and *Blake's 7* on multiple occasions, as well as *Carry On* films and a large number of sitcoms, but this was his only work with Cleese.

Andrew Leeman,[15] the namesake of the corpse in this episode, was a friend of John Cleese, and had advised him on many aspects of the hotel business. He worked at the Savoy Hotel and had his own hotel (The Feathers in Woodstock), as well as working as a restaurateur at Morton's and Langan's Brasserie. Cleese has told many versions of his conversations with Leeman over the years. The *Times* obituary[16] for Leeman stated that Leeman's partner Maxine White introduced him to Cleese and they became friends over their shared loves of backgammon, food and wine. In 1977 Cleese and Leeman went on holiday *"to avoid the Queen's Silver Jubilee in London"* and Cleese asked him about his worst hotel management experience. Leeman told him about having to discreetly remove a dead body from a

Savoy bedroom. The *Daily Telegraph*[17] obituary refers to Leeman's response to the question: *"What's the worst problem you had when you used to work at the Savoy Hotel?" Quite straight-faced he replied, "oh, the stiffs.""* Cleese questioned this and was told that it was a frequent occurrence – elderly guests would arrive at the hotel with a bottle of pills and overdose in the night, knowing that the Savoy would treat them well and kindly. The staff would enter the room, find the body, and *"pick up the phone and say, 'We've got another one.'"* Then Leeman or other managers would have to arrange removal of the body to an undertaker, usually via the service elevator. Cleese was gleeful about this idea: *"it's just wonderful. And then you put a doctor in the hotel and it's kind of a joy."* They named the corpse Mr Leeman *"in Andrew's honour"*.

An unpleasant detail that Andrew Leeman would definitely have advised on: dead people *leak*. The idea, therefore, that any decent hotel would remove a corpse from room 8 and almost immediately check Mr Ingrams into the same room is unthinkable – there would be very little time to change the sheets, let alone the mattress, and the room would not have been aired. The desire to mock journalist Richard Ingrams, via this guest, is clearly the driving force for this scene. For our own comfort, we can assume that someone misspoke when allocating Mr Ingrams to room 8, that the bedding *was* dealt with appropriately, and that this re-use of the room simply stems from a practical desire to avoid creating a second bedroom set for the day's filming. Of course, there's also the argument that this is *not* any decent hotel, but – despite its many minor faults – Fawlty Towers does *not* appear to be unsanitary, unclean, or even a particularly unpleasant place to stay, proprietors aside.

John J Hoare, on his Dirty Feed website,[18] directs readers to the first episode of *Doctor in the House, So Why Do You Want To Be A Doctor?*, which also deals with the attempted concealment of a part-cadaver – specifically an arm – which two medical students need to hide, inadvertently causing a policeman to faint in a very similar manner to Miss Tibbs. Hoare argues that Cleese – working on *Doctor in the House* with Graham Chapman – had already sown narrative seeds for this episode before he even met Leeman. The manhandling of a corpse is also an element in classic farce, seen in such diverse productions as Joe Orton's *Loot* and the 1989 film *Weekend at Bernie's*.

First Broadcast
26 March 1979[1] – The Anniversary

The sign says: FLOWERY TWATS[2]

In this episode we meet:
The elusive Audrey (Christine Shaw[3]) who has been on the phone in practically every other episode. We know lots about her already including that she's had a hysterectomy, her husband George can be violent, and they have a troubled marriage.

Roger and Alice Terry (Ken Campbell[4] and Una Stubbs[5]), who are long-suffering friends of the Fawltys. Roger should have been played by Julian Holloway[6] but was replaced at short notice when a one-week delay in filming meant Holloway could not play the part.

Arthur and Virginia (Robert Arnold,[7] Pat Keen[8]), likewise. Virginia is a nurse.

Reg and Kitty (Roger Hume,[9] Denyse Alexander[10]). It's really quite impressive that as many as three couples consider Basil a friend.

Physical comedy: Polly imitates Sybil. Basil carries a protesting Polly up the stairs. Basil follows Sybil in the car then hops up and down in the drive. Basil fakes leg pain to stop Alice going upstairs. Sybil slaps Basil. Terry moves all the pans while Manuel is prepping his meal. Terry and Manuel wreck the kitchen. Basil locks Sybil in a kitchen cupboard.

Sets: Hotel lobby, bar, Basil and Sybil's bedroom, kitchen, office.

On the menu: cake with *"lots of extra marzipan"*, nuts. Gin and tonic, medium sherry, gin and it [*aka* sweet martini – gin, vermouth, bitters].

Not on offer: paella, especially paella with mince in it. Gazpacho, chicken Andalus [chicken in a saffron-based sauce], eggplant Espanol [fried aubergine, *Berenjenas a la Importancia*], Franco fritters [presumably a product of Terry's fevered imagination at this point]. Eel pie.

First Broadcast 26 March 1979 – The Anniversary

Polly wanted an advance on her wages to buy a car, and Sybil said it would be ok but Basil has said no, even though she 'only' wants £100.[11] She first asked the Fawltys three weeks ago, and promised that the debt would be repayable over six weeks from her wages (we can assume this means a little over £16.50 a week or close to all her available cash).[12] Terry tells her to ask Basil again, pointing out that *"me and you practically run the bleeding place for them"*. Manuel has been shopping for paella ingredients so he can cook it for the Fawltys' dinner that night, at Basil's request. Polly asks if Terry knows about this plan, aware that it may be impinging on his territory.

Sybil is very unhappy: it is the Fawltys' 15th wedding anniversary (17 April 1979) but Basil seems to have forgotten for the second year in a row. It is implied he was given quite a short shrift when he forgot the previous year. Basil, on the other hand, is very happy, entering the kitchen humming *Ode to Joy*. He asks Polly if she knows the poem[13] it was based on. Sybil and Basil snipe at each other. Sybil points out that *Polly* doesn't forget things – she is dropping a very heavy-handed hint to Basil, who then claims his memory isn't very good. Sybil is clearly very upset. After she leaves the room he quips *"Do I detect the smell of burning martyr?"* Basil is winding her up, is not afraid to let the staff know it, and he actually hasn't forgotten at all. Polly reminds him and he confesses that he has a plan, involving friends, a meal, and champagne. She asks if it wouldn't be simpler to boil her in oil. *"Yes, but not as economical."*[14]

Manuel asks about dinner and is told it should be at 9pm that night – we know, from *Waldorf Salad*, that hotel guests cannot usually have dinner after 9pm, so this is obviously going to be an intimate dinner *à deux* for the Fawltys alone, once the guests have been banished from the dining room. For Basil this is an impressively romantic gesture, even if it is mostly formed from fear of haranguing and reprisals.

Polly asks about the money again and Basil fobs her off. She clarifies that she only has until this weekend to buy the car and he seems surprised. Polly is annoyed. Terry comes back and asks about the paella ingredients in the kitchen. We don't see Polly's response to this, but we can guess. Sybil is *"just a little bit tense"* and finally asks Basil outright if he knows the date (he lies) and if he knows it's their anniversary. He eventually looks at the newspaper to confirm the correct date. *"Does that stir any memories in you, Basil?"* *"Memories? Agincourt*[15]*?"* She slaps him, but he continues guessing: *"Trafalgar*[16]*? Crecy*[17]*? Poitiers*[18]*? Yom Kippur*[19]*?"*

Terry accosts Basil and complains about Manuel cooking that evening. Terry can cook it, but Basil tells him he should let Manuel do it. Terry explains that he is a trained chef, and he has been to catering school. He is insulted that he has not been consulted or asked to cook the anniversary meal.

Manuel alerts Basil to Sybil leaving the hotel just as she drives off in their red Maxi. Basil gives chase in the car park then collapses in despair on the drive and is nearly run over by their friends Roger and Alice. He claims to be smoothing out a bump in the drive when they ask him if he is alright. Bob Spiers reminds us in commentary that Roger was a last-minute substitute, and so this external shot of his arrival had to be reshot after the rest of the outside filming. Inside the hotel, Basil greets them properly, not having had time to think of a convincing lie to put them off. Although Manuel ingeniously suggests that he should claim that the surprise aspect of a surprise party is that Sybil is not there, at Polly's prompting Basil makes up a story about Sybil being ill. Roger finds this hilarious – *"Syb ill!"* Manuel gets the joke and responds *"Man well!"*. His English has progressed to making puns.

This story does not work on the visitors, however, and Alice insists on seeing her despite his description of Sybil's apparently disfiguring illness. Basil diverts her into the bar to have a drink by faking his old war wound pain again. Alice attempts to call Sybil on the hotel's internal phones but again Basil dissuades her by saying first that she's having a sleep and then that Sybil has lost her voice. The lies compound. Alice wants to know if the doctor has been, but he says the doctor hasn't been yet. Roger – correctly – surmises that they've had a row. Polly arrives and attempts to help Basil by saying that the doctor suggests Sybil stays in bed for a few days, but this contradicts Basil's story so they fumble over a story involving a dentist and *his* wife. Basil gives Alice and Roger their drinks. Roger toasts cheerfully and irreverently: *"up yours, Basil"*. They make small talk until more friends arrive: Virginia and Arthur, who have brought a cake. Alice and Basil explain to the others that Sybil is ill; Roger suggests that the cake would cheer her up. Basil has to put everyone off yet again, despite their earnest efforts to see her. Basil explains that Sybil has lost her voice and is *"very puffed up"*.

Manuel complains that Terry is interfering with his cooking preparations. Polly tells the guests that Sybil's legs are puffed up, though Basil briefly misunderstands and thinks that Polly's legs are. Basil then claims her face is also puffed up. Virginia is a nurse who asserts that she will examine Sybil, as she sounds quite ill. Basil has forgotten this fact and has to strenuously dissuade her. *"She's ill isn't she, what's the bloody point of looking at her?"* Polly then explains that the doctor *did* in fact come this morning and that it might be serious. Reg and Kitty arrive and claim to have seen Sybil in the High Street in her car. Basil panics and claims that this is another woman who drives a red Maxi, is from the North of England, and merely looks like Sybil. They are sceptical – they know the Fawltys' car isn't outside, they are doubtful about the doppelganger story – but eventually they accept his assertion that Sybil is in bed. Basil gets huffy at the implicit accusation that he is not good enough for his friends, since they clearly insist on seeing Sybil as well. He offers to refund their petrol for the visit, as it has obviously inconvenienced them so much. They make conciliatory noises to him, trying to be kind. Basil claims the puffing up started after Sybil saw the doctor, so Virginia insists again on seeing her to find out how serious her illness is.

Basil gets confused again and starts to gabble incoherently: *"It's perfectly Sybil. Simple's not well. She's lost her throat and her voice hurt. The doctor came and said it was a bit serious. Not a lot. A bit."* Basil gets upset at the persistence of the friends and at their not believing his story – which is of course all lies, so they are right to be sceptical. He challenges them to come and see Sybil if they think he is a liar, calling their bluff. They all insist that it is OK, they do not need to see her after all, but eventually the friends talk themselves into wanting to just peep in and see her. Basil asks Polly to come with him to prepare Sybil to receive visitors, and she quickly realises what his plan is. She objects vociferously. He picks her up and carries her bodily up the stairs and into the Fawltys' bedroom, in one of the most physical scenes between Booth and Cleese in the whole show.

With the aid of one of Sybil's wigs and her bed jacket, Polly is persuaded into portraying the puffy Mrs Fawlty. Polly and Basil argue about the ridiculous situation and she likens it to a Marx Brothers movie. Basil threatens her: *"You'll never waitress in Torquay again!"* – as if he has the power to stop her moving to another hotel. She is adamant that she will not comply with his demands. This is the most angry we will ever see Polly be, a surprise after her peacemaking efforts in previous episodes. After a knock on the door causes Basil to fake a heart attack, she realises that she can get the £100 from Basil this way. He agrees to pay her if she helps him, and she gets dressed up while Basil deals with the increasingly upset Manuel, who is still rowing with Terry over the paella. *"He call me ignorant, wog[20], motherboy, crump."*

Basil delays the friends at the bedroom door until he is sure "Sybil" is ready for visitors. He claims she is writing notes to tell him some messages he can pass on to their friends. He runs downstairs to the bar, find an ashtray for Alice, where he starts drinking wine from the bottle out of desperation. Manuel interrupts to complain that Terry has put mince in the paella even though it is a fish recipe, and he spills wine on himself in his agitation. Manuel is now extremely upset – again, this is the most angry behaviour we have seen from him (so far).

Roger again opines that the Fawltys have had a row and that Sybil is sulking in her bedroom, not wanting to see them. Virginia is sympathetic to Basil, who is apparently finding life difficult with his wife unwell. He gives the friends some crisps and nuts which get spilled on the hall floor, so he goes to fetch a brush. Roger takes the opportunity for a pun: *"a Basil brush! Broom broom!"*.[21]

Basil throws Manuel into the kitchen, not wanting to listen to any more of his complaints. When he returns upstairs Basil falls onto the crisps. After some discussion of the wallpaper and carpet – *"one of them will have to go and my money's on the carpet"* says Roger; *"read a lot of Oscar Wilde,*[22] *do you?"* counters Basil – the Major appears with his golf clubs, ready to play a round. He is told that Sybil is ill, and so attempts to see her himself. Basil turns him around, however, and lets the friends into the room instead. It is pitch black with all the lights off (Polly has removed the bulb from the central fixture so it does not work when the switch is pressed). Basil puts on a dim table lamp at the other side of the room, to aid their subterfuge. "Sybil" is in bed,[23] wearing the wig, sunglasses, and has cotton wool in her mouth to simulate the puffiness and account for the difference between Polly and Sybil's face shapes. "Sybil" refuses some cake – Polly gesturing that she cannot open her mouth – and then the cotton wool accidentally emerges. Her friends wonder what the white stuff in her mouth is, and Basil says it is foam, implying she is rabid. Basil sees Sybil driving back into the car park, from the window. He screams quickly, and runs downstairs to Reception to greet her and prevent the others from seeing her. Sybil has come back for her golf clubs and is very upset at how unloving he is and how awful their marriage is – *"Fifteen years I've had with you. When I think what I might have had."* She leaves again and he agrees with her cheerfully that it's for the best. Appeasing her now would add an extra layer of complication to his lies so letting her leave, still angry, is his optimal choice even though he will pay for it later.

The friends leave "Sybil's" bedside but not before Virginia attempts to feel her glands and Polly hits her. Basil, who has returned in time, tells her off. *"Don't hit our friends!"* as if this is something Sybil always does. He offers everyone drinks, but they make their excuses and start to leave.

Sybil and Audrey are in the car, and Audrey consoles her – men are all the same, they sigh. She reminds Sybil that she didn't get her golf clubs, so Sybil returns to the hotel lobby just as all her friends come downstairs nursing their injuries. Basil pretends she is the doppelganger and introduces himself. Manuel and Terry's disagreement bursts out of the kitchen as a brawl, and Basil takes the opportunity to shove them and Sybil back into the kitchen. He locks Sybil in a kitchen cupboard, promising to explain shortly, and returns to the lobby, shutting the kitchen door on them all. Polly comes back downstairs as herself, and Basil says *"piece of cake"* to her. *"Now comes the tricky bit."* The episode ends just as he goes to explain everything to Sybil, sort out the warring chefs, and attempt to salvage something of his anniversary plans. Good luck, Basil!

First Broadcast 26 March 1979 – The Anniversary

Above all else, this episode casts a new light on the Fawltys' marriage. Basil may have forgotten the couple's anniversary last year, but he obviously learned from the experience, and has planned a decent evening for Sybil. His ploy, pretending he has forgotten, is definitely not a smart one and the inevitable result is chaos and tears. But if all had gone well – if he had warned Terry and negotiated Manuel's dinner preparations properly, if he had told Sybil the truth and welcomed their guests... a lovely day would have been had by all except Polly (who might have had to wait a lot longer for her money). For a change, Polly is the most active collaborator in the disaster, as her attempts to help make things worse, and her eventual agreement to assist Basil is effectively blackmail. Jodi Taylor: *"It's obvious that they still care – there's no apathy there. It's conflict, and conflict can be helpful. They have a relationship – she hasn't killed him."*

Written after the Booth-Cleese divorce, this episode gives Polly much more agency than earlier episodes. There is more physical interaction between Polly and Basil, and perhaps it exercises – if not exorcises – some of the demons from their own marriage.

The storyline sounds ridiculous when explained in any other context, but when it comes to the Fawltys, ridiculous is believable. Basil is not an irredeemable man, clearly, and loves his wife – or at least, he loves keeping the peace with his wife – enough to make nice arrangements. But the moment things start to spiral out of his control his ability to create utter chaos out of order kicks in. If he did not lie, if Polly did not attempt to help him lie, if – like most sitcom plots – he simply *communicated* with his friends and his wife, all would have been well.

Steve Punt is not a fan of this episode. *"The one I really don't like is the one where Polly dresses as Sybil. Why don't their best friends understand the relationship? It doesn't hold up as a scenario."* It is a point worth examining – why do these friends of the couple, who have known them for a long time and are clearly tolerant of their foibles and quirks, not understand that Basil is prone to exaggeration and lies, and that Sybil's temper is a significant part of their marriage? The seemingly flippant Roger is the only one who sees the truth, almost from his first line, and it's laughed off. When Basil denies the accusation, the others believe him – but where's the evidence?

Spiers notes that as Ken Campbell was put into the show at the last minute, after the delay in filming caused by industrial action, he was significantly behind the rest of the cast who had had time to work together to rehearse the performance well. He puts in an excellent performance under these constraints – it helps that Roger's character works well if viewed as a man who likes to joke around and interject funny remarks regardless of any conversation other people are having. Cleese thinks the delay helped the rest of the cast relax, having an extra week to get into the parts, and that Campbell's addition didn't detract from that.

The delay in filming was caused by the industrial action that would also nearly scupper *Basil the Rat*. John J Hoare[24] sets out the timeline:

> 31 January: *The Anniversary* location filming
> 8 March: BBC strike starts
> 11 March: Intended studio date for *The Anniversary*
> 14 March: BBC strike ends
> 18 March: Actual studio date for *The Anniversary* (intended for *Basil the Rat*)
> 26 March: TX date of *The Anniversary*
> 20 May: Actual studio date for *Basil the Rat*
> *So surely the location remount to add Campbell must have taken place between 14 March and 26 March...*

The BBC's Written Archives[25] confirm the 18 March recording date, giving Bob Spiers and crew just a week to get the episode ready for broadcast, complete with new outside footage, which is required as Ken Campbell is seen in the car park when Roger and Alice arrive.

First Broadcast
25 October 1979[1] – Basil the Rat

The sign says: FARTY TOWELS[2]

In this episode we meet:
Mr Carnegie[3] (John Quarmby[4]), a health inspector who doesn't like the hotel kitchen.
The unnamed hotel cat.
The named hotel rat – sorry, hamster – Basil.
An unnamed departing guest (Stuart Sherwin[5]). who doesn't want to buy a picture.
The very posh Ronald (David Neville[6]) and Quentina (Sabina Franklyn[7]), who would really like some veal.
Mr and Mrs Taylor (James Taylor, Melody Lang[8]), who do not get to eat their veal.

Not seen: Geoffrey Boycott.[9] Wittgenstein.[10] George Orwell.[11] General Franco.[12] Flying pigs.

Physical comedy: Polly slaps Manuel about, for a change. Manuel cowers from Basil: *don't hit me, always you hit me!* There is a lot of looking under tables. Basil jumps about when he learns the cat is fine. The Major takes a knee to the groin.

Sets: Lobby, kitchen, Manuel's attic bedroom, the upstairs landing, bar, dining room; outside the back door of the kitchen (not seen before), the shed.

On the menu: Lamb, plaice, green salad, bread roll, Windsor soup, paté, lobster.

Not on offer: ratatouille with extra rat – that was just Manuel's misunderstanding, we hope. Veal, veal substitute (allegedly made of soya beans and '*essence of cow*'). Eel escalope.

The Fawltys arrive home in a red 1976 Austin Maxi.[13] They are squabbling about going out: Sybil 'never gets out' and her friends think Basil is 'peculiar'. They wonder how the Fawltys ever got together – as do the audience.

Mr Carnegie has been inspecting the hotel kitchen, something Sybil knew but Basil did not. He has a very long list of issues with the hotel, which is deficient in: cleaning of surfaces, appliances, floors, utensils; replacing filters; storing food safely; washing hands and overalls; the prevention of smoking in the kitchen … and there are two dead pigeons in the water tank. Although he *threatens* to report the hotel and recommend closure, the tolerance on these issues is clearly quite generous. He will return tomorrow to see how they have been rectified, and to inspect the rooms.

Terry "*thought we was in trouble*" but believes the kitchen can be cleaned very easily and that it is not an issue. "*The better the kitchen, the filthier it is.*" Sybil tells them off for gossiping and sends Basil off to get Manuel to help him sort out the list. Basil visits Manuel in his bedroom, ordering him to remove the pigeons from the water tank on the roof. Manuel does not entirely understand, thinking Basil means pigs – "*pig-e-on*" – which of course cannot fly. "*Pigeon, like your English!*".

Basil spots Manuel's pet hamster – which is a rat. No, says Manuel, it is a filigree (pedigree) Siberian hamster, but Basil confiscates it anyway. The Ladies see them arguing in the lobby and reassure Manuel that Basil can't get rid of his pet. They volunteer to host the hamster in their room – but are understandably startled to find out it is a rat. They shriek and run away. Basil passes some guests and, embracing the lie, assures them that he is carrying a hamster. Polly explains patiently to Manuel that it is, despite everything he believes, a rat. Basil takes the rat to the kitchen to show Sybil but she tells him to get rid of it and suggests that he put the rat to *S-L-E-E-P*. After some argument, Polly and Manuel leave the hotel, carrying the rat's cage.

Basil confirms to Sybil that he has removed the pigeons and they are ready for the inspector. Manuel returns to the kitchen with a long face and black armband, in mourning for the loss of his pet. Basil suggests that Manuel goes to the cinema or something to cheer himself up. "*Depression is a very bad thing.*[14] *We didn't win the war by getting depressed, you know.*" This is unusually cheerful – and helpful – for Basil. When Basil has left the room Polly returns and tells Manuel he is overdoing the sadness – and he perks up. He is not really depressed: just play-acting to make Basil believe that he has complied and killed his pet. He takes some food out to the shed where he calls for Basil… which we now realise is the name of the rat.

Polly is failing to sell a picture to a departing guest when Manuel rushes in to tell her that the rat has gone missing. He left him in the shed but let him out of his cage, without thinking about the consequences. Polly calls him a *dago dodo* but then alerts him (in Spanish) to the presence of Mr Fawlty before he lets the metaphorical cat out of the bag.

The Major goes into the bar and spots the rat on a table by the nuts. He rushes upstairs, ignoring Basil who is inspecting the lobby flowers. He returns with a large gun – Basil notices and follows him, questioning him quietly and calmly. He reassures the Major that there are no Germans staying this week, assuming that the Major had misheard *"vermin*[15]*"* – but the Major still tries to tell Basil about the rat. *"He was sitting there, eating the nuts."* Basil returns to the kitchen to find Terry casually cleaning behind the fridge – obviously he is really looking for the rat. Polly is under a table in the dining room, quietly calling *"Basil"*. Manuel, who has been under another table, attempts to creep away while Basil is mocking Polly in a high squeaky American tone redolent of Minnie Mouse – *"Oh, I've got a friend who'll take him, Mr Fawlty"*. Polly lies to Basil that rats are homing creatures, and Terry attempts to help. Basil is not convinced.

Basil puts a box of rat poison on the fridge after liberally coating a piece of raw veal and leaving it by the fridge door. Mr Carnegie returns and Sybil greets him. He decides to start his inspection with the water tanks in the roof, which Basil is relieved about, as he has actually completed that work. They are about to go upstairs when there are gunshots in the bar – Basil blames the television for exploding again – as if this is a common occurrence in the hotel – and Polly emerges into the lobby with a large butterfly net. The Major thought he saw the rat again, but they did not catch him or successfully shoot him. Basil wrestles the gun from him in the bar and takes it back to the lobby. Spiers notes that there is a bad edit at this point and that it doesn't quite work, but most viewers don't notice anything wrong.

Basil tells Mr Carnegie that the Major was shooting at a starling. Manuel is distraught at the idea that they have shot his hamster, saying that they tried to *"kill Basil"*, but Polly intervenes to cover, describing Basil-the-rat as Basil-the-ratatouille to avoid Carnegie understanding her actual meaning. *"Chef calls the ratatouille Basil because he puts quite a lot of basil in it."* Manuel is even more upset, despite Terry's reassurance that he has not made ratatouille at all. Manuel knocks over a tray of veal by the fridge and they pick it all up again. Meanwhile Basil attempts to explain the situation, rather futilely, to the Major, quoting George Burns: *"Say goodnight to the folks, Gracie"*. This is an allusion to *The Burns and Allen Show*[16] and the 'ditzy, forgetful' character played by Gracie Allen. The Major is even more of an airhead than she is.

The piece Basil had poisoned is not visible to the staff or the audience. The cat[17] tries to eat some of the veal, just as Polly serves two cooked pieces. Basil is horrified to hear that Terry has picked up and cooked *all* the spilt veal, and so rushes to reclaim the dishes from the diners, claiming it is off and that it isn't even veal. Basil brings the veal back into the kitchen only to find Mr Carnegie there, so briefly returns to the dining room in panic, before sneaking back in behind the health inspector's back. He knocks the rat poison off the fridge before Mr Carnegie can see it. The inspector finishes his formal inspection, perfectly satisfied with Sybil's explanations and receipts for the work yet to be done. To Basil's horror, he requests lunch – he saw some veal being prepared earlier, and would like that. Basil and Terry try to put him off, to Sybil's confusion. They assert that the veal is Norwegian, although Sybil insists it is Dutch. Terry backs Basil up, and Mr Carnegie says he has never heard of Norwegian veal.[18] Basil says that that's because it's not very good, and recommends lobster instead.

Terry points out that if the cat had a slice of veal and the cat is still OK, the veal it nibbled is not the poisoned one. Polly confirms that the cat is fine, and Terry trims the veal before cooking it. Mr Carnegie accidentally sits on one of the two plates of veal Basil had hidden in the dining room. Basil slaps Manuel and blames him for the issue after rescuing the other plate. Polly brings the inspector his veal and a salad. Basil sees the cat retching in the yard and sprints to retrieve the veal from Mr Carnegie before he can eat it. He claims it is not hot enough but burns his hand on the plate so claims it is not big enough, instead. Terry cooks some of the other veal, using the same logic – if the cat is *not* OK, then that slice *was* poisoned and the other pieces are fine. The cat is fine – Basil does an impression of the retching, and Sybil points out that it's just fur balls – so Basil recalls the second piece of veal as well, telling the Inspector that they can't be seen to be bribing or influencing him with preferential treatment. The Major greets *"the rat inspector"* before remembering and correcting himself – the *starling* inspector.

The rat appears in the dining room,[19] and Manuel stares under the table, so Ronald thinks he is looking at Quentina's legs and is outraged at the impudence. In the kitchen, Polly, Sybil, Terry, and Basil are debating the state of the veal and trying to resolve the logic problem of which one might be edible. Manuel tells Basil that the rat is in the dining room at table 7, so Basil goes to look. Ronald complains to him that he wasn't being listened to – but Basil is distracted and doesn't pay attention either, to Ronald's annoyance. When told that Manuel was seemingly interested in Quentina's legs, Basil bends down to have a look as well. Basil calls Polly to take the order while he continues to look for a fictional bread roll under the table. They see the rat and Basil sends Manuel to get a box to put it in, to the guests' bewilderment. *"We have a bread box... for any bread that has gone past its prime."* Basil restrains Ronald when he attempts to look under the table himself.

The guests attempt to order but are outraged and sceptical when told that the veal is already off. Basil claims that it is a typo on the menu and should say eel. The

First Broadcast 25 October 1979 – Basil the Rat

rat is now in Quentina's handbag[20] and Manuel attempts to retrieve it. Sybil brings Mr Carnegie some veal, which the other guests notice. Ronald and Quentina try to leave, and ask Polly to recommend a restaurant while Basil surreptitiously tries to rescue the rat from the handbag. He fails to do so and is noticed, and the guests understandably get even more upset. Ronald threatens Basil, as he's had quite enough. *"You're getting my dander up, you grotty little man."* Polly ingeniously says that there has been a bomb scare, so that is why they want to search the bag and were previously looking under the table. The rat scurries across the lobby[21] and into the dining room, where Manuel starts searching for it. He successfully catches it and puts it into the biscuit tin, but the Major takes the tin before Manuel can remove it from the dining room successfully. Mr Carnegie orders cheese and biscuits, and Basil brings over the cheese trolley. Manuel is running to and fro looking for the tin at this point. They cannot initially find the biscuits – when the Major obligingly hands over the tin, Polly offers it to the inspector. He opens it and a (puppet) rat[22] is seen in the biscuits – *"the biggest laugh* [Spiers] *ever heard on the show"*. Polly switches the tins and re-offers the biscuits to the inspector, minus rat. He looks on incredulously as Basil drags Manuel out by his legs while Sybil notes casually that it is starting to rain again.

◦≡◦

This episode was inspired by a letter from a viewer who had stayed in a hotel where the manager had hunted a rat with a shotgun but, once he found the rat, could not bring himself to kill it. Sybil's final line about rain relates to a cut scene where Polly and Sybil attempt to distract and relax Mr Carnegie by discussing the weather.[23]

This episode's recording was delayed by industrial action,[24] and was eventually broadcast seven months after the rest of series 2. A number of sources claim that it was originally scheduled for broadcast on Monday 19 March 1979, as episode five of six. Industrial action by technical staff at the BBC from Thursday 8 March to Wednesday 14 March 1979 meant that no episode could be recorded on Sunday 11 March – without sets there could be no episode – so it was replaced with a short-notice repeat of *Gourmet Night*. The remaining episode, *The Anniversary*, was delayed by a week (requiring the short notice recasting of Roger and some additional external filming) but was eventually ready to be shown in its original slot on 26 March. Basil is seen reading a newspaper with a headline[25] referring to this industrial action during *The Anniversary*. However, as we know *The Anniversary* took *Basil the Rat's* studio slot after initial delay, *Basil the Rat* must always have been intended for recording on 18 March as episode six, the series finale.

The delay meant that Bob Spiers felt he could ask, "*cap in hand*", for a second day of studio filming, and extra pre-recording time in order to improve some of the special effects for the rat. By modern standards the effects are not impressive, but for 1979 the rat on a string is quite effective; the puppet that pops up in the biscuit tin, maybe less so, but it is still a fan favourite. As a result of that extra time, it proved possible to record the show in front of two separate audiences on the afternoon and evening of filming, and then edit them together to get the best version of the episode. All the delays meant that the viewing audience were looking forward to this episode more than any previous one, according to Spiers, and he felt that the extra time put into the production paid off: this is one of the sleekest episodes of the twelve with "*the biggest laugh we ever heard* [for the puppet rat] ... *we jumped in the gallery at that one.*"

Steve Punt: "*Basil the Rat is an object lesson in how to structure a farce. It has a fantastic structure, it really builds. Every joke is topped by another. There's a terrible prop puppet rat – and it's the funniest thing in the world because you've seen the real rat nibbling the nuts, then a beautiful prop stage rat. The audience are laughing so much that you almost miss it when the rat swivels* [to Mr Carnegie]. *It's so rare to see the punch line to a whole 40 minute plot that has that much perfection to it.*"

John Cleese, as Basil, introduced the debut episode of *Not The Nine O'Clock News*[26] which had been scheduled for 2 April 1979, 'replacing' *Fawlty Towers*, but as *Not The Nine O'Clock News* was in turn delayed due to the 1979 General Election,[27] the full impact of the joke was lost – it was eventually broadcast on 16 October, 9 days before the last episode of *Fawlty Towers* was shown. Andrew Sachs, as Manuel, appears briefly at the end of the first episode as well.

From 10 August to 24 October 1979 ITV were also on strike, so the delayed broadcast of *Basil the Rat* benefited slightly from increased viewing figures: viewers had only had two channels to choose from for the previous three months so had got into the habit of watching BBC as their default choice. On 25 October, although the strike had formally ended, the choice was still not much better. ITV was not yet back up and running a full schedule in all regions, and the regular autumn schedule of new shows would not begin until Monday 29 October. As a result of the delay and the increased viewing figures, a repeat of *The Psychiatrist* at Christmas 1979 was the first episode of the show to reach the top 10 viewed shows in any week.

This episode aired three weeks after John Cleese made an appearance in *Doctor Who* (series 17 serial 2, *City of Death* episode 2) – coincidentally broadcast on the same day as an episode of *Basil Brush*. His fellow guest star, Eleanor Bron, was a long-standing collaborator with Cleese, David Frost, Peter Cook, and other Footlights alumni, and Douglas Adams, a long-time fan of Cleese, had

First Broadcast 25 October 1979 – Basil the Rat

co-written the serial. 3 days earlier he had also appeared in *Ripping Yarns* s2e2, on 17 October 1979, a show written by his old friends Terry Jones and Michael Palin.

Cleese claims this is his favourite episode. *"In terms of confusion and chaos and frenzy it's almost the most consistent... Once the rat poison gets introduced we might be talking about a serious problem like the death of a human being, which increases the fear... In farce there is always something happening that the protagonist has to cover up."* The jeopardy and stress in this hotel ranges from the hotel being closed down for breaches of public health, to a potential murder charge. *"As farce performance goes, this is about as good as it gets... as funny as I can do."* He attributes the lack of a series 3 to the perfection of this episode – when people asked if they would do a third series, he simply couldn't see how they could live up to this one.

Memories

The show has a large number of celebrity fans[1] from film director Martin Scorsese and US sitcom supremo James Burrows to former US President George Bush[2] and Beatle John Lennon. It has been sold around the world and viewed regularly for fifty years now. Ricky Gervais and Stephen Merchant claim that its success is the reason the original (UK) version of *The Office* is also only two series long – although it has 14 episodes to *Fawlty Towers*' 12, as it had a Christmas episode and a one-off short for *Red Nose Day*. *The Young Ones* similarly had two series of 6 episodes, 1982-4. Light Entertainment producer Paul Jackson:[3] "*If 12 episodes was good enough for John Cleese, it's enough for* [The Young Ones]. *Everybody knew that was it.*" These shows illustrate what TV Tropes calls 'British Brevity:'[4] "*most notable is* Fawlty Towers; *one of the more famous and well-regarded sitcoms – and indeed television series of any kind – ever made, and there were only ever twelve episodes, from two seasons made four years apart.*" Get in, make your point, and get out again before it all goes wrong. Director Edgar Wright,[5] who worked on the similarly brief *Spaced*: "*There's a thing that everyone talks about called 'The Curse of* Fawlty Towers*' ... network executives really bemoan the fact that John Cleese set that bar with only 12 episodes of* Fawlty Towers *... then [said] 'I can't write anymore. I'm very happy with the 12 episodes... I'm done with it'.*" He feels Cleese and Booth have made TV companies wary.

MAURICE GRAN[6]

I did watch it from the off because I was a huge *Python* fan, a big Cleese fan. I knew Cleese from *The Frost Report*, and I was also a big fan of *I'm Sorry I'll Read That Again*, on the radio. So I would have watched it, and of course I would have watched because he stole the idea from us.

1973-74, Laurence [Marks] went along as a local journalist to write about the drama group, Player Playwrights, where you could watch plays being performed or read. it was for writers, actors, people who just wanted to be in the audience. It cost 5p, might have gone up to 10p later. You got a cup of coffee at half time and a biscuit, so it was a cheap night out. We started going there, writing bits and pieces, and getting laughs, and so between 1974 and 1980 probably went every Monday night in term time. It was like an education really. When I was a student and I attempted to write for the Revue I just had no idea, I just couldn't. Even though I'd written short stories, student journalism, it didn't seem to be a transferable skill. By the osmosis of going to that sort of thing, I sort of got it. I always say to anyone who wants to write any form of drama, find a group, find some other people. It's a lonely enough calling, but if you can find people who are as stupid as you and want to do it, then that's what you should do.

So at that time, I remember there was a pub round the corner that we used to go to on a Monday night and two or three of our stillborn shows were kicked around there, and one was called *You Can't Get The Wood* which was set in a hotel in 1945. We had an owner who was obsessed with improving the standing of her establishment – that was the only similarity, it wasn't farcical. But when we heard about [*Fawlty Towers*] we were both annoyed and flattered. Not that we thought he was listening – he was so tall he couldn't have been listening, we'd have noticed.

What did I think of it? I thought he was fantastic. I thought – and I still do to a small extent – that his secondary casting was a bit broad for my liking. His primary cast was so on the nose and a lot of his secondary cast was, but some of his secondary cast knew they were in a sitcom. I don't think I appreciated the difficulty of writing farce – the technical difficulty of writing farce, and the technical difficulty of a farce a week. It made me laugh. I loved the cruelty, I loved the relationship with his wife. At the time I found the character of Polly a bit too straight and I don't know if that was his co-writer's input – if they had the idea that you need one character who was not mad? She could deliver a comic line but I remember thinking at the time she could be a bit funnier, she hasn't got a comic trope, she hasn't got a Thing.

If they just said she was absolutely fine except she was claustrophobic, then you could keep locking her in wardrobes. I think they missed a comic beat. I think [John Cleese would] accept that he's a megalomaniac, so he wasn't that bothered that Polly didn't get the funny lines.

It's better on re-watching. Is it better on re-watching because it's such a sturdy structure? Or because it's a great *tour de force*? I think the answer to both those questions is yes. Is it better because there's so relatively little top class quality comedy now that you really appreciate it? It dates back to a time when you could watch *Fawlty Towers* on a Friday and *Porridge* on a Thursday and *Rising Damp* on a Wednesday and so on. I don't believe in golden ages as a rule, but I do believe that the mid-70s was a golden age for sitcom and I wouldn't be a writer of comedy but for the joy that those shows gave Laurence and me back in the day. Maybe we *under*estimate it.

And of course it created this really annoying myth that no comedy is any good if you do more than 13 [episodes]. It's a great sop to lazy writers, or writer-performers who don't have much to say really. Also I suspect that if the Cleese/Booth marriage hadn't split up there might have been more episodes.

What is the legacy of Fawlty Towers? That's a wonderful question of the sort I hate to answer. Anything you say is going to sound stupid. It has many legacies, not least it's left us a very enjoyable show, that – when you stumble on it at half past eleven on BBC 4, when you come in from the pub, you're happy to watch it. I think what it is, it's one of those shows – I would put it on a par with *Porridge* and *Rising Damp*, and to some degree *Dad's Army* and *Yes Minister* – that remind people that multi-camera three wall shows in front of a studio audience are part of an important and fabulous art form that has been traduced in recent decades by commissioners who are scared of it or don't understand it, and who know – and I can't blame them for this – that four cheap comics, or six cheap comics and one expensive comic – equals a panel show. And you can make seven panel shows for the money that it takes to make one sitcom episode. But we won't be sitting here in 20 years time talking about series 73 of *8 out of 10 Cats Does Who The Fuck Gives A Shit?* And you can quote me on that!

His regular ensemble, like the two little old ladies and the Major, they're great comic creations. The more I think about it the more I chastise myself for being rude about his secondary casting. Occasionally there was someone who came in and you thought "are you in the right show?" and that was just because they didn't pick up on the vibe. There were some terrific moments. The scene where Fawlty is being very offhand with someone – the conman – until he reveals he's Lord Melbury – the way Cleese contorts himself into a slavering Uriah Heep is something that should be turned into a gif and John Cleese should be made to watch it all the time. *This is what you did. No one else can do it. Why did you stop?* Because he was a comic genius and we are entitled to be annoyed with our geniuses when they somehow start to underrate their talent. Maybe the revival, if it gets made, – we talked up the B'Stard reboot [the proposed 2017 *The New Statesman* revival] but talk is much cheaper than studios. If it happens, I hope it's *funny*, that's all.

STEVE PUNT[7]

My parents watched the first series of *Fawlty Towers* [Steve's 13th birthday was the week of the first episode]. They were *Beyond the Fringe* and *Monty Python's Flying Circus* fans. At teatime on BBC1 they would put up the programme guide, including 10.40pm *Python* and I'd say "why can't I stay up to see the circus?" I remember hearing them laugh at it. I preferred *The Goodies* initially, as it was more suitable for my age. But you always want comedy that's a bit older than you are – that's the aspirational part. You want to aspire up – part of the thrill was watching what your parents didn't want you to watch. I remember discovering Derek and Clive through recordings – we forget now how important comedy albums were. A lot of the coolness of *Monty Python* was judged through the albums (which were much filthier but more accessible[8] than broadcast TV for 1970s teens).

John Cleese had *Python* cool. It was a niche show – on BBC2, never on before 10.30pm. To make a sitcom might have been considered an unusual move. But Cleese also had a track record in sitcom, working with Les Dawson [*Sez Les*] which I liked. He dominated mainstream comedy.

The 1970s British cultural history of sitcom is mostly comprised of BBC shows – *The Fall and Rise of Reginald Perrin, Dad's Army, The Good Life*. ITV shows like *Bless This House* felt more like a life that I recognised though: it was ahead of its time. *The Good Life's* Tom and Barbara Good were the straight men to Margo and Jerry Leadbetter, but in *Bless This House* the lead roles were the funny ones. *Man About The House* is worth re-watching – it's much better than you might remember. *George and Mildred* is another guilty pleasure. People love watching couples argue – across the country they would argue about Basil and Sybil. She is more than equal to him. She only really loses her temper once, in *The Builders*.

The setting for the show was something out of the ordinary, despite seeming sedate from a 21st century perspective. Hotels weren't what ordinary people did, day to day. It was a slight remove from reality, and a microcosm of 'little Britain'.

Basil is a vicarious character – he says the things we'd all like to say, and he has a mechanism for just exploding. *Thank you so much!* There's something in it that is resonating deeply with audiences still, like *The Office* – it's something deeper than just "oh, a funny boss". Something about Basil Fawlty resonated with the British public, more than just him being an angry hotelier.

For someone my age [61 when interviewed in 2024] it does belong in the top ten sitcoms. If you grew up in the 70s it was part of your world and vocabulary and references, which it isn't for our kids. They've seen it, they've heard the phrases, but it's not the same. I can't think of many sitcoms that made me actually laugh out loud as much as *Fawlty Towers*. I'm overly biased because I'm a comedy writer, perhaps, but I think that it's very rare to see TV comedy that has had six weeks spent on it, like six one-act plays. There aren't that many comedies that are *that* densely constructed. It deserves its place – it's not easy, what he was doing. In TV terms, it's a multi-camera show, a complicated show in a large set, with a live audience. All comedy is hard, but single camera, one shot at a time, one scene at a time – that's easier.

Sitcom is a strange hybrid form of comedy, emerging from extended sketch shows and radio comedy, and ~30 minutes is a very short timeslot. Most sitcoms are 28 minutes [BBC] or 22 [ITV/C4 or US format] so there's no flab. Very little happens, or it's mostly verbal. *Fawlty Towers* on the other hand has a main plot, a sub-plot, and sometimes a third – they tangle, and climax.

TV of that era has lasted – people had to remember it, to talk about it and dissect it [because it was a live event]. There are plenty of Basils around, still.

JASPER FFORDE[9]

I watched it on first broadcast, as I was at boarding school. I watched it either in the TV room or with my houseparents, which was a good way to watch. It was a very social activity, and everyone was sort of fancying Polly. We didn't fully understand high farce but recognised it as an uncontroversial comedy.

I knew about *Monty Python* – they were pre-eminent in comedy – but I had been too young to watch until the final, Cleese-less, season four [October-December 1974]. When *Fawlty Towers* was advertised in the *Radio Times,* with pictures, it was fully expected to be something we would like. This is going to be clever, to be funny. I had learned Monty Python sketches by heart by then, via records my friends and I owned, listening at school. Our expectations were met.

It was not cutting edge, it was not breaking *new* ground at the time – unlike *Monty Python*, which was a major influence on me and confirmed that it was "ok to make bizarre connections".[10] *Fawlty Towers* was traditional high farce, in the classic sitcom tradition. At heart, *Fawlty Towers* is tightly written and well performed and part of a Golden Age of British sitcoms. *Fawlty Towers* has become a cultural institution – *"I know nothing"*. It has become internalised to UK culture now.

The Pythons by 1980 were a busted flush – *Ripping Yarns, Fawlty Towers, Holy Grail* were good but then it gets patchy – *Brian* was ok, *Meaning of Life* could have been better. [They have given us] fractured shards of pure genius.

The legacy of *Fawlty Towers* will doubtless ebb and flow down the years as public tastes change and alter. It may be trimmed for content, criticised and momentarily cancelled for the disrespect of foreigners, the deaf, the old, and those with dementia. But notwithstanding, it will endure. Art of high quality always does. And so long as the British understand the complexities and absurdities of their own national identity and can laugh at their own failings, the series will not only endure, but become, like all great artworks, revered.

NB: Fforde believes he may have encountered the real Basil, hotelier Donald Sinclair, when he was taking pictures for O Level Photography, knowing that the

Sinclairs lived in the building he was photographing. *"A man came out and told me to piss off. Was it him? I like to think so."*

JODI TAYLOR[11]

As a writer, the thing that always strikes me about *Fawlty Towers* – not surprisingly – is the consistent quality of the writing, which I think set a standard which lasts to this day. The cast were all magnificent, of course, but it's always the writing that's a standout for me.

I understand it was based on a hotel in Torquay where they actually stayed, and Basil was based on a real person. What always made me laugh was when they wanted to take the show to the United States the producers wanted to write Basil out because they didn't think the American audiences would either like or understand him. *Fawlty Towers* without Basil! The cast was perfectly balanced, with the four of them, and they played off each other beautifully. I think to have added a fifth, or to take one away, would have spoiled the balance.

Cleese always said he wasn't going to do a third series, he was seriously concerned about over exposure. The BBC tend to flog things to death don't they? We had how many years of *Last of the Summer Wine*[12] – *Casualty*'s still going, *EastEnders* – everything's run for 40 years or more. I would not have liked to see *Fawlty Towers* lose its edge and dwindle into conventional comedy. [Apart from *Fawlty Towers*] 1970s & 1980s comedy was very Benny Hill-ish and women were either nurses in short skirts or harridans and nags – it was all very stereotypical.

[Regarding a revival] I would say let it lie. I've always been very much a *quit while you're ahead* kind of person. Stop at the top of your game. Never be the last to leave the party. The thing is not to make any of them *sad* – quit at the top of the game, you don't want to see the characters getting sad, lost, bewildered.

STEVEN MOFFAT[13]

It's always important to have humour. If the audience laughs, you have said something to them that they know is true. A joke is just truth at speed – a high-impact insight. So there is no difficulty in marrying comedy to a serious subject. In fact, I would argue that's where comedy belongs. Basil Fawlty was very serious about running that hotel, and we did not see him having a good time. From his point of view, Fawlty Towers *was a drama series.*

GEOFFREY PALMER[14]

It's nice to have that in the CV.

DAVID KELLY[15]

I've been 52, 53 years on stage and yet... Those nine minutes in The Builders *makes me recognised all over the world.*

MICHAEL PALIN[16]

Fawlty Towers *survives because it's brilliantly made, brilliantly written, immaculately performed precision comedy.*

From his diaries: *24 October 1975: ...the last of* [John's] Fawlty Towers *series had me laughing as long and loud as anything since* Hancock and the Vikings. *26 February 1979: marvellously constructed, very funny... it makes me want to give up! 27 February 1979: ...congratulate* [Cleese] *on last night's disgustingly funny* Fawlty.

ROWAN ATKINSON[17]

[Basil is] *on the edge of mania and that is very funny, particularly from the educated middle-class 'behave well' perspective. When you see someone portraying someone from that background pushed to the limit of sanity and good behaviour. The repression.*

GRAHAM LINEHAN AND ARTHUR MATHEWS[18]

[Fawlty Towers is] *at least ten of the best farces ever written – a definite influence* (Linehan), *sheer greatness* (Mathews).

The pair argue that every good sitcom has a 'daft' character – in *Father Ted* it is Father Dougal Maguire, and in *Fawlty Towers* it is Manuel. Actor Ardal O'Hanlon, who played Dougal, claims that he drew inspiration from Manuel and from Laurel and Hardy.

JOHN LITHGOW[19]

[Would you do a British comedy show?] *I feel like I've already done one:* Third Rock from the Sun. *We did everything we could possibly do to rip off* Fawlty Towers, *including hire John Cleese.*

JOHN LENNON[20]

In John Lennon's final interview with BBC Radio 1 he talks about being a fan of *Fawlty Towers,* and professes disbelief that it was filmed in one day – something

Spiers was very proud of. "*I love* Fawlty Towers, *I'd like to have been in that...* Fawlty Towers *is the greatest show I've seen in years – they have it over here now. God, it's great. What a guy ... I saw him explaining how he only gets half an hour to do it ...* [they] *produce it once a week – what a masterpiece! A beautiful thing.*"

LISE MAYER[21]

We were determined to make [the Young Ones characters] *all really unpleasant. If you look at* Fawlty Towers, *none of them are really likeable. The audience are predisposed to like main characters so you don't actually have to make them sympathetic.*

LARRY GELBART[22]

We are so tranquillised by the TV set today. Even our insults in the insult humour shows are on a lower level. That's what is so marvellous about Cleese – the way he abused Manuel, cars, moose heads.

MARVIN KITMAN[23]

Fawlty Towers *is a funny funny show, which should always be on. It's an educational tool, an example for the new generation of sitcom writers of how sitcoms should be done.*

It's a model[24] *for future generations. It should run forever as a demonstration of how to write sitcoms, a continuous loop of all 12 episodes culminating in the 'rat' episode.*

DAVID MITCHELL[25]

On the surface, it may all be jokes and antics, but look at Fawlty Towers *– it is the greatest sitcom ever in my opinion but that marriage* [Basil and Sybil's] *is extremely bitter and unhappy. It is a very un-jolly scenario.*

Criticism of Fawlty Towers

No matter how well-loved a show is, how stellar its reputation, and how well it does in polls, there will always be naysayers and critics. *Fawlty Towers* was not initially the hit that more recent viewers might expect. *Monty Python* fans were not expecting a straightforward sitcom from Cleese. His friend Iain Johnstone[1] overheard producers saying *"oh dear, have you seen this new script Cleese has done? Oh it's terrible"*. A BBC Comedy Script Editor, Ian Main,[2] infamously dismissed the pilot script in a May 1974 memo,[3] calling it *"a collection of cliches and stock characters... a disaster"*, and Jimmy Gilbert, Head of Light Entertainment, reputedly told Cleese[4] to *"get them out of the hotel more"*. Gilbert remembered it[5] slightly differently: *"I was interested in anything John wanted to do for me."* He loved the script but was surprised at the staid hotel setting. Cleese convinced him that remaining in the hotel worked, as it could only build up the pressure around the characters. JHD was one of the few people who was very keen on it from the start – he was banned from reading the pilot script in bed, as he was laughing too much. He found the script in the office and said[6] *"I'm going to do this or die."*

John Lloyd[7] says[8] that *Fawlty Towers* was seen as a *"bizarre aberration"* at the time. His – and Cleese's – friends Douglas Adams and Graham Chapman went to the pilot taping and shared a taxi home, saying it was *"embarrassing and awful"*. The expectation among Cleese's peers seemed to be that by opting for a straightforward sitcom he was selling – or wimping – out somehow. Cleese recalled a *Daily Mirror*[9] review as being fairly typical: *"Long John Short On Jokes"*, a review printed after the second episode aired and quoted repeatedly ever since, including in 2024 interviews. Other reviewers were much more generous, however.

Steve Punt: *"The critics were all thinking that the Python team needed to be taken down a peg, whereas I, at 13, thought it was the best thing* [Cleese] *had ever done. They were queuing up to kick Cleese:* "he thinks he can master sitcom, does he?" *It's not standard, it's not set in a living room, it's not trying to be fashionable. It's an old-fashioned farce. The public were way ahead of the critics – the critics are always looking for something to write about, but the audience are looking for something to* laugh *at."*

The *Evening Standard* quoted Cleese in their preview of episode 1: *"low comedy with fast movement"*. The *Sunday Telegraph* reviewer Philip Purser, writing for the 21 September edition, found the episode *"puts up the blood pressure"* but ultimately thought it funny. He summed up Basil in a damning sentence: *"gaunt, hen-pecked, permanently harassed, by turns rude and cringing"*. A few weeks later[10] he added that, *"Cleese is outrageously funny as he hectors, wheedles, misconstrues every action, screams ... and hurries hither and thither on those long splayed legs."* *Fawlty Towers* was, he said, a situation comedy that drew humour from *"the head and the bowels"*. Sachs was sufficiently upset by Peter Buckman in *The Listener* that he quoted the review in his autobiography nearly 40 years later: Buckman highlighted the potentially racist dialogue.

Peter Fiddick in the *Guardian* on 18 October 1975 could not be happier with the show, calling it the undoubted hit of a season packed with comedy, *"something out of a new mould"*. The *Evening Standard,* in the person of Oliver Pritchett,[11] were more cautious initially,[12] calling the first episode's plot *"thin and obvious"* but praising the performances, particularly Cleese, and tentatively giving it three stars with a promise to return to reevaluate it before the end of the series. By 1979, Bill Grundy[13] in the same newspaper was calling it great comedy and boggling at the fact that *The Psychiatrist* was only *"the eighth episode ever"*. Sylvia Clayton[14] in the *Daily Telegraph* on 18 October 1975 likened Basil to Tom of *Tom and Jerry*, frenetic and flailing. Strangely her colleague Sean Day-Lewis[15] made several errors in his review a week later. He says the hotel was *"created and run by John Cleese and Connie Booth with the skilled support of Prunella Scales"*, an intriguing way to view the relationship between the Fawltys and Polly; he calls it a five-part series – which episode did he miss? – and he claims that the scene that had him *"crying with laughter"* was when Basil, Manuel and the Major *"got mixed up with an antelope head"*. Peter Fiddick calls the same episode *"one of the most amazingly funny programmes... it must certainly come back."* He added that he *"literally, laugh*[ed] *till I cried"*.

The show averaged only 1.8-2.6 million viewers on first showing, though this rose to 7 million three months later – undoubtedly due to word of mouth and good reviews, though also the difference in autumn and winter viewing habits played a part – and by contrast reached 12 million when repeated again a year later. However it was always going to be niche when compared to BBC1 mainstream entertainment. A big show like the Royal Variety Performance in November 1975, one month after the end of the first series, drew 22.6 million viewers effortlessly, a figure *Fawlty Towers* could not achieve until the 10th anniversary in 1985. *Fawlty Towers* never made it into the week's top 10 viewing figures on first broadcast, and while it is longer-lived than many sitcoms, it was a slow grower.

Overseas sales were good, however, and critics were more generous: Danish reviewers Ralph Oppenhejm and Claes Kastholm Hansen are quoted in *The Fawlty Rhetoric of National Character*:[16] *"The truly convincing fun of the day was to be found in the English series* Fawlty Towers, *a crazy farce with breathtaking acting and true situational comedy"* (Oppenhejm, 29 July 1979); "Fawlty Towers, *which is aired at an inconvenient time, is one of TV's little good deeds. For once a series in which the canned laughter does not seem like an attempt to persuade the viewer. The hotel owner John Cleese is screamingly, wonderfully crazy"* (Hansen, 5 August 1979).

Critical charges levelled at the show over the years include racism (both overt and more subtle examples), sexism, and – while clearly played entirely for comedy, not cruelty – the casual classism and ableism displayed can also be uncomfortable for some viewers. For others, it's simply not that funny. The critic A A Gill recalled[17] his mother Yvonne Gilan appearing in an episode of *Fawlty Towers* when he was younger, in a 2015 *Evening Standard* interview with Hermione Eyre. *"'When my mum was asked to do it, she showed me the script and I said, 'This is terrible!' He grimaces. 'That was my first piece of criticism.'"* [18] Cleese's own friends weren't entirely keen at the start either.

Sexism in the scripts comes out mostly in Basil's prudishness but it is refreshing to learn that at the time he was not regarded as sexist behind the scenes. There were not very many women working in mainstream TV comedy writing at the time – the most obvious being Carla Lane[19] (*The Liver Birds, Butterflies*) writing sitcoms and Victoria Wood[20] performing her own sketches and songs – so Connie Booth getting equal credit for what was clearly equal work is a good start. Carol Cleveland,[21] who had worked extensively with the Pythons, feels[22] that the show was good for women: it had *"wonderful female characters, strong women"*. Terry Jones, often cast as women in Python shows himself, agreed: *"women save the day, time and again. Polly saves Basil from Sybil, Sybil saves Basil from his customers. Basil is sexist, but* Fawlty Towers *is not."* This phrase mirrors Mark Lawson's evaluation and defence in the *Guardian* 4 years later: "*Fawlty Towers* isn't racist. Major Gowen is."[23]

Comic actress Miriam Margolyes has been quite critical of the 'Cambridge sexism' she experienced in the Footlights club. She told[24] Morwenna Banks[25] and Amanda Swift that *"they're not actually interested in women. They play all the women's parts ... in bold caricature. The only one who's allowed women any prominence is Cleese in* Fawlty Towers*"*. The writers bemoan that – in 1987 – it was *"not widely recognised"* that Booth had played an essential part in constructing the series. They suggest that this is because Cleese/Basil is the comic to Connie/Polly's straight 'man', but also wonder if it is that *"people are generally reluctant to accept women writers"*. 1970s and 80s comedy was *dominated* by male writers.

This does not seem to be exactly the case in 2025, 38 years later, but there are still relatively few mixed-sex writing relationships to compare: married couple Jan Etherington and Gavin Petrie wrote *Second Thoughts*[26] and its sequel *Faith in the Future* for Linda Bellingham; another couple, Pauline Devaney and Edwin Apps, wrote *All Gas and Gaiters* for Derek Nimmo 1966-71, but under a joint pseudonym (John Wraith), while Charlotte Bingham and Terence Brady wrote some episodes of *Robin's Nest,* and the short-lived sitcom *Yes, Honestly.* At the start of the 1980s Lise Mayer wrote cult favourite *The Young Ones* with Rik Mayall (with whom she was in a relationship at the time) and Ben Elton. Simon Pegg and Jessica Stevenson (now Hynes) wrote cult hit *Spaced*[27] together, and Caroline Aherne[28] wrote *The Royle Family*[29] with Craig Cash and Henry Normal, though neither group features a couple; Daisy May Cooper and her brother Charlie wrote *This Country*[30] more recently. Booth & Cleese remain the single most prominent married/divorced couple in British sitcom writing, however. Lane wrote solo, as have Hynes (*Up The Women),* Wood *(dinnerladies),* Phoebe Waller-Bridge *(Fleabag),* Michaela Coel *(Chewing Gum)* and Jennifer Saunders *(Absolutely Fabulous).* Female writing partnerships such as Dawn French and Jennifer Saunders are less common in sitcoms than in sketch comedy, although the duo wrote *Girls on Top* with Ruby Wax, and Saunders wrote *Jam and Jerusalem* with Abigail Wilson. Germaine Greer, who had been in the Footlights club herself, found it hard to write for her own performances and believes that women, particularly British women, "*work on other people's material"* from birth: fitting into moulds and taking on responsibilities that men feel freer to abandon. Banks and Swift argue that [British] men are more able to be *silly* as a result of this internalised solemnity on the part of women. This line of argument explains the silliness and surreality of *The Goons, Monty Python's Flying Circus,* the comedy club acts that led up to *The Young Ones* and the *Comic Strip Presents* family of related shows, *The League of Gentlemen (*another all-male comedy troupe who played all the female parts themselves), Banks's own sketch-show collaboration with a group of men, *Absolutely,* and Aherne's sketch show collaboration, *The Fast Show.* Booth and Mayer (both Americans) found it much easier to unleash the silly side of their sense of humour, not having to contend with innate British reserve and expectations, and – perhaps relevantly – living the other side of the Atlantic from some family members, so not feeling the same pressure to behave and be 'ladylike'.

Basil Fawlty is an unabashed snob and a prude – a flawed man with many neuroses relating to sex and class. The impression given is that Sybil is slightly posher than he is – she has better manners, certainly – but he would like to be upper class if he could. He treats guests he perceives as lower class with outright hostility; he fawns over an apparent Lord in the opening episode *A Touch of Class,* and dismisses the CID officer who will eventually alert Sybil to the truth. In *The*

Hotel Inspectors (s1e4) he similarly attempts to ingratiate himself to the guests he believes to be judging him. He judges an unmarried couple harshly in *The Wedding Party* (s1e3) – and of course many of the audience would have done the same at the time. Today the prudishness seems ridiculous, and an unmarried couple sharing a hotel room would raise no eyebrows at all, but at the time it was still low-key scandalous.

Basil is overtly rude and unpleasant to the equally unpleasant Mrs Richards in *Communication Problems* (s2e1) – she refuses to switch on her hearing aid to save the batteries, but he doesn't display an understanding attitude (to no one's real surprise). This episode's plot also relies heavily on the Major's slow decline into senility – he cannot remember information reliably enough to be Fawlty's cover story for a gambling win; when he does remember why he's holding money, he returns it at just the wrong moment. The Major's shown to be mildly absent-minded and bewildered in other episodes but only in this one does it cause actual calamity for Basil. In conjunction with the flippant attitude to deafness it looks more intentional than it perhaps really is: one example of casual ableism can be excused as funny, two can feel targeted.

Although some flaws are more obvious to modern audiences, *Fawlty Towers* did suffer criticism at the time for its portrayal of non-British characters in a still heavily racist 1970s society. Andrew Sachs, himself a German immigrant, did not dislike the character of Manuel: *"If it's insulting to the Spanish, what is Basil to the British?"*[31] but viewers did feel affronted on his behalf, particularly as the non-fluent immigrant was the constant victim of repeated verbal and physical attacks from Basil Fawlty. Basil constantly belittles Manuel's ability to perform simple tasks, his language skills and his country of origin, and denies him basic employment rights. Despite this, Manuel continues to want to please his irrational and intolerant manager, looking up to him as a mentor. Manuel is a sympathetic and kind character, and viewers can identify with his desire to please. Immigrant viewers particularly identified with his efforts to fit in, and to learn English through careful practice with colleagues and self-improvement books. He can be seen as aspirational. He is a victim and whipping-boy to Basil, but everyone else treats him with some respect.

Davidson in the *Independent* wrote that Manuel was perceived as an overtly racist stereotype, a bumbling figure who causes angst in critics and viewers – but he remains the most popular with audiences despite this – or perhaps because of it.

It is worth noting that Spanish television did buy and broadcast the show, re-dubbing Manuel as an Italian – perpetuating their own local prejudices about immigrant labour. French and Catalonian TV make him a Mexican. The perceived insult to Spanish people did not put them off, nor did German audiences find the show's treatment of their nation completely off-putting (although their later attempt at a remake did not feature an equivalent for the episode *The Germans*).

The hotel has other minority workers and non-British characters, of course. Polly, with all the privilege of a pretty blonde whom much of the audience knows to be an American (but played as canonically British), is attacked much less than Manuel, and is far more capable of standing up to her tyrant boss. She can use both her intelligence and her 'feminine wiles' to win arguments, without the disadvantage of a language barrier. Manuel struggles to keep up with her almost as much as he does with Basil, but she is much kinder to him. She recognises his effort with the language, and places herself between Manuel and the Fawltys as Manuel's ally and protector.

The single American character in the show is a guest, Mr Hamilton [played by *Canadian* actor Bruce Boa], who arrives at the hotel with his British wife in *Waldorf Salad* (s2e3). The late-night arrival means Mr Hamilton 'flashes the cash' to get his dinner when Basil baulks at keeping the chef on – a stereotype of Americans in the 1970s was that they were all much richer than Britons. For Americans travelling outside the USA for leisure, the cliché might have been justified, as by definition they had the money to spare – particularly when this is contrasted with the currency restrictions[32] British travellers were subject to when holidaying. Audiences can be forgiven for siding with Fawlty over Hamilton, a man embodying a cliché they fear might be accurate in real life. Fawlty becomes very defensive at any perceived criticism of England or his hotel and, while he is always wrong-footed by *any* guests managing to highlight gaps in his knowledge, when his opponent is not English his response is amplified in ferocity and volume. He is clearly very upset by the patronising and brusque manner of Mr Hamilton, who in turn deserves much of the aggressive behaviour Basil exhibits towards him. When Ugly American meets Rude Hotelier neither comes out of it well, but Basil has the advantage of familiarity and sympathy – the audience knows why he behaves this way and perhaps how he feels. Poor Mrs Hamilton attempts to mediate but both men effectively ignore her. Mr Hutchinson in *The Hotel Inspectors* also draws Basil's ire as an example of an exceedingly pompous and over-correcting man. He strikes even Basil as unnecessarily petty and pedantic. The audience *delight* in Basil's ultimate triumph over him, even if it does end badly when the real inspectors are identified.

Kurt, the Greek chef hired for the night in *Gourmet Night*, is – unusually for 1970s comedy – *not* the target of homophobic jokes, other than Basil's clichéd "*they invented it!*" when Polly explains his sexuality as background to the emerging kitchen crisis. Kurt is written to be the target of jokes about his inability to cope with rejection (Manuel is not gay and tells him so, rejecting his 'love') but modern viewers may find these scenes more uncomfortable than intended, with hints of homophobia on top of mild xenophobia. Steve Punt points out[33] that Cleese "*of course had worked with Graham Chapman, gay and an alcoholic, for years by this point.* Kurt is *a sympathetic character, drowning his feelings in alcohol. There's no mocking.*" We can feel sorry for him without effort.

Unusually, it is *Sybil* who demonstrates an anti-Irish stance when dealing with *The Builders* (s1e2). She favours Stubbs, an English builder, over O'Reilly and his Irish crew; Basil wants to save money and hires O'Reilly anyway. Sybil has some justification in favouring Stubbs, as O'Reilly has not completed a previous job, but she makes an unexpected out-of-character direct attack on O'Reilly and not Basil, usually the focus of her ire. A string of stereotypes and insults emerges:

> [to Basil] *He's shoddy, he doesn't care, he's a liar, he's incompetent, he's lazy. He's nothing but a half-witted, thick Irish joke!* ...[to O'Reilly] *I have seen more intelligent creatures lying on their backs at the bottom of ponds. I've seen better organised creatures than you running around farmyards with their heads cut off.*

Ultimately she is proved correct, as O'Reilly's cut corners nearly cause a catastrophe in the building, but we can expect that any modern version would remove the Irish slant from the scene. There's no reason to pit England against Ireland here, except to play off stereotypes that the viewing audience will happily enforce through their own prejudices. 1970s relations between England and Ireland were uncomfortable at the best of times and English audiences may have agreed with Sybil without much urging.

The most problematic episode for a modern audience is *The Germans* (s1e6) which rather impressively manages to illustrate three different examples of racism and xenophobia in one half-hour. This episode has been edited for 21st century broadcast and in the stage script, removing the worst lines, but other issues remain. Sybil's hospital doctor is black, and we see Basil's visible surprise and involuntary physical response when he appears on screen – he shrinks away from him on first sight. Basil does treat him politely and respectfully once they speak, and his main reaction to the conversation is a childish glee at the thought of the pain Sybil will be in after her treatment, but his initial recoil and facial expressions – Cleese's mastery of physical comedy demonstrating much more than any lines could say – do not sit well today.

Feelings about editing this episode to remove the Major's use of two racial slurs are mixed. Trevor Phillips,[34] former chairman of the Equality and Human Rights Commission: "*I am against the removal of these kinds of references. If you think the terms are unacceptable do not play the episodes. Do not tamper with the works of writers who created them at a particular time in order to make yourself feel better."* Louis Mahoney,[35] the actor playing the doctor in question, and an anti-racism campaigner, said the episode needed to still be seen because it satirised the attitudes of people who used racist language. He told *The Times* in 2020: *"I don't think there was anything wrong with* Fawlty Towers. *My feeling is* [the Major] *said what he said because he believed it. I don't think he was a nasty man and I think if he said the n-word it should be said very loudly because that's what offensive people say. It's mocking people who endorse his views."* Cleese feels the same way. He told *The Age*[36] newspaper in 2020, in response to news of UKTV editing the episode, that there was a *"really admirable feeling that we must make our society less discriminatory* [but] a *lot of the people in charge now at the BBC just want to hang on to their jobs ... they pacify* [complainants] *rather than standing their ground as they would have done 30 or 40 years ago."*

Armando Iannucci, writer and satirist, told the BBC in 2020[37] that reactions to satire and offence should be tempered carefully. *"I think it's important that we don't do a nervous reaction and diss everything from the past. There is an understanding... that attitudes, language, behaviour, tolerance was very different... I'm more concerned with ... what we do coming forward."*

Impressionist Rory Bremner told the Daily Mail[38] *"It's quite clear that John Cleese was ridiculing colonial attitudes. The laugh is at the Major's expense, not the races mentioned."* Steve Bennett, editor of comedy website Chortle, wrote that he understood *"the need to remove words and scenes that sound appalling to modern ears ...*[when] *repeated on terrestrial TV, which comes uninvited into the living room. But on-demand is different ... viewers are warned beforehand about questionable content.* [Retaining] *such scenes is useful to give an insight into how attitudes have changed."*

Kamm and Newmann,[39] in *British TV Comedies,* argue that Shakespeare could stand to be cleaned up as well: if the BBC thinks that *Fawlty Towers "could be offensive to contemporary audiences and* [can be] *tampered with to suit the dictates of political correctness, these productions are* [not thought to be] *autonomous works of art".* They believe there is a danger in changing TV comedies which give *"a voice to dispositions and anxieties at the time of production"* and expose the subject to laughter, not reverence. Oliver Goldsmith[40] wrote in *Sentimental Comedy* (1765) that morally upright but dull comedy might spell the death of the more entertaining comedy of manners *"which did not praise virtues but exposed human follies to ridicule".* Stewart Lee, stand-up comedian, argues[41] that taboo-breaking demonstrates what we *"stand to gain if we step outside restrictions of social convention and polite everyday discourse"* – something Basil definitely does at times, and his audience wishes they could do. Vicarious comedy always has a place as catharsis for its audience.

Cleese often refers to the Major with affection despite all the controversy. *"We loved this guy who was in his own world... never understood what was going on* but always added his own insane interpretation of it." The Major's erased line is a slur that simply will not be broadcast on TV today, but it took until 2013 for it to be edited from any BBC broadcast, and it was still available in full on streaming services well into 2023. [At time of writing *Fawlty Towers* does not appear on any UK streaming service, however.] When the episode was finally edited, Mark Lawson wrote a defence for the *Guardian*[42] arguing that the Major is a clichéd product of his time, so he uses non-PC language without thinking. His use of the n-word is in a spirit of pedantry rather than vitriol – he tells Basil about a woman who described a cricket team with an *inaccurate* slur, and so he corrected her – using another slur, but again, without thinking or apparent ill-intent. He appears to focus only on her "*factual error*", and not the insult behind it. Lawson strongly defends Cleese and Booth as writers – they are sending up people like the Major.

> *The joke depends on the audience first thinking that, when the Major rebukes his companion "No, no, no", he is condemning her for inflammatory language, when it turns out that he is simply a particularly pedantic racist.*

Cleese[43] confirmed the intention:

> *If you put* [racist words] *into the mouth of someone you want to make fun of you're not broadcasting their views, you're making fun ... The Major was an old fossil left over from decades before. We were not supporting* [his views]... *If people are too stupid to see that, what can one say?*

He discusses[44] language in a wider context:

> *The woke people...miss something quite badly. The meaning of a word depends on its context. If I use sarcasm... I'm meaning the opposite of the words I'm actually saying. If you don't get irony... if you take it seriously, you completely misunderstand the intention of the writer or speaker.*

This argument holds if we are able to view the show through a completely satirical filter: every awful piece of behaviour demonstrated in the show is mocking one type of person or another. Snobs, racists, tourists, con-men, grumpy old women – everyone is fair game. Fawlty's concussion removes a filter from his conversation – he is not normally a polite man at the best of times, but without full control his attempts to avoid mentioning the war wind up upsetting and hurting at least one of his guests quite badly. And if this was completely out of character for Fawlty, we might understand and forgive him the out-of-character moments – he's only human, after all. But we've also seen five episodes before this one, each confirming that Basil is *always* a horrid man at heart: injury only enhances his nastiness.

In an episode that also appears to exercise decades of pent-up anti-German sentiment – it was first broadcast thirty years and six months after the end of World War II, when many veterans were still in their 40s and 50s – it is sometimes difficult to see the funny side of the satire. For every dozen *"Alf Garnett is a figure of fun, not a hero"* arguments, there's a viewer thinking *"but he spoke for me"* – and so it can be with *Fawlty Towers*. The Major's "benign racism" – *"he didn't really mean it"* – and Fawlty's atrocious behaviour – *"but it was the head injury making him behave so badly"* – can sum to an aggressive and unpleasant whole: this episode is comic, but some people truly did – *do* – think and say these things, and we can't be sure they know it's satirical. Responses to the occasional withdrawal and editing of this episode range from anger that it existed in that form in the first place (and relief that it's been edited), to anger about giving in to "woke" sentiments and the need to censor the past, regardless of anyone's feelings. It would be wonderful to think that everyone always knew the intent was satirical, but cynicism and experience unfortunately suggests otherwise. Cleese is not immune to this himself: he has railed against "*wokeness*" and the editing of the episode, although some critics feel that censoring the Major was not only necessary but shouldn't have ever been needed – even in 1975 Cleese should have known that the attitudes were unpleasant and caused upset to some of his audience. Steve Punt argues that there is no way Cleese *"couldn't know it was offensive even then"* [in 1975], and that it wasn't necessary for the Major to use that language at all – his casual racism is demonstrated just as well without it. It is perfectly possible to demonstrate the attitude without the words, as the edited version of the episode demonstrates.

Thomas Leatham, writing in FarOut, in 2022,[45] says that it is *"beyond evidence that such words have caused deep offence to those that they have historically been aimed. Despite being under the guise of comedy, as Cleese says, only being there so the people who use them so wantonly can be derided, they have a historical context that cannot be ignored"*.

We cannot ignore the feelings of those who watched in 1975, and we must not ignore the feelings of those who will watch in 2025. It is testament to the genius of the show that it has been watched consistently for 50 years; it deserves to have its flaws acknowledged too.

The last word in the episode is given to one of the German characters, observing the chaos Basil has caused and the climax of his absurd behaviour: *"However did they win?"* The audience is intended to – and generally does – share their disbelief, thankfully. We *know* that Basil is not representative of the English, or the British, as a whole. But he *is* a warning: if you turn the English up to 11 and annoy them enough, this is what might emerge. We all have bad days, but we (mostly) know how to keep our temper when pictures fall off walls, food goes off, colleagues make mistakes, the unexpected happens, our spouses irritate us, our cars break down, our tradespeople let us down, the wine is corked, our guests are irrational and petty, and our fear of screwing up leads us to make other mistakes. And if our collective fear of turning into Basil Fawlty has held society together for nearly five decades, long may it continue.

Cultural Inheritance

There are many ways in which the influences of *Fawlty Towers* can be seen in everyday life today. It has been assimilated into British, especially English, culture and it is a building block for writers and comedians working in the UK and elsewhere.

THE SCRIPTS

The characters and plots of *Fawlty Towers* have become a useful cultural shorthand, especially among those of us who internalise scripts and can't help using favourite lines in conversation, almost against our will. Mealtimes in a family of sitcom fans might involve *"the soup"* in an affectedly posh voice, the dismissive *"We're fresh out of Waldorfs"* if you ask for salad, or perhaps a condescending *"chef has just opened the tin"* when dithering about a dessert choice. This tic is not limited to *Fawlty Towers* fans of course – serving or choosing fish often triggers *"today's fish is trout a la creme, enjoy your meal"* around *Red Dwarf* fans; you'll hear *"just the one, Mrs Wembley"* when offered a drink (*On the Up*); and beware the suggestion *"Sausages... sausages and plants and goldfish"* (*The Young Ones* – this is the meal that neil pye *(sic)* cooked on the first night in the student house) when asked what might be for dinner. Sounds nasty? Whatever you do, don't request a cappuccino from a *Blackadder* diehard.

Fans – and now their descendants – will use lines without even remembering what they are from, as they have become part of everyday speech. Few remember that everyday familiar phrases started life as sitcom, radio, sketch comedy, or music hall catchphrases. On the internet today you can find people 'discovering' recycled phrases anew, and misattributing lines to the newer creators. *"Mind how you go"* is often attributed to Sir Terry Pratchett – and he certainly did use it, but he got it from *Dixon of Dock Green*,[1] shown on TV in his own youth. *Fawlty Towers* has reached the same level of cultural osmosis, so people now forget that there is an older source. *"Let's hope it's nothing trivial"* in *Gourmet Night* can be found attributed to Cleese – omitting Booth – in a number of sources, but the writer Irvin S Cobb coined it at least 40 years earlier. People also hear lines they've known 'all their lives' and mis-attribute to a fictitious older source, assuming that Cleese and Booth couldn't have coined *all* of these great jokes themselves.

Many people have absorbed Manuel's *"I know nothing"* or Basil's *"Don't mention the war"* into their personal lexicons, the same way that they will use *"Listen carefully, I will say this only once"* or *"I have a cunning plan"* (*'Allo 'Allo* and *Blackadder,* respectively). They do *know* that they're quoting a TV show, but the phrasing has become so enmeshed in the vocabulary, so embedded, that it completes itself before the conscious brain can intervene. We simply don't say *"I mentioned it once but I don't think anyone noticed"* if we have the opportunity to say *"I mentioned it once but I think I got away with it"*. If you say *"I know nothing"* in just the right tone of voice, people just *know* that you mean to convey that you know something and have been told to forget all about it. My own immigrant father *"learned* [English] *from a boook"* – which of course has to be said with Sachs' exact intonation and elongated vowel.

Jodi Taylor:[2] *"I was at work and the person who was supposed to be my assistant and treat me with respect, as I pointed out to her… I did something more than normally stupid and she turned round to me and said* [in Basil's tone of voice] *"sackless bint!*[3]*" and I've been waiting for an opportunity to use that ever since!"*

Steve Punt:[4] *"I will say to my wife 'I say, he doesn't look quite the ticket'. Even the kids quote it: they will say, in that tone of voice, 'I'll have the soup ... and a pate'."*

Prunella Scales' particular way of saying *"ooh, I know"* (a habit mimicking Connie Booth's real life vocal tic, along with her distinctive laugh) is both ridiculous and infectious, and it's frighteningly easy to find yourself doing it without realising. Basil's riposte *"then why is she telling you?"* has been in the thoughts, if not mouths, of many frustrated listeners to such calls.

There's a particularly satisfying dopamine hit from completing a quotation or reference accurately. Internet communities are full of people providing the next line as a collective social activity – these were called cascades at the peak of Usenet activity (1990s), and are frowned upon by staid authority figures. *"In Usenet usage,*[5] *a cascade is a series of trivial follow-up postings, usually with each addition consisting of a single-line rhyme or comment. Not only do such postings not substantially contribute to any discussion, they involve the wasteful quoting of an entire article with minimal additions…filling a newsgroup with garbage postings."* In an era when we no longer pay per kB for downloads and most people in North America and Europe have unmetered access, it is far less disruptive to play such games. A Reddit or Facebook group may trade lines for days. Google for *"Fawlty Towers quotes"* and your social media platform of choice will return many results. Contributors[6] will often editorialise as well: *I will say* 'back to the world of dreams*' at work;* 'Would you like the hotel moved a little to the left?' *This is my go to when asked about pointless shit; when the Americans complain that they* "had to take a little back street called the M5", *and I thought to myself that he should've gone on the M3 to Popham and then the A303...*

The show is a reliable fallback for newspaper stories in quiet periods, and clickbait websites that rely on external material for hits – 10 best *Fawlty Towers* lines, 20 reasons *Fawlty Towers* is the best UK sitcom, and so on. Impressionist shows have lessened in popularity in the last two decades but every 80s and 90s show had a Cleese moment, whether it was silly walks, Basil Fawlty, or Basil Fawlty doing a silly walk (as in *The Germans*).

Steve Punt: "*TV of that era has lasted because people had to remember to talk about it and dissect it after each show* [because there were no repeats or recordings]. *Fawlty is easy to do impressions of, and Michael Barrymore*[7] *nicked the character wholesale. Fawlty became a stock part of people's cultural knowledge and impressions, our reflex responses. That helped develop the legend. ITV viewers (and the country did divide into BBC and ITV households at that time, sometimes for practicality, sometimes for class reasons) hadn't seen the show but they all saw the impressions. But this does lose something, as do clip shows: You watch the highlights but not the build-up. So you lose the whole impact if you only see the 'best bits'.*"

THE AWARDS AND POLLS

Channel 4 ran a series of polls on *100 Greatest...* In 1999 *100 Greatest TV Moments* ranked *The Germans* 11th out of 100. In the 2001 *100 Greatest TV Characters*[8] poll, Basil was ranked second only to Homer Simpson. The 2004 TV show *Britain's Best Sitcom*[9] ranked the show only 5th in a long list, but it would rally. In a 2012 Lovefilm[10] poll, *Fawlty Towers* came second to *Blackadder* as Best TV series ever. In 2017 TV channel Gold[11] asked comedians to name their funniest shows, and *Fawlty Towers* topped the poll. The British Film Institute's top 100 TV shows, judged by 1600 industry professionals,[12] named *Fawlty Towers* as the top show in 2000. There has barely been a comedy poll since 1975 that hasn't mentioned *Fawlty Towers*. A slightly more niche award is the NatWest Car Insurance 'Momentous Motoring Moment,[13]' awarded in 1999 to the infamous car-thrashing scene in *Gourmet Night*.

John Cleese as Basil would win a TV BAFTA for Best Light Entertainment Performance in 1980, beating Andrew Sachs as Manuel, and previous winners Ronnie Barker (*The Two Ronnies*) and Penelope Keith (*To The Manor Born*). He had previously been nominated for *Monty Python's Flying Circus* in 1970 and 1971, losing to Eric Morecambe and Ernie Wise (*The Morecambe and Wise Show*) in both years, and for *Fawlty Towers* in 1976, when he had lost to his old friend, Ronnie Barker (*Porridge*).

The show itself won Best Scripted Comedy in 1976, with the award going to John Howard Davies, as director/producer, and again in 1980, with the award going to Bob Spiers and Douglas Argent, director and producer respectively. Cleese *was* given a Film BAFTA for Best Actor at the 1989 awards, for *A Fish Called Wanda* – arguably a successor of sorts to *Fawlty Towers,* though not as obviously related as his earlier *Clockwise.*

Andrew Sachs won a Broadcasting Press Guild Award in April 1976 for his role as Manuel, and the show won Best Comedy, but the BPG is an industry specialist group of UK media journalists and not well publicised. John Cleese won the Royal Television Society Programme Award for Outstanding Creative Achievement for *Fawlty Towers* in 1976 and was also given the 1976 BBC TV Personality of the Year[14] for a wider body of work. *Fawlty Towers* won a Variety Club Award in February 1977.[15]

The 1979 Montreux Light Entertainment Festival was a surprise loss for *Fawlty Towers. The Kipper and the Corpse* had been submitted by the BBC, but the jury rejected it for a prize. Roger Wilmut quotes[16] an unnamed Swiss TV executive: *"Funny foreigners may be a joke to the English. But not to us. We are your funny foreigners. Manuel is a character in dubious taste."* The Monty Python team as a whole had been presented with the Golden Rose in 1971, would win an honorary Golden Rose in 1995, and were eventually inducted into the Montreux Hall of Fame in 2005, at the 50th Golden Rose awards – but *Fawlty Towers* remains unrecognised. Perhaps its 50th anniversary in 2025 will improve that?

The Hyatt hotel chain used episodes of *Fawlty Towers* as a business training tool – illustrating exactly how *not* to treat your customers – and the show won a Queen's Award for Export Achievement as a result. The London Hilton and British Holiday Inn hotels used *Gourmet Night* as training material for "what *not* to do" in a catering crisis. This was not surprising to anyone who had seen any Video Arts customer care training material. Cleese had been running Video Arts,[17] with Anthony (Tony) Jay since 1972, and was very used to producing training films with contrary and awkward customers. The key, he said, was to think about how you were *supposed to* treat customers... and then Basil would do the opposite. As a bonus: when Cleese was absent from the company – writing, rehearsing and filming *Fawlty Towers*, for large parts of 1974-5 and 1978-79 – Jay needed a second person to work with, and in stepped Jonathan Lynn. This collaboration ultimately gave us *Yes, Minister* in 1979 and *Yes, Prime Minister* in 1980, invaluable contributions to the British comedy lexicon and catalogue – an unexpected legacy of *Fawlty Towers.*

BASIL THE MONSTER

In May 2003 Basil Fawlty was recognised as the most 'Monstrous Boss on British' TV by the UK Satellite Channel UK Gold, just beating David Brent from *The Office* (BBC2/BBC1 2001–2003). 'Basil Fawlty' has become shorthand for a particular type of frustrated manager, and his name is used in a wide variety of contexts – the allusion is usually enough to paint the picture the writer wants.

> Andrew Hill in the *Financial Times*: *"David Brent and Basil Fawlty Personify Britain's Hapless Managers."* FT.com 2017
>
> Sean French in the *New Statesman*: *"Conspiracies Very Rarely Succeed. Basil Fawlty Is the Best Guide to the Way the World Really Works (Real World Intrigue Not as Complex as in Movies)."* vol. 129. 2000.
>
> Robert Macfarlane in *The Observer*: *"Even Basil Fawlty Wouldn't Check in: Seedy, Venal, Mesmerising – That's Just the Hotel Owner. The Guests Are Odder Still."* 2001

The first article is about UK businesses and the increase in "accidental managers", promoted but not trained, and so varying in competence. The allusion to Fawlty and Brent is not too tenuous – both are terrible examples of management – but Fawlty was *not* an accidental manager. He *chose* to open the hotel.

The second is a piece of writing about how (mainly) military accidents happen just as often as successes – the real world is a farce, when we look at the facts. There is very little reference to comedy at all in this article, but we still understand from the title and the in-article name-drop what French means – situations which spiral into tragedy or disaster through "comic" error occur much more often than true conspiracies do. Missiles misfire, buildings collapse – "you couldn't make it up", as the saying goes. Basil Fawlty would agree wholeheartedly with this premise, and we as viewers and readers understand what French means by using his name here.

The third article is a review of the novel *Hotel Honolulu* by Paul Theroux. Neither the review nor the novel has anything to do with *Fawlty Towers* – but again, we know from the headline that the hotel in question *must* be bad if even Fawlty wouldn't stay there. The shorthand works.

Less offensively, Basil Fawlty can be useful for a reviewer trying to explain a character or performer's rage, frustration, or physicality. Comedian Rhod Gilbert in particular attracts a number of allusions: *"Gilbert makes Basil Fawlty look as serene as the Dalai Llama* (sic), *so emphatic does he get when making his valid points he just couldn't let lie."*[18] *'Man who makes Basil Fawlty look like a Pilates* teacher."[19] "It is like watching Basil Fawlty on fast forward combined with an Alex Ferguson hairdryer moment." [20]

Comic magazine *Viz*[21] featured Basil and Manuel as regular characters Roger Mellie and Sid the Sexist on their cover in August 2024. The magazine had previously featured the show in a number of articles. Co-editor Graham Dury is a fan[22]: *"I remember coming upon Fawlty Towers by chance on BBC2 one Friday night in 1975 and I was gripped"*. The cover was prompted by the stage play. It is and is not connected to any story in the issue, it is simply an opportunity for an homage to a show the magazine staff love. The attention to detail in the image is impressive – a labour of love by co-editor and artist Simon Thorp.

HOTEL HELL

There is a huge selection of articles using *Fawlty Towers* as a byword for poorly-run businesses:

> Matthew Vincent in the *Financial Times*[23]: *"Ryanair Resorts to the Fawlty Towers School of Man Management."* The article criticises Michael O'Leary (sometimes called 'the Fawltyesque' Ryanair CEO – we can assume the allusion is to his irascible and sometimes crass manner,[24] as he's demonstrably far more successful than Basil!) for taking every opportunity to extract cash from his customers (*£20 to keep the chef on*), providing a sub-standard service, and manipulating pilots into shifts and routes they don't want: *"And this is an offer they cannot refuse. "We don't need their agreement," he noted, in a tone redolent of Fawlty Towers' finest hastily revising the dinner menu."*

The Economist wins the most tenuous namedrop, with *Euro Towers or Fawlty Towers?*[25] This is an article about the European Central Bank with no allusion to the show at all, beyond the implication that the ECB may be rather chaotic. A more shocking European story appeared in *The Guardian*[26] in 2003: controversial Italian politician Silvio Berlusconi *"rounded on German MEP Martin Schulz and suggested he play a guard in a film about Nazi concentration camps. It was a Fawlty Towers moment, mentioning the war in the most inappropriate context imaginable – the symbolic site of European reconciliation and integration."* The headline *Europe stunned by* Fawlty Towers *gaffe: Nazi jibe leaves governments dreading Berlusconi's EU term* couldn't be more appropriate. Berlusconi mentioned the war and he did not get away with it.

Even *Farmer's Weekly* gets in on the act with *"Those Basil Fawlty Moments"*,[27] the headline for a benign column about very minor mishaps at a rural B&B. A guest locks himself out of a room, the hoteliers borrow a JCB from a farmer to get back in through the window, a dog walker observes them "breaking in". In real life the situation resolves easily – the hotelier in the JCB bucket identifies himself, the dog walker is satisfied, the guest eventually gets back in to his room (though not before the hotelier has been slightly scared by his wife's control of the JCB). The sub-editor (for they usually devise the headlines) knows exactly what they have done with this headline – the reader has been led to expect a tale of calamity and chaos; the reality is rather milder. But we can all imagine how Basil would have handled such a situation – the anecdote is reasonably close to the section of *The Psychiatrist* where Basil climbs a ladder, after all.

Fawlty Towers is also handy for headline writers who want to imply chaos and mistakes in any situation: MP Teresa Gorman's building issues were even likened to *Fawlty Towers* by her local Essex council, according to her[28]: *"The Council says we've built a version of Fawlty Towers but that is completely untrue."* She and her husband spent £300,000 on restoring a listed Essex home but allegedly forgot to obtain planning permission.

Academics use the show for similar purposes: a paper about academic research errors entitled *Verification of Citations: Fawlty Towers of Knowledge?*[29] does at least mention the show, though only in passing. In 2000 a piece of academic innovation was heralded with the headline *Move over Fawlty Towers:*[30] *"Strathclyde University is combating Basil Fawlty tendencies in the hospitality business with an innovative CD-Rom education programme from its Scottish Hotel School."* Believe it or not, this *was* groundbreaking technology at the time.

Advertising and Marketing professionals also reference the show:[31] Because Rowan Atkinson decided to set *The Black Adder* in mediaeval times to avoid any comparison with *Fawlty Towers*, "Fawlty Towers' *success became the essential unintended ingredient that created the genius of Blackadder. The sad truth is most experts would have looked at the available data and tried to do another* Fawlty Towers. *It would have been terrible. A pale imitation."* While market forces demand we try to copy what we know works, creativity requires us to think of something different, and may result in a much better outcome.

Allusions to the hotel and to the sitcom are sometimes hard to distinguish from each other, but at other times there is no doubt. Hotels around the world must dread online reviews that mention *Fawlty Towers* in any way: *Worse than Fawlty Towers! Fawlty Towers was luxury compared to this place! Disgusting – Fawlty Towers springs to mind!* These are all genuine TripAdvisor review headlines, complete with exclamation marks, though we'll refrain from naming and shaming the hotels in question. Simon Hoggart[32] wrote about[33] 'the worst hotel in Britain' in the *Guardian,* pointing out that *"articles about such places are always illustrated by a picture of John Cleese as Basil Fawlty. But that's unfair. The point about* Fawlty Towers *was that it had pretentions. Basil and Sybil wanted it to be the finest hotel in Torquay, but it was the clientele who let them down."* The hotel itself – as with the *Gleneagles* before it – was actually perfectly fine, the odd wobbly wall or disappearing door aside. The problem was almost all in the management: while some of the real hotels branded this way are undoubtedly mismanaged, few are run by a hotelier quite as bad as Basil.

Hotels *deliberately* named Fawlty Towers have appeared in places like Otautau, New Zealand; Cape Town,[34] South Africa; Florida,[35] USA; Rome,[36] Italy; Yangshuo,[37] China; W Australia, Zambia, Belgium – but all are serious hotels, trading only on the name and, thankfully, not the reputation.

In Sidmouth, 30 miles along the coast from Torquay, hotelier Stuart Hughes changed his name by deed poll to Stuart Basil Fawlty Hughes. He was elected as a member of the East Devon District Council, representing the Raving Loony Green Giant Party, in 1991. The party headquarters was Hughes's hotel in Sidmouth – also named *Fawlty Towers.*

The hotel industry is well aware of the issues, of course. Emily Boxall wrote for *Investors Chronicle:*[38] *What can the hospitality industry learn from* Fawlty Towers? *"The exhausting series of disasters that took place every episode will resonate with the current UK hospitality industry, which lost approximately £200m every day during 2020... to bounce back the industry can perhaps take some tips from Fawlty's abominable example."*

For instance, she notes, self-service works. The Fawltys' guests could not get what they wanted from the hoteliers, but today they could provide their own drinks and food: Airbnb thrived during the pandemic. Vegan food was not well catered for by hotels like *Fawlty Towers,* but modern hotels thrive on vegan and vegetarian offerings. Foreign guests are much better handled today, and overseas revenue from North American visitors grows rapidly. Germans must quarantine (this article was written in 2021*)* but this allows them to avoid *"idiotic hotel owners"*. Manuel represents the low-skilled overseas workers who have been prevented from moving to the UK, post-Brexit, as immigration prioritises *"the brightest and best"* over low-skilled workers. Hotels and other industries are struggling to fill summer vacancies as a result of that policy.

A *Guardian* article[39] in 2019 explored the link between *Fawlty Towers* and Brexit further. Alex Clark argues that the show was a warning to us – *"an ensemble piece about isolation... the impotence that results when the world as we wish it to be is so agonisingly at odds with the world as it is. It is the Brexit mindset incubating in the shabby surroundings of a down-at-heel hotel that has seen far better days."* Clark draws attention to the role of Manuel as a final victim of imperial Britain and a past some British want to return to – where it is OK to control and abuse non-Britons. Fawlty has negative responses to young people, sexuality, immigration, race, and social climbing (unless it is his own), and he yearns for the past when Britain was best and didn't need the rest of the world – like many outspoken Brexiteers. But of course Basil does not get what he wants, and he is forced to adjust his expectations and live in the real world.

Legal scholar Neil Cobb writes about a legal case in *Gay couple's break like Fawlty Towers: dangerous representations of lesbian and gay oppression in an era of progressive law reform*. [40]

The trial and judgement was printed in the *Daily Telegraph*: "*A gay couple's stay in a country hotel took on, in the words of a judge, 'elements of Fawlty Towers' when first they were told to sleep in separate beds, then locked out overnight and, finally, threatened with a beer tap that they mistook for a handgun.*"[41] Cobb elaborates on how the judge likened the hotel proprietor to "*something akin to cantankerous Basil Fawlty from the classic UK TV sitcom Fawlty Towers*". This view, Cobb argues, undermines the seriousness of the case as it "*presents a comedic interpretation of the hotelier's actions that refuses to take seriously his discriminatory behaviour*", risking the perception of other incidents of discrimination in the same vein as "*harmless and ephemeral... underpinning the comedy of the scene for the judge is an implicit (and comprehensible) assessment of the relative power of the couple in this archetypal bed and breakfast scenario.*" Hotel proprietors have more power than their guests and should not use this to discriminate; the reporting of such behaviours should not be trivialised with comedy.

Michael Apter reflects on the synergies in the situation: a hotel is a place of opposites – a 'home' that is simultaneously not a home, somewhere to stay but not remain, a place where hotel staff live and also work, a public and private place – especially for the owner. Hotels are run for the convenience of guests but are "*also patently run for the convenience of the owner*". Paul Davies: "*Fawlty Towers mercilessly satirises the hotel industry and tourist service, both of which were perceived as exemplifying the British disease of chronic inefficiency. The so-called 'British Disease' was a derogatory term for what was believed to be a relative decline in Britain's economic power throughout the twentieth century.*"

Fire safety is not inherently funny, and *Before Grenfell: Fire, Safety and Deregulation in Twentieth-Century Britain*[42] is, as you'd expect, a sobering read. Chapter two, *How red tape saves lives: the law on fire precautions in Britain since the 1970s,* is serious, but inevitably addresses the portrayal of the Fawlty Towers fire preparedness. It is not critical of the hotel: "*Whereas Basil fails to grasp the seriousness of the fire drill and of maintaining precautionary equipment, his staff (with the exception of Manuel) are well trained in the use of extinguishers, and his*

guests are prepared to briefly interrupt their holidays to participate in the drill."
Ewen notes that it was Basil's legal duty to carry out the fire drill, under the 1971 Fire Precautions Act, and that guests were significantly more likely to encounter a fire in a hotel than at home. The portrayal of the guests as more than willing to participate rings true to life.

THE NAMESAKES

Britain has a strong tradition of naming and anthropomorphising vehicles – *Brum, Gumdrop, Boaty McBoatface* – and every year a new wave of witty names will hit the newspapers. Gritters, for spreading grit on snowy and icy surfaces, particularly lend themselves to this punny practice, and the roll call includes *Dr Snow* and *Coldfinger* (Scotland trunk roads), *Usain Salt* and *Nicole Saltslinger* (Leeds), *Spready Mercury* (Dumfries and Galloway), and *Andy McFlurry* (Edinburgh). Even Minnesota, USA, have got in on the act with *Edward Blizzardhands* and *Ctrl Salt Delete*. To this list, in 2020, Manchester added *Basil Salty*. Doncaster held a public vote, shortlisting the same name, in 2017 – but *David Plowie* just pipped Basil to the post. There are a number of claims to a Scottish *Basil Salty* too, but no local authority appears to own him.

Basil Fawlty is one of the long list of names guessed by Wade Wilson (Ryan Reynolds) when he is trying to deadname the character Ajax, in the 2016 film *Deadpool*. In the same year, the *Blood and Wine* expansion for *The Witcher 3: Wild Hunt* introduces a character named Barnabas-Basil Foulty. He is the majordomo of a property owned by the player's character – i.e. the steward of a property, or the manager. In *Jumpin' Jack Flash*, Whoopi Goldberg's character identifies herself as *Sybil Fawlty* in a phone call. Hospital comedy *Scrubs* puts Basil's name on a medical chart in a blink and you'll miss it reference.

When the original Gleneagles hotel in Asheldon Road, Torquay was finally demolished it was replaced with a block of 36 retirement flats, eventually named Sachs Lodge after Andrew Sachs's death in 2016. A blue plaque[43] on the building marks the importance of the site. However you can still stay in *a* Gleneagles Hotel, Torquay – in 2025, this is run by the Best Western group. No pets are allowed – not even a hamster or annoying small dog – and there are TVs in every room. It won't be quite the same experience, but you should get a good night's sleep.

OTHER APPEARANCES

John Cleese portrayed Basil in a 1980 special[44] for the British rock band Queen. Basil is seen at a bar and is asked what he thinks of Queen. He shows disgust and calls the music "*rock rubbish*". He asks, "*What do you need that for when you've* got Beethoven?... ban it now." Cleese also reprised the role of Basil for the song "Don't Mention the World Cup",[45] an allusion to *"don't mention the war"* from *The Germans*, for the 2006 FIFA World Cup. The aim of the song was to reduce tension between English (and Australian) fans and their German hosts.

Cleese turned down a mock-Basil cameo in a show about Richard Wagner, but did work again with Andrew Sachs and Prunella Scales for Video Arts training films and Amnesty International charity performances. Scales and Cleese worked on sketches for *The Human Face*[46] – not as the Fawltys, but as very similar characters. Scales starred in Tesco commercials as a Sybilline creature, always complaining or having some kind of issue with the store while her long-suffering daughter looked on, while Cleese made adverts for Sainsbury's at the same time – a gift for journalists and critics who love to pit them against each other. Cleese appeared as Basil in a 2016 TV advert for Specsavers[47] during which, in a reference to *Gourmet Night,* Basil accidentally attacks an adjacent police car, mistaking it for his own. Andrew Sachs, as Manuel, promoted a lot of products including building societies and Australian wine Yalumba Carte d'Or:[48] *"I bring you car door".*

In 2008 Basil and Manuel appeared as aged versions of themselves in *We Are Most Amused.*[49] *"I can't really say no to John, he's so much bigger than me."* Andrew Sachs and his stepson John considered creating a sitcom based entirely on Manuel – *Perrin* writer David Nobbs was approached to write it but declined – and the idea eventually fizzled out. In September 2000 he began a one-man show named *Fawlty Years On* initially, then renamed *Life After Fawlty*. It included a monologue on how to survive being a Spanish waiter, as well as poetry recitation and reflection on his life and career.

In the *Secret Policeman's Third Ball,*[50] Stephen Fry and Hugh Laurie present a 'Silver Dick'[51] award to 'Jim' Cleese, a revered elder statesman of comedy – the sketch forming an early UK comedy roast.[52] They claim that the award is in recognition of a career that includes a comedy show that ran for *"a whole twelve episodes before being taken off"*. Fry and Laurie discuss with him the idea that the BBC cancelled the *"heartwarming comedy classic* Fawlty Towers *… just when it was starting to get good"*, and jab at him about his 'messy divorce' from *"the woman who was chiefly responsible for writing your scripts"*. *"Michael Barrymore doesn't even bother to do you anymore."* They imply he is bitter, old, and despairing. *"We all want to see* Basil Brush[53] *back on television."* Cleese weeps on stage as Fry and Laurie mock him and claim he is nothing without his dead parrot.

The New York regional paper *Newsday*[54] started a Basil Fawlty for Prime Minister campaign – in a mock election he won 63% of the vote. Columnist Marvin Kitman[55] was an enormous fan of the show and mentioned it whenever he could, from the first US broadcasts well into the 1990s. He called the show[56] *"the definitive guide to hotel management and relaxed personal living... people who saw it for the first time* [in 1993] *are still laughing* [in 1996]". He campaigned for repeat showings of *Fawlty Towers* on local public service broadcasting channels (PBS) from the 1970s to the end of his days on the paper. Channel 13, his local station, had declined to show the second series in 1979 *"because it wasn't funny enough"*, a judgement he would crusade against until they finally showed it in September 1980. He wrote about having lunch with Cleese in summer 1996, asking him about a reunion show. Cleese was not forthcoming, so Kitman encouraged his readers to *"unsheath* [their] *mighty pens"* and write begging letters (his contact details were published at the end of every column) and he would pass these on to Cleese personally.

(DON'T MENTION) THE DINING EXPERIENCE

(I'm mentioning it once but I think I'll get away with it.) In 2016 John Cleese was alerted to the existence of the *Faulty Towers Dining Experience*[57] (note spelling), which was operating in Australia without his permission or knowledge. He was not happy, although it was subsequently established that legally, the concept did not need his or Connie Booth's approval. This version of the show had been established since 1997 in Australia, and arrived in the UK in 2008[58] – it had obviously escaped Cleese's notice in its first 13 years.

> *"After waiting 20 minutes for my starter... the lady next to me had fished the chef's false teeth out of her appetiser and Sybil had used a balding man's head as a mirror to adjust her hair... I realised I was in for an evening of authentically awful Seventies-style chow."*
>
> Journalist Ellen Stewart reviews[59] the Dining Experience and is only disappointed by the food.

Other entrepreneurs have had similar ideas. By 2006 a UK firm was marketing a more passive version to holiday-makers:

> Basil! Superbreak Goes Fawlty[60]: "*Customers can experience the hospitality of Basil, Sybil and Manuel at seven hotels offering Fawlty Towers packages, in Superbreak's latest programme. Guests can watch a cast perform a range of classic sketches. Another option is to stay at the Hotel Gleneagles in Torquay, which inspired the comedy series.*"

In the interactive experiences, guests arrive at a hotel or restaurant and are greeted rudely, before a series of chaotic events ensue and 'ruin' their meal.

People like to be abused and treated badly when they are expecting it and if it's funny. You can book a stay in any of a series of seaside and country hotels, following the Dining Experience on tour and having the 'full Faulty experience' each weekend if you so wish. For instance, the Fawlty Towers Weekend[61] experience in Warrington, June 2024, would cost £250 per person for the experience and an overnight stay: *You will be greeted by Basil, Sybil and Manuel who will check you in... Afternoon Tea will be served with the help of the Fawlty Towers Team.* [In the evening] *the Fawlty Towers Show will commence, and you will enjoy a fabulous 3 Course Meal.* Rival company *Fawlty Towers – Dinner is Served* do a similar circuit around the UK with a range of shows, featuring some original material e.g. *Basil's Twin.*[62] The *Fawlty Towers Tribute Show*[63] can be hired for murder mysteries, weddings, and other formats – you get Basil, Sybil and Manuel as standard, Polly and the Major for an extra fee.

One wonders if the root of Cleese's ire was that he didn't think of it first. In 1976 he had discussed opening a restaurant himself – allegedly[64] to be named Basil's, in Knightsbridge. He would partner with his friend and hotelier/restaurateur Andrew Leeman, the inspiration for *The Kipper and the Corpse* – but ultimately it would come to nothing.

QUIZ SHOW STAPLE

"Can't we get you on Mastermind, Sybil? Next contestant, Sybil Fawlty from Torquay, special[ist] *subject: the bleeding obvious."*[65]

Fawlty Towers is extraordinarily popular for quiz shows and feats of memory – its very short episode run, just twelve half-hour episodes, does not hurt here – especially in shows where contestants can revise in advance e.g. *Mastermind.* In 2018 producer Mark Helsby wrote[66] for *Radio Times*: "Thirty-two people wanted to do *Fawlty Towers* last year [2017], 19 wanted *Blackadder* [26 episodes], and 22 wanted *Father Ted* [25 episodes]."

Compared to the most popular US sitcoms such as *Friends* [236 episodes], *Frasier* [264 episodes *before* the 2023 reboot added another 20], or other British long-runners like *Only Fools and Horses* [64 episodes], *Birds of a Feather* [128 episodes], or *The Last of the Summer Wine* [295 episodes over 37 years], *Fawlty Towers* provides a short and easily memorised 6 hours of comedy – ideal for the quiz show competitor who doesn't necessarily care about the topic memorised as much as how memorable it can be. This *Mastermind* story, highlighting how they had to say no to everyone to make it fair to all, was spun by news media as a *ban* on *Fawlty Towers*: *Mastermind has banned Blackadder, and Father Ted from its specialist subjects list*[67] in the Metro, *Fawlty Towers among subjects banned by*

Mastermind as questions run out[68] in the Guardian. *Mastermind limits use of Harry Potter and Fawlty Towers,*[69] the BBC version of the story, was less stern but still made it clear: contestants would be asked to name another specialist subject.

Celebrity Mastermind has no such ban, and among those who have tackled *Fawlty Towers are* writer and presenter Adil Ray[70] on *Fawlty Towers*, comedian Fred MacAulay[71] on *Fawlty Towers (Children in Need* special); former MP Anna Soubry[72] on *Fawlty Towers*. In conversation with the author, Ray described his performance as *"awful!!!!"* and would not be drawn further!

On regular *Mastermind,* before the 2018 'ban' heat winner Gregory Spiller[73] scored 16 points in 2012, with questions such as *"What is the punch line to Mr Johnson's joke in* The Psychiatrist, *which Sybil finds extremely funny and Basil doesn't?" "Erm... 'Pretentious, moi?!'"* (correct). He got only one question wrong: *"Mrs Peignoir tells Basil that she thinks beneath his English exterior throbs a passion that would make Lord Byron look like... what?"*[74]

Junior Mastermind too had a round on it in 2005: host John Humphrys and the contestant (James) discussed the original *Mastermind* line from *Basil the Rat* between rounds. *Only Connect*, a fiendish quiz known for not pulling punches, loves to use *Fawlty Towers* for questions. They stumped a team in the 2013 semi-finals with pictures of celery, apples, and walnuts – the sequence ending in grapes for the *Fawlty Towers* specific version of a Waldorf salad. As host Victoria Coren Mitchell explains to the teams: *"You'd have to be such a fan of the relevant thing* [to get this]...*The customer ordering the Waldorf salad asks for celery, apples, walnuts and* grapes, *which you don't often find in a Waldorf salad. The* wrong *ingredient. You were supposed to think of the classic sitcom."* Another episode had her questioning the logic of the team who correctly put together the group 'Sachs, Berkeley, Cribbins, Cleese', as they had immediately discounted Scales and Booth, the deliberate red herrings which the show puts into every wall game. A particularly difficult question, which a team guessed correctly at clue 2 for extra points, began *Noriega, Toynbee.*[75] Full question and answer in footnotes!

University Challenge, Eggheads, and *The Chase* are among many other shows that use *Fawlty Towers* for material – the harder the quiz, the more obscure the reference.

Pointless has a less traditional quiz format – instead of question and answer interactions, contestants have to find examples of answers that fit a category, or decode a series of clues to decide which is likely to score the least points. For example, on 19 October 2018 a round of haikus included:

> A Torquay hotel,
> A man from Barcelona.
> Don't mention the war!

While it *does* meet the syllable and phrasing requirements, it isn't strictly a haiku.[76] Regardless, it met the criteria for being easily guessed by the polled audience and the contestants. Unfortunately for the contestant who chose it, 84 of 100 people polled knew this one. In March 2010 the show asked contestants to name two of the eight characters who appeared in more than one episode of *Fawlty Towers*. The contestants guessed the Major (scoring 32 points) and Miss Tibbs (5 points). The others were then named to wrap up the round: Miss Gatsby scored 4 points, Terry the chef 11 points, Polly was worth 40 points, Sybil Fawlty 58 points, Manuel 80 points and Basil Fawlty 82 points. When the question was posed again but requesting the actors' names, in August 2011, the contestants opted for Andrew Sachs (37 points) and Prunella Scales (29 points). The rest of the list was not too surprising: Gilly Flower and Renee Roberts were both Pointless answers (that's a good thing for the contestants in this format, though less good for actors' egos), Brian Hall and Ballard Berkeley both scored 1 point, Connie Booth 21 points, and John Cleese 79 points. It's slightly surprising that so few people remembered Booth, whose name appears on the opening credits of each episode, and we can only assume that the 21 people who couldn't remember John Cleese don't really care for sitcoms.

INSPIRATION

Characters that may owe something to Basil include Del Boy,[77] David Brent,[78] and Victor Meldrew[79] – people with flaws they cannot overcome, people who do not know that they are funny. Meldrew is funniest to the audience when he loses his temper and chaos takes over. Basil, like Harold Steptoe[80] and Reginald Perrin,[81] is a man approaching middle age, contemplating the life left ahead of him and the years behind him, and finding both wanting. He has little agency to change this, however.

Other shows that acknowledge debts to *Fawlty Towers* include *French and Saunders, Father Ted,* and *Cheers* – James Burrows, co-creator of *Cheers*, confirmed in his 2022 memoir[82] that it was a direct influence: "*We loved the outrageousness of it... I adored* Fawlty Towers, *because that character was so brazen... The main action would take place in the hotel bar. The structure was similar to that of* Fawlty Towers *in that the stories would walk into the bar.*"

The character of Arnold Rimmer in *Red Dwarf* isn't a middle-aged man[83] but he embodies all the aspiration, snobbery, and frustration of Basil Fawlty. His ability to shift the blame from himself to anyone or anything around him is extremely familiar. Bernard Black in *Black Books* similarly blames the world for his woes, although alcoholism and apathy prevail over aspiration. It is impossible for any writer to avoid unconscious influence, and it's difficult to rule out influence even when it's negative, such as Rowan Atkinson's assertion that *The Black Adder* was set in the fifteenth century to *avoid* any comparisons with the show. Although some comparisons may only be in the mind of the viewers, not the writers, it's still tempting to see a bit of Basil in any angry Englishman.

Even children's television gets in on the act: s1e15 of *Count Duckula*,[84] '*Hardluck Hotel*', features a tall snobbish hotelier wearing a tweed suit, loud tie, and large moustache, who would rather read the newspaper than help his guests, and who quickly chivvies Duckula out of the lobby on arrival: "*pop up to your room now sir, you're making the foyer look untidy*". He explains that Chef gets the economy breakfasts out of the way at 6am, to make room for the super luxury guests who have paid more. Duckula complains that there are no furnishings in his room – "*well you* were *told that it was room only*". When it is confirmed that Duckula cannot pay his bill, he is made to do the washing up and act as hotel bellboy. The episode even features a Manuel-worthy linguistic joke – delivering a meal, his knock on a bedroom door is answered with '*Entrée*'. Yes, says Duckula, the meal *is* on a tray.

The black comedy *The White Lotus*[85] features a hotel resort manager named Armond (Murray Bartlett) who similarly bears a strong resemblance to Basil, both physically – tall and slim, he sports a large moustache, a similar haircut to Cleese in *Fawlty Towers,* is often seen with a manic fixed grin, and dresses surprisingly smartly for the location – and temperamentally. He is sarcastic, antagonistic towards guests, and quietly despises his job and everything that goes with it. He has to deal with errors and calamities in the hotel, but as he has no support staff or spouse, no Polly-equivalent to bail him out of catastrophes, things spiral badly for him. The *White Lotus* wiki[86] includes the very Fawlty line: "*As his personal issues mount, he fails to provide the level of service expected of his position.*" Armond, unlike Basil, has a history of drug use, and eventually succumbs to the turmoil. There but for the grace of Sybil goes Basil.

Fawlty Towers – The Play

Romney Green Players[1] put on *The Hotel Inspectors, Communication Problems,* and *Waldorf Salad* in 2006, "*one of the first amateur groups[2] to tackle* [the] *classic series."* Other AmDram[3] groups similarly presented the show in the same era, after the scripts were first licensed for public performance. A Leighton Buzzard group[4] presented *A Touch of Class, Communication Problems,* and *Basil the Rat* in 2015 and the NODA[5] reviewer noted: "*This is not a time for personal interpretation or making it 'your own'. The public wants a carbon copy of the original. That's no easy feat – its amateurs playing professionals playing characters they have created. Every idiosyncrasy, mannerism and vocal intonation must be recreated."* The Dubbo Theatre Company[6] produced amateur stage versions of several episodes 2013-15, and their version of *The Hotel Inspectors*[7] is available to watch on YouTube. These were all direct adaptations of the show's scripts, faithful in every detail, and prove the point first made in a TV studio in December 1974 – these are not just sitcom scripts but short-form theatrical farces, fit for repeat performance.

A REALLY PROFESSIONAL JOB

In August 2016, in the Roslyn Packer Theatre,[8] the first professional performance of *Fawlty Towers – the play* took place. John Cleese collaborated with theatre director Caroline Jay Ranger, who had worked with the surviving Pythons on *Monty Python live at the O2* in July 2014, to bring the show to the stage after years of being asked to do so. "*There have been many requests ... to adapt* Fawlty Towers *for the stage. I now sense the time is right and I'd like my Aussie actor friends to be my collaborators on the world premiere of this epoch-shattering event, a watershed in the history of Australian theatrical culture. Or not."*[9] Cleese was impressed with the success of the Python show, and the initial commercial success[10] of Eric Idle's *Spamalot!,* the stage musical version of *Monty Python and the Holy Grail.* The *Fawlty Towers* show would tour Australia until the end of 2016, but was not then extended.

It was popular with the audiences that saw it but not particularly stunning at the box office or well received[11] by critics,[12] who weren't convinced that the show was even necessary. *The Daily Telegraph*:[13] "*It is a somewhat reassuring surprise* to find that many of the gags are still funny. Yes, it is riding on the coat-tails of its source material, but this is why it ultimately works." The Australian *Daily Review*[14] wrote: "*It's a meticulous, detailed and undeniably successful recreation of the TV series, even if it never entirely justifies its own existence*". The *Guardian*[15] gave it only two stars (out of five): "*There's nothing new or exciting enough to make a compelling case for Fawlty Towers as a play.*" Cleese defended the play on Twitter,[16] but it was not enough to prolong the life of the show, and the proposed New Zealand tour was cancelled. There was no move to the UK or USA for the play. Cleese blamed the *Dining Experience* for the poor box office performance in Australia, though that seems unfair.

There was much speculation about a musical version in the 2010s, after the rise and rise of the jukebox musical (e.g. *We Will Rock You, Mamma Mia*) and the beginning of the plundering of vintage sitcoms for new stage shows, but Cleese rejected the concept, and the many offers he had received, telling Australian TV broadcaster ABC: "*It would slow it up too much. That kind of comedy has got to play to* [a] *frantic pace. If you stop for songs, it wouldn't work.*" Mark Lawson[17] wrote: "*Instead Cleese turned the sitcom into a lukewarmly received stage play with no songs*", referring to the 2016 Australian version of the play.

Without the cooperation of and collaboration with Connie Booth, would it even be possible to create new material that is substantially different from the old scripts? And in an increasingly nostalgic world, do people actually *want* new material, or do they want the comfort, the familiarity of the lines they know and the plots they already understand? Booth *is* credited for her part in the writing of the material used in *Fawlty Towers: the play*, but in Australia in 2016 and in London in 2024, the theatre advertises only *John Cleese's Fawlty Towers*. His name sells the show to those who know him but not the series – and there are still many of those around.

The concept of an 'uncanny valley'[18] – the point, on a 'rough to flawless' scale, where people find almost-perfect copies creepy and off-putting rather than familiar and comfortable, and consequently consider them worse than visibly imperfect copies – isn't usually applied to theatre, but some reviews invoked it to complain about the too-strong similarity between screen and stage. The plots of three episodes were 'cannibalised' to form the plot of the new show, like Frankenstein's monster. The Australian *Daily Telegraph*,[19] somewhat at odds with the UK newspaper of the same name, loved this aspect of the show: "*While the actors weren't cast in their roles to impersonate as such, they are visually perfect, costumes, makeup, mannerisms all aping the originals without ever being cartoonish or creepy.*"

The debut cast were praised in all reviews, though, and of course the writing – barely changed from the television version – was held in high regard. The main objections seemed to be that John Cleese was making money[20] from old material and that there was nothing new in the production. Cleese had taken a known fan favourite and simply repackaged it, a 'lazy' effort. But audiences like the familiar, thankfully. *The Sydney Morning Herald* speculated: *"Opening night revealed a show with obvious commercial (and West End) potential"* – but it would be eight years (and one global pandemic) before the London debut.

THE LONDON SHOW[21]

The set is simplified – stage right is the hotel reception desk, with a smaller desk signifying the office downstage right, although there also is a door to the office upstage; at the back is the hotel's external door; the stairs occupy upstage centre and rise to a mezzanine with a single bedroom. This room is flanked by an image of the original hotel (Wooburn Grange) on its right and the hotel sign on its left – a sign which changes from **Fawlty Towers** to **Watery Fowls** in the interval, to the audience's audible delight. Downstairs again, the dining room (four tables) occupies the usual place but with no dividing wall, so the action can move freely from the lobby to the dining room and back. Upstage, the kitchen doors. We can see a kitchen unit through these when they are opened, but it is offstage space otherwise.

Cleese provides the voiceover at the start of the play, telling audiences to behave themselves properly. The hotel decor is roughly similar to the show – cream and black paintwork, pale green walls and lurid 70s carpeting. The script is an amalgam of episodes – we first meet Mr Hutchinson, the small pedantic spoon salesman, so we know we are beginning with *The Hotel Inspectors*. The cast seed Sybil's ingrowing toenail operation and the concurrent fire drill, so the audience – if they know the show already, for many do not – can recognise *The Germans*. Then Mrs Richards arrives and we acknowledge the start of *Communication Problems*. Mr Walt from *The Hotel Inspectors* gets some lines that would otherwise have gone to Mr Johnson in *The Psychiatrist*, curiously – no other lines from this episode are used but presumably they were judged funny enough to stand alone (where can one find French food? In France, of course). No real hotel inspectors have arrived yet. Mrs Richards' plot goes as straightforwardly as the source episode's, Mr Firkin gives Basil the racing tip, and the Major and Basil discuss women/dragons without the offensive lines (he does mention taking a woman to watch cricket but she simply disappears off to tea with the Major's wallet, and is never heard from again). Cleese wrote in *The Daily Telegraph*:[22] *"We haven't* [updated] *the script except to cut a speech in which ... Major Gowen uses the N word. At the time, in 1979* [it was actually 1975]*, everyone knew that it was the attitudes themselves that were the butt of the joke, but we've taken this bit out anyway because it's not worth the trouble."*

The biggest audience laugh of the first half goes to Basil and Polly miming the horse name – 'small', seen simply as a dick joke, is funny to audiences everywhere.

There were quite a few first-timer audience members at the performance I saw in July 2024 – some who were new to the show completely and some who had seen one or two episodes in the past. They weren't necessarily expecting all the plot points and observed that it was easy to hear when a majority of people knew the laughs were coming and when they were unexpected for others. Some of the jokes that went down particularly well were visual or non-plot related, open to everyone. The suitcase-upstairs card cues for Manuel, for instance, got a very big response.

A sample of audience members, some of whom had seen all the episodes before:

We wondered if there'd be new material, but it's good to hear the old material too.

We can't see the joins unless we know where they are. It flows really well.

I didn't expect all the different plots but it works!

Act 2 introduces elements from *Basil the Rat* as the Major sees a rat in the bar and goes to get his gun. We are told that the Germans are arriving, and the mildly xenophobic dialogue about Germany is given to the Ladies rather than to the Major, rendering it slightly more benign by removing the military aspect from the conversation. The Major does threaten to shoot the Germans, but it's both less aggressive and also more alarming than the on-screen version, somehow – this version of the Major is not established as xenophobic or racist, so this behaviour comes more out of the blue than it did in the original episode. Sybil goes off to hospital after resolving Mrs Richards' money and vase plot points. Basil attempts the fire drill, with Mrs Richards taking the lead female guest role in that dialogue. The moose falls on Basil, and Mr Walt drags him away. Retaining Mr Walt at this point allows Mrs Richards to mix him up with Mr CK Watt, the manager she has imagined after her confused conversation with Manuel, a nice bonus laugh for old and new audiences alike. The hotel inspectors appear quietly before Basil returns, bandaged, in time to greet the German guests. Adam Jackson-Smith points out[23] that Basil is *trying* to be kind to the Germans, at least in his interpretation of the role, and is not being xenophobic. The plot of this section follows the same line as the episode, and then a loud bang goes off in the kitchen – something has exploded. Manuel comes out, on fire, and the rat rushes across the stage. [To avoid spoiling it in this paragraph, please read this footnote[24] if you do want to know the ending.] Cue Basil's anguished meltdown, and the curtain.

Some of the more melancholy aspects of the Fawltys' relationship are included, bringing quiet reflective moments to the show – the *manacled/we used to laugh* dialogue, *'there goes your life mate'*, and the sadness of a not-quite-failed relationship. But overall the play is an amalgam of classic farce plots, upbeat and funny even as everything is going wrong for Basil.

The cast are very good – *Basil* can sing in tune, and is more limber and active than Cleese, leaping up and down and dancing as well as goose-stepping and hopping about. *Sybil* has nailed the laugh and aspects of the voice although her dialogue seems somehow cruder and coarser, on stage. She isn't as sympathetic as screen Sybil and the dialogue highlights her flaws more. *Manuel* is very good – he has the physicality of Sachs down pat. *The Major* is a decent interpretation – and crucially, rather less sad in his portrayal of dementia. It is a portrayal of an absent-minded but kind man, not a rapidly failing one. *Polly* is an uncannily accurate version of Connie Booth's character. Victoria Fox (Polly) told me she grew up watching the show with her father, a memorable shared family experience, and so it was "*an acting dream*" to be in the show. She was able to meet Connie Booth in May 2024, when Booth attended the play with husband John Lahr. In April 2024 Lahr had told the *Daily Mail*[25] that Booth would not be commenting on the play, and in 2023 she had expressed some disbelief to the same newspaper: "*I'd have appreciated learning about the project from John rather than reading about it in the papers. Because a previous American reboot of* Fawlty Towers *had failed some years ago, I was surprised that another was being planned.*" But she seemed to enjoy the experience and had multiple photographs taken with the play cast including Fox.

Manuel's Turkish-born actor Hemi Yeroham talked about experiencing the show for the first time after being cast and how much he liked it when he got to know it. He was not able to watch the show growing up, and so he did indeed learn it from a book, rather fittingly. Rachel Izen relishes the role of Mrs Richards, an older woman who says exactly what she thinks and has no compunction about it. She doesn't need to be restrained or polite, she can say what she thinks – a "*glorious*" role to play.

Adam Jackson-Smith is a good physical likeness for Cleese, but also nails the air of repressed anger. He is grateful to Cleese for his direction on the character. He told the BBC[26] in July 2024; "*He's a real force of nature with a real eye for detail with the direction. He just wants to make it funnier all the time. John has been an incredibly generous spirit and a really great and useful voice in the room.*" He also joked that each one of us has a Basil inside and that he was "*chanelling my mini Basil*". Cleese jokes in a number of interviews[27] that he could "*do it better*", but Jackson-Smith says he welcomes the tips. When asked if Basil is a victim or a monster, he says that Basil's heart is in the right place but he is "*100% in the wrong job. Something that is not public facing*" would suit him better. Anna-Jane Casey, as Sybil, didn't think she was right for the part initially but wept[28] when she got the part. Paul Nicholas was excited to play the part, and pointed out that the audience will have forgotten some of the material before they see it, which makes it funnier when they hear and remember it.

As a theatrical-style sitcom performed originally as half-hour plays with minimal exterior filming, the play works well – audience reactions include some very knowing laughs when each new plot element is introduced. People like working out what will happen, but they also like recognising what they already know. It is a very satisfying mix of known and unknown, and the plot elements that have made it into the show are all ones that we know work on stage because of the way the show was written and filmed originally. Dispensing with the hospital plot of *The Germans*, for instance, removes the need for a second set, extra parts, and largely unnecessary exposition – the new-to-this audience doesn't really need to know *why* Sybil is absent for the fire drill, simply that she *is;* the familiar audience knows enough to fill in any blanks from their own memory. The show isn't *quite* at the level of being able to simply quote one line and have the audience fill in the rest, *a la* numbered jokes or audience sing-a-longs, but it's close enough.

Broadway World's[29] Aliya Al-Hassan loved the show: "*The performances come off as imitations, rather than any move to bring novelty to the parts. But the audience would leave disappointed if Sybil didn't cackle like a drain on the phone or if Basil didn't jump from obsequious servitude to abject rudeness within the same breath*" and that sums up the predominant audience response – they want to see the familiar played as close to the original as possible, including impersonations if necessary.

Maurice Gran: *I haven't seen it. I've heard it's really well done. If it tours I'll definitely watch it. If I happen to be in London with a spare evening and they've got some tickets at the Leicester Square booth, I'll go and see it. Am I going to spend £100 to see it? Not sure. It really depends on how well and how deftly it's done. It depends on the needlework. When we had a very successful stage revival of* Birds of a Feather, *we decided to write a brand-new self-contained story, nothing to do with stitching things together, because I think if you're going to ask people to spend £150 on two tickets, two gins, and a babysitter, I think you should offer them something new – but maybe we should offer them something old. The proof of the pudding is in the audience, and it's had a great reaction. I would always prefer to write something new for my characters, as we did with* The New Statesman *as well. With Fawlty on stage, it has to be done with accuracy and affection, but it can't be a tribute act or a clone. It's quite a difficult path to tread.*

Jodi Taylor: *I have seen the stage version of* Drop the Dead Donkey[30] *and thought it was excellent – it was the original cast excluding Henry and Alex* [David Swift and Haydn Gwynne] *who are sadly no longer with us, and there was a nice little tribute to them at the end, which was really well done. Most of the audience were my age because we remember the original.* [The sitcom transfers to stage well] because most of it is fairly static, and exactly the same on stage. *I* think *I* want to see Fawlty Towers *on stage, but I'm slightly terrified of Basil. I might be watching from behind the sofa.*

The British Sitcom History podcast[31] were not impressed. Gareth Allen and Allen Turing discussed the opening night in a May 2024 episode and felt that it was not really understandable as a concept – *"it's like going to see a cover band"* rather than the original. Watching other people perform the material isn't something they enjoy. Turing points out that the cast list gives away the main plot points – Mrs Richards, Mr Hutchinson – and is not particularly impressed with the finale. *"It's the absolute lowest possible effort adaptation from screen to stage."* He notes that the cast are doing a great job and are obviously happy, and that Paul Nicholas being the only 'name' doesn't hurt the show – it's the material that sells it, not the cast. A farce works better on stage than on TV, but sadly this material is not the most farcical – they contrast it with *The Goes Wrong Show*, which uses many classic farce tropes to great success, both on stage and on TV. The pair acknowledge that *Fawlty Towers – The Play* is not pretending to be more than simply three episodes put on stage, but regret that a fan, someone with passion, didn't get the chance to create something bigger and better from the source material. For those who hadn't seen the original often or recently, it *was* a pleasant enough show – just a let-down for life-long fans.

The Spectator[32] called it a museum piece: *"It's like returning to a seaside funfair after half a century and finding all the rides unchanged and the staff more or less as you remember them."* Steve Bennett, writing for comedy website Chortle,[33] called it *"a period piece about the frustrations of the post-war generation, though it is none the worse for that, just like an Oscar Wilde comedy is always going to be rooted in Victorian mores"* and a *"masterclass-level comedy"*. It's dated – but not too much. It's familiar – but maybe a little too much. It could be better, and it could be much *much* worse. It has been confirmed that it will get a regional UK tour after its West End run ends in March 2025, and a trip to see it should be worth the effort.

Adaptations and Revivals

From the final minutes of *The Germans* critics and viewers clamoured for more *Fawlty Towers*. It took three and a half years for series 2 to arrive, and from the final minutes of *Basil the Rat* the clamour started again – but with Cleese and Booth divorced, everything they planned to say about hotel management or human frustration said, and the *Monty Python* team enmeshed in the post-release controversy of *Life of Brian* and subsequently the production of *The Meaning of Life*, there was no prospect of a third series.

Cleese had hoped for a film[1] to wrap up the story for once and for all: Basil and Sybil would fly to Spain to see Manuel, who had returned home after his time in Torquay, but the plane would be hijacked and diverted back to Heathrow. Basil – naturally – would not be able to stand this and would hijack the plane himself, returning it to Spain, where he would then be arrested and spend his entire holiday in prison. Unfortunately, Cleese could not find a way to make this *funny*, so the idea was abandoned before it was written. *"I don't think I ever mentioned it to Connie."*

The first remake off the mark was *Hotel de Botel*,[2] made for Dutch TV and written by British scriptwriters Lawrie Wyman and George Evans.[3] The main character, Koos Overwater, was played by singer, comedian, and actor André van Duin.[4] Koos worked at the Ruimzicht hotel with his brother Bob (Allard van der Scheer), Bob's wife Kitty (Ronny Bierman), and dog Woef. Koos's girlfriend Suzanne (Corrie van Gorp) was also a series regular. The second episode was *The Wedding Party*,[5] but not much else is known about it now. At least one episode is available on YouTube,[6] though only in Dutch. It's debatable how close to a genuine remake this is – it doesn't credit Cleese and Booth, but contemporary reviews do say it is a remake, and there are definite similarities: the brothers get trapped in a lift, there's quite a lot of physical violence, and more in that vein. Bob has the most Basil characteristics, hitting his brother in a rage, and being grumpy with guests; Koos is more random – appearing in a scuba diving outfit, covering a guest in goop, scaring little old ladies in the hotel lobby... he is the chaos to his brother's rage.

When *Fawlty Towers* was remade for American television – an inevitable move in a culture of trading sitcoms[7] – the character of Basil Fawlty was transformed beyond recognition. In the 1978[8] remake *Snavely*,[9] Basil's character is recreated as loud-mouthed Henry Snavely (Harvey Korman[10]) with Betty White[11] in the Sybil role. Cleese felt that it was abandoned because the producers felt it was *too* mean-spirited – thus missing the point of Basil. There is a tradition in US sitcoms that everyone should have at least one redeeming trait but of course Basil does not, really, and this was at odds with American expectations.

Snavely Manor, the hotel, has a similar look to Fawlty Towers – very yellow decor, the familiar reception desk, even an animal head ready to put up on the wall. Petro[12] the almost silent hotel assistant – an Albanian refugee – needs the same flashcards as Manuel and puts his finger on a menu to show the chef an order. Betty White's Gladys is much cheerier than Sybil. Henry, her husband who originally inherited the hotel, talks over her more aggressively than Basil does. He is a penny-pincher – rationing the toilet paper so the guests don't waste it – and openly shouts at guests. He is less snarky than Basil, but also less funny as a result.

The pilot episode covers the plot of *The Hotel Inspectors* in the first half. The Snavelys give their own bedroom to the pernickety guest Mr Bishop, assuming him to be one of the inspectors. The hotel's waitress is named Connie,[13] in a nod to Booth, and she's studying hotel management. Henry accuses Gladys of 'fooling around' with a guest – much nastier in tone than Basil's acknowledgement of Sybil's open flirting – although he's wrong. The Major is now a grumpy ex-Chief of Police[14] accused of rape – an uncomfortably dated joke that turns out to refer to a false accusation but isn't any funnier with that elaboration. Some of the original material survives – the peas *were* fresh when they were frozen, as frozen vegetables tend to be – but the delivery is extraordinary when viewed through British eyes. The movement of Mr Foley[15] (the Mr Walt equivalent) from the 'wrong' table is more physically aggressive than the UK version. The explanation of Mr Bishop's non-inspector status happens much earlier in the plot, and he's barely been active at all by the time Henry wants to kill him, halfway through the episode. By the time they get to their punch-up, triggered by a bill presented in the dining room (why would a guest pay for dinner separately like this?), Snavely already knows he isn't the inspector, and suspects another guest in the same room of being the inspector. Why would he lose control and take it out on him in front of a witness, especially one he believes to be the real inspector? Mr Bishop threatens to sue the hotel.

In the second half of the episode Snavely attempts to hold the fire drill – the same burglar alarm confusion is used with similar effect – to impress Mr Foley and to convince him that the hotel is safe. The Chief fetches his service revolver, and Gladys tends to Mr Bishop. Petro has evacuated the hotel already, so Snavely demonstrates the two alarm bells to him. Connie refuses to escort the guests out via the fire escape, as '*last time the Chief tried to give me a sobriety test*' – a nonsensical line to 21st century British viewers but likely referring to the 'walk and turn' test, an opportunity for the Chief to leer at her from behind as she walks. Petro sets fire to the kitchen and alerts Snavely in exactly the same way as Manuel, while the guests are all at the bottom of the stairs – they all witness Snavely pushing him back into the kitchen, and the subsequent smoke plumes. Snavely empties a fire extinguisher onto Mr Foley, who denies being an inspector. Gladys efficiently puts out the fire, and Snavely claims credit for saving Petro's life. The real inspectors arrive at the hotel and Gladys spots them. Mr Bishop and Mr Foley tell Snavely what they think of him before he yells at them. Gladys alerts him to the inspectors' presence, and he groans while she comforts him. Very un-Sybil-like behaviour. There was no second episode. Cleese said[16] that the stars *"played it too slow and were embarrassed by the edgy dialogue"*. They are almost entirely unbelievable and uncomfortable to watch, and the changes to the dialogue ruin most of the jokes. Cleese was surprised that they did not ask him for assistance or help in any way.

Steve Pratt in the *Northern Echo*[17] called Snavely *"manic"*, but also described the affable Gladys as *"domineering"* – this doesn't come across strongly in the pilot episode.

Newhart,[18] a hotel comedy with Bob Newhart[19] in the title role, is often suggested as a *Fawlty Towers*-inspired comedy, if not a direct remake, but it bears little resemblance to the show. Newhart was clear[20] that he didn't want it to be: *"Let's not make it a* Fawlty Towers. *Because first of all, I'm not John Cleese — I'm not that physical a comedian. Secondly, I don't want to be accused of doing a rip-off. And thirdly, I think that's an English form. I don't think there's any counterpart over here."*

There was a second *Golden Girls* star in the next attempt: *Amanda's [By The Sea]*[21] starring Bea Arthur. The gender-swapped Amanda Cartwright has a similar demeanour to Basil, and some snappier comebacks. She fawns over the judge who arrives at the start of the first episode, upgrading his room once she knows who he is. Aldo[22] the waiter – *'he's from Toronto'* – similarly needs flashcards for some instructions. The hotel lobby resembles *Fawlty Towers* much more than *Snavely*'s lodge did, as does the kitchen and upstairs landing. A new character sets up the financial precariousness of Amanda's hotel – he wants to buy out the hotel and demolish it, setting up an arc for the series – something *Fawlty Towers* didn't need. The first episode, like *Snavely*, uses *The Hotel Inspectors* for source material, and some lines from *Communication Problems:* the Mrs Richards character – Mrs Davenport[23] – complains about her lack of sea view. The *only sane man* character is Amanda's son Martin Cartwright,[24] who has been to hotel management school. His spoiled wife Arlene[25] – who plot-drops in every line – is set up to be at odds with Amanda. Amanda accidentally hurts a new guest before Aldo announces that the oven is dead – she instructs the chef to use a grill ('Hibachi') indoors.

The potential-inspector guest checks in for the same room she has given to the previous guest, so she explains a farcical room swap plan to a bemused Marty.

There is, unsurprisingly, a fire in the kitchen as a result of the improvised cooking facilities. Amanda announces a change of menu to the diners – they will now be offered frozen shrimp salad. The room swap means she cannot let anyone leave the dining room. She sends the chef to a nearby restaurant for 10 meals. Arlene – effectively a pointless character, adding nothing to the plot and not providing much comedy – bursts in to explain that she has resolved a clothing crisis. Aldo sends a guest to his room – off screen there is a scream as Amanda 'thanks' him for this work, as she and Marty have not yet facilitated the room swap. On the landing she and Aldo move luggage and rooms in a spot of classic 'door comedy' that results in her being shut in a closet. Disgruntled guests tell her and 'the hotel critic' everything that is wrong with the hotel, and she unburdens herself to him – but he's a golf journalist. The grumpy Mrs Davenport is the real hotel critic. All of this is familiar but not, and it tries a *little* too hard to be funny. Arthur has the same manic energy and similar delivery to Cleese, and her delivery flips from polite snark to angry just as easily. She tells lies to cover herself just as comfortably. As adaptations go, it could be worse. It did get a full – by British standards – season of 13 episodes, but ratings were not good. The final three episodes went unaired, and it did not get a second season. Jerry Stiller[26] makes an appearance in the second episode, but apart from him, Arthur herself, and Alan Alda's father Robert,[27] there are no really big names in the show. It doesn't fit the same niche as *Fawlty Towers*. The staff and family dynamics in the hotel just don't work as well as the Basil-Sybil relationship – Amanda's son and daughter-in-law have no plausible signs of being in a romantic relationship, bizarrely – and while the show gives Amanda a romantic arc and a happy ending, this is not what a Basil-analogue deserves.

Robert Gore-Langton:[28] *"The Americans tried their own version called Amanda's By The Sea, it was ... a disgraceful travesty of the spirit of the original."*

Pratt: *"The manager ... was a woman but just as formidable as her male counterpart in Snavely."* Arguable, as Amanda appears less aggressive but more intelligent than Snavely.

Sir Terry Pratchett had watched *Amanda's*[29] without disliking it particularly, but was not keen on remakes in general: *Why the hell did anyone think a pale UK version* [of The Golden Girls] *was needed? The Golden Girls was a great show, because it was about four great actresses. It didn't *matter* where it was set.* And the same was true of *Fawlty Towers*.

In June 1993 there was suggestion[30] that Raquel Welch might take on the role of Basil in a remake – *"I'm underestimated as a comedienne"*. Nothing at all came of this, which is probably for the best.

In 1998, Basil became Royal Payne[31] (geddit?), husband to Connie[32] (another nod to Booth), and co-proprietor of the Whispering Pines Inn. Manuel and Polly became Mo[33] and Breeze.[34] *Payne* was a critical and audience failure, and only eight of its nine[35] episodes were aired. Cleese approved of the attempt, however: *"they tried to get away from doing* Fawlty Towers *the way we've done it ... no point reproducing what had already been done."* He noted that maybe 2-3% of Americans at that time had seen *Fawlty Towers* on broadcast TV, leaving 97% who could come to *Payne* with fresh eyes and no expectations. Ironically it would get a better audience in the UK – where it was shown on ITV in full – than in the USA.

In 1991 Pakistan's PTV made *Guest House,* a *Fawlty Towers* inspired show set in the Welcome Guest House, Islamabad. Rauf Khalid[36] directed all 52 episodes of the show, which featured the Shameems and their three employees, and their persistent meddling in the affairs of their guests. It differs from *Fawlty Towers* in a number of ways; most significantly, the hotel employees seem to be kindly disposed to most of their guests and meddle because they care.

In 2000 German TV company RTL discussed making a version. Germany had seen and loved the original show: it had been shown with subtitles on SAT1 and was also available as an import on VHS. An RTL spokesman said *"German audiences were ... keen on the slapstick elements. 'Don't mention the war' did not cause offence"*. Sachs was initially approached to reprise Manuel, speaking German but in a Spanish accent. The proposal was to remake 11 of the original 12 episodes, omitting *The Germans* – although this had been shown before, it would make no sense translating it exactly as it was written. The producer Rudiger Jung points[37] out that to make the guests British and the impersonation of Churchill simply wouldn't work. *"...few in Germany feel the kind of lingering hostility ... that prompted Fawlty ... To make the scene convincing* [the hotelier] *would have to be an outright neo-Nazi. And that would lose him the tenuous sympathy of the audience."* All comedy in the scene would be lost, no matter what is done to change the setup – it's simply not possible to adapt it and retain the humour. *"The rule is: Don't mention the war. But for entirely different reasons."*

The show was set at the North Sea holiday resort Sylt[38] and featured all German stars. It was filmed in summer 2001 as *(Hotel) Zum letzten Kliff (Hotel on the Last Cliff)*. Sylt is known for its impressive – but crumbling – cliffs. The Basil character was played by a big name in German sitcom, Jochen Busse,[39, 40] and was significantly older than Cleese had been in 1975. The Major became an academic – less controversial and more relevant to German culture – and Manuel an immigrant from the former Soviet Union, named Igor. It is the only remake to actively involve John Cleese as consultant, and he allegedly appears in one of the episodes. Unfortunately, only the pilot episode was aired – Cleese claiming that the network thought it was too expensive to show in full – and the rest appear to be lost.[41]

THE ORIGINAL FAWLTY TOWERS HAS BEEN TRANSLATED INTO MANY OTHER LANGUAGES

- Czech: *Hotýlek* ("The little hotel")
- Danish: *Halløj på badehotellet* ("O-hoy at the seaside hotel")
- Dutch: *Hotel op stelten* ("Hotel on stilts")
- Finnish: *Pitkän Jussin majatalo* ("Tall Jussi's inn")
- French: *L'Hôtel en folie* ("The hotel in madness")
- German: *Das verrückte Hotel* ("The crazy hotel"); *Zimmer frei* ("room vacant")
- Greek: *Ένα τρελό, τρελό ξενοδοχείο* ("A crazy, crazy hotel")
- Hungarian: *A Waczak szálló* ("The Waczak hostel")
- Italian: *Basil e Sybil* ("Basil and Sybil")
- Norwegian: *Hotell i særklasse* ("A hotel in a class of its own")
- Polish: Hotel Zacisze ("Hotel Tranquility")
- Portuguese: *A Grande Barraca* ("The great shack")
- Slovak: *Hotelík* ("The little hotel")
- Swedish: *Pang i bygget* ("A blast in the building")

John Cleese claims to be astonished at hearing himself dubbed into other languages: *"I've seen myself in Japanese and it's incomprehensible to me how this stuff translates, but it must."* The universality of the situation means it will always translate though – as long as we have hotels and social aspirations, we will have hoteliers with aims their guests cannot meet.

NOT A SEQUEL

There is no official sequel to *Fawlty Towers*: not even *Clockwise*,[42] although most viewers feel it is related in spirit if not in intent. Many people believe – incorrectly – that the scene where Basil thrashes his car with a tree branch (*Gourmet Night*) occurs in this film. The *Radio Times*[43] called it *"less a narrative than a series of sketches"* adding that Cleese *"unravels here much like Basil Fawlty, from a simmering starting point to a climax of epic proportions"*. Ewan Gleadow wrote[44] *"Although giving up on Fawlty Towers at its height was a masterful move from John Cleese that assured its stance as a culturally relevant comedic force, for the remainder of his career, he would chase characters that felt similar to Basil Fawlty. His best shot at that is* Clockwise*"*.

NOT A SEQUEL EITHER

A Fish Called Wanda.[45] It does have a number of things in common with *Fawlty Towers* including many of the same actors, quite a lot of hopping about, and a failed attempt[46] at a remake with Cleese's daughter Camilla.

REPEATS AND REBOOTS

The first series significantly increased viewing figures between the first and last episodes and was granted an almost immediate repeat barely 10 weeks later, starting from Tuesday 6 January 1976. In September 1976[47] it would make a move to Sunday nights on BBC1 and an earlier time slot (8.15pm), making it accessible to a younger age group who had previously been excluded by the 9pm watershed. In June 1978 *The Germans* was shown on BBC1 at 8pm as a standalone episode. Series 2 started in February 1979, but as we know, it was disrupted by industrial action. Because the *Radio Times* went to print before the show had been recorded, Julian Holloway appears as Roger in the cast listing[48] on 19 March 1979, and the episode name is not given – but we know now that the episode broadcast on that date was a repeat of *Gourmet Night,* its fourth showing overall. The final episode was broadcast as a special in October 1979, and then repeats for that series started as well – from Wednesday 5 December on BBC1, again at a pre-watershed time (8.25pm). *The Psychiatrist,* shown on Thursday 27 December as part of the traditional Christmas schedule, scored the highest viewing figures the show would achieve until 1985. It would be shown again as another standalone episode in July 1980, before 8pm. By Christmas 1980 *Gourmet Night* was being shown as a "Christmas Comedy Classic" on Christmas Day itself.[49] Series 2 was repeated in full in February-March 1981. In June 1982 it was the turn of *The Hotel Inspectors* to be randomly repeated at 7.15pm – getting earlier and earlier. The series would be repeated regularly through the 1980s, gaining a 12.5m audience for its 10th anniversary in November 1985.

In 2023 Cleese, then preparing for the 2024 stage play, gave a round of interviews in which he claimed that he would – once again – be attempting to reboot the show. Not everyone was convinced, for exactly the same reasons Cleese had given in 1979 for ending the show. "*There are two reasons for the public's wariness. First, that the show simply won't be funny. 12 episodes were enough, so rich was its comedic virtuosity. The reboot doesn't have a chance, says just about everyone. It can only tarnish the memory.*"[50] Secondly, and more controversially, John Cleese was being perceived as a man "*on the wrong side of a culture war*", railing against 'woke culture' and the changed sensibilities of the 21st century audience. The withdrawal and editing of *The Germans* had made him defensive and prickly. He is on record on multiple occasions as saying that he disagrees with censorship and 'modern snowflake sensitivity' and will not offer any new show to the BBC, which he feels has betrayed him and/or British comedy by being overly attentive to changing audience attitudes.

On Alan Carr's *Chatty Man* show in May 2014 Cleese threw nuts and drinks at Carr, who eventually retaliated. Interviewed[51] 9 years later Carr still found the behaviour *"obnoxious"* and felt bad *"because he's a comedy legend. But he's an odd man"*. Carr then asked the journalist, Charlotte Edwardes: *"Please tell me they've scrapped that* Fawlty Towers *reboot – that's going to be awful. Do something else. Do maybe a garden centre? Don't do* Fawlty Towers." *Guardian* columnist Stuart Heritage addressed[52] the suggestion of the reboot written with Camilla Cleese, calling it a *"nauseating idea"*. Feelings about rebooting such a beloved show are mixed – everyone wants there to be more, but no one wants the disappointment of a poor imitation. The ratings for *The Legacy of Reginald Perrin*, nearly 20 years after the death of Leonard Rossiter who played the titular character, were poor and the reviews were worse, despite the return of most of the main cast and the addition of the excellent comic actress Patricia Hodge. Nothing could really save the concept without the central character. Heritage makes the same point about *Fawlty Towers*: *"Cleese won't have the same support staff around him. Andrew Sachs is dead. Prunella Scales has long since retired on health grounds.*[53] *Connie Booth ... doesn't appear to have anything to do with this new project."* And indeed, Booth went on record[54] to say that she had not been consulted and wasn't – it was implied – particularly pleased. *"I'd have appreciated learning about the project from John rather than reading about it in the papers."* Heritage admits that a remake in the 1980s or 90s would have been welcomed, but that the ageing Cleese, huffing and puffing on X/Twitter and GB News, is not likely to write a show we want to see. That sentiment, and Carr's pleading, is echoed in other similar articles. Make a new show, by all means. Rework the old material. But don't take a chance on a substandard reboot and ruin the legacy of *Fawlty Towers*.

Bibliography

THE SHOW

Cleese, John and Booth, Connie. *The Complete Fawlty Towers.* Methuen, 1988.

Cleese, John and Booth, Connie. *Fawlty Towers: The Builders, The Hotel Inspectors, Gourmet Night.* Contact, 1977.

Cleese, John and Booth, Connie. *Fawlty Towers: Book 2 [A Touch of Class, The Wedding Party, The Germans].* Contact, 1979.

ABOUT THE SHOW

Apter, Michael. *Fawlty Towers: A Reversal theory Analysis of a Popular Television Comedy Series.* Journal of Popular Culture, 1982.

Banks, Morwenna and Swift, Amanda. *The Joke's On Us: Women in Comedy from Music Hall to the Present Day.* Pandora/Routledge, 1987.

Bright, Morris and Ross, Robert. *'Fawlty Towers': Fully Booked.* Bay Books, 2003.

Chapman, Graham. *A Liar's Autobiography: Volume VI.* Eyre Methuen, 1980.

Gore-Langton, Robert. *John Cleese: And Now for Something Completely Different.* Chameleon/Andre Deutsch, 1999.

Greenall, Annjo K. *Gricean Theory and Linguicism: Infringements and Physical Violence in the Relationship between Manuel and Basil Fawlty.* Journal of Pragmatics, 41.3 (2009) 470-483.

Holm, Lars Holger. *'Fawlty Towers': A Worshipper's Companion.* Leo Forlag, 2004.

Jeffries, Stuart. *Mrs Slocombe's Pussy.* Flamingo/Harper Collins, 2000.

Davies, Paul. *Class and Other Hotel Matters in Fawlty Towers* in

Kamm, Juergen and Neumann, Birgit. *British TV Comedies: cultural concepts, contexts, and controversies.* Palgrave Macmillan; 2015.

McCann, Graham. *'Fawlty Towers': The Story of Britain's Favourite Sitcom.* Hodder and Stoughton, 2007.

Palin, Michael. *Diaries 1969–1979: The Python Years.* Weidenfeld and Nicolson, 2007.

Ross, Robert. *The Monty Python Encyclopaedia.* Batsford, 1996.
Sellers, Robert. *Raising Laughter: How the Sitcom Kept Britain Smiling in the '70s.* The History Press, 2023 edition.
Wilmut, Roger. *From Fringe to Flying Circus.* Methuen, 1980.

BY OR ABOUT THE CAST

Cleese, John. *So, Anyway.* Random House, 2014.
Cribbins, Bernard. *Bernard Who? 75 Years of Doing Just About Everything.* Constable. 2018.
Fielder, Harry with Saunders, Clive. *Extra! Extra! My Life as a Film and TV Extra.* Self-published. 2012.
Ransom, Teresa. *Prunella: The Authorised Biography.* John Murray, 2005.
Sachs, Andrew. *I Know Nothing!* The Robson Press, 2014.
Scales, Prunella and West, Timothy. *So You Want To Be An Actor.* Nick Hern Books, 2005.

RECOMMENDED VIEWING AND LISTENING

Fawlty Towers Remastered, the DVD (and subsequent Blu-ray) release.
Fawlty Towers Re-Opened, 2009. Documentary, excerpts from which are included in the DVD release.
The audio commentaries recorded for the DVD release, and the audiobook/LP record versions of the show.
The Secret Policeman's Ball (1979).
The Secret Policeman's Third Ball (1987).
John Cleese and Andrew Sachs: We Are Most Amused (2008).
John Cleese: Specsavers advert (2016).
Prunella Scales: Tesco adverts (1995-2004).
Prunella Scales: *Children in Need* sketch (2007).
Monty Python's Flying Circus, particularly s2e4 (Architects Sketch), s3e5 (Travel Agent), s3e11 (Off Licence).
Prunella Scales on Desert Island Discs[1]
John Cleese on Desert Island Discs[2]
What's Funny About[3]... Fawlty Towers?[4]

Endnotes

FIFTY YEARS OF BEING FAWLTY

1. https://www.independent.co.uk/arts-entertainment/arts-to-hell-with-basil-1619527.html
2. https://www.bbc.co.uk/news/entertainment-arts-38507022
3. Guardian, 24 Oct 1992.
4. Davidson, Andrew. *To Hell With Basil. The Independent*, 13 May 1995. https://www.independent.co.uk/arts-entertainment/arts-to-hell-with-basil-1619527.html
5. NB: Unless otherwise noted, all comments from original cast and directors (John Howard Davies, known as JHD, for series 1; Bob Spiers for series 2), are from the 2009 DVD release, "Fawlty Towers Remastered". Audio commentaries from John Cleese and directors are original to that release; interviews with the main cast and some commentators are taken from the Tiger Aspect documentary Fawlty Towers Re-Opened (2009), included on the DVD and Blu-ray releases and noted here as FTRO.
6. Office of National Statistics. Total population 52m, minus 14m under-19s.
7. A show that started on the Home Service (s1) and the Light Service (s2-5).
8. FTRO.
9. https://www.chortle.co.uk/news/2016/07/07/25239/james_gilbert%2C_the_man_who_commissioned_fawlty_towers%2C_checks_out_at_93
10. The narration on FTRO – read by Stephen Fry – incorrectly gives this date as May 1971.
11. 1909-81. *"Donald Sinclair died in 1981 from a heart attack and stroke when some workmen he'd upset painted his patio furniture and car gunmetal grey during the night." Fawlty Towers*, Graham McCann.
12. *A Liar's Autobiography* Vol VI, Methuen, 1980.
13. Cynthia would later appear in *A Fish Called Wanda* and *Fierce Creatures* with her father, and her half-sister, Camilla Cleese.
14. *TVZone* 151, May 2002.
15. Under the pseudonym Jonathan Cobbald. The scripts were later published under his own name.

16. Lost for years, it was found in 2009.
17. *Ronnie Barker: A BAFTA Tribute*, BBC2 23 December 2010.
18. Best known as Compo in The Last of the Summer Wine.
19. These would be re-adapted in 2015-19 with Aiden Turner in the lead role, and Ellis appearing in a guest role.
20. *Open house with Gloria Hunniford*, Thames TV. 25 February 2000.
21. Essay in *British TV Comedies: cultural concepts, contexts, and controversies*. Ed. Juergen Kamm, Birgit Neumann.
22. Interview with the author 2024.
23. Born 1944, and 79 at time of writing, so 5 years older than Ballard Berkeley was in 1975.
24. Ours was brown, with a psychedelic purple and orange paisley carpet. The interior decor in Fawlty Towers itself mirrored that belonging to its viewers, with patterned carpets that didn't match the patterned wallpaper, and lots of fussy design touches like coving and dado rails.
25. David Frost; topical comedy written by a host of writers from David Nobbs to Tim Brooke-Taylor and the future Pythons. BBC1 March 1966-Dec 1967.
26. The Class Sketch was written by Marty Feldman and John Law, and broadcast on 7 April 1966. Ronnie Barker wrote three subsequent sketches for the same trio.
27. One of the most quoted sequences of the film, an absurd piece of wordplay featuring Terry Jones as a knight determined to see a fair trial for the accused – Booth – against all odds, including her guilt.
28. August 1963-June 1966, s1-5 on BBC1; 2 series on BBC radio (Light Service) May 1965-June 1967.
29. Series 1 ran from April-May 1975; series 2 will start 6 weeks after s1 of *Fawlty Towers* ends.
30. There was a little fanfare for the show but not excessive – the 13-19 September 1975 edition of the BBC listings magazine features *The Explorers* on its cover, an expensive documentary show narrated by David Attenborough. Younger viewers may not be aware that the Radio Times had a monopoly on BBC listings at that time – newspapers could show only that night or the following day's schedules. The proliferation of listing options we are used to today – and inclusion of both BBC and independent channels in the same magazine – would not happen until the 1990s.
Fawlty Towers would appear on the cover for the start of series 2 in February 1979, and again in May 2014.
31. Born 1939, Nightingale was a contemporary of Cleese at Cambridge, which he mentions in the interview.
32. S1e5 *Advanced Criminal Law,* Oct 2009. Jeff Winger (Joel McHale) is merely thanking Professor Ian Duncan (John Oliver) – a Brit. Abed Nadir (Danny

Pudi) – a media-savvy nerd – cannot resist the response; Duncan plays the trump card. Nothing more needs to be said.
33. For this author? 2014 and "maybe 1994" respectively.
34. Admittedly having a baby the day after episode 3 (*The Wedding Party*) and her own birthday the following Friday (*The Hotel Inspectors*) were pretty good excuses.
35. *Upstart Crow*, s2e4 "*Food of Love*", 2017.
36. The worldwide web as we know it would not be dreamt up until autumn 1990; email existed in 1971 but only for users of the same computer! It was in limited commercial use in the late 1980s, but the average Briton wouldn't encounter it until the late 1990s.

THE HOTEL AND INHABITANTS

1. Born 1939 and contemporary of Cleese at Cambridge Footlights. FTRO.
2. S1e1 *A Touch of Class*.
3. S1e6 *The Germans*.
4. Another seaside town, in Dorset, 100 miles along the coast from Torquay. With Cleese himself being from Weston-Super-Mare, it's not hard to guess at why all these characters live along the coast. Even the infernal Mrs Richards comes from Brighton.
5. All able-bodied young men aged between 18 and 21 in Great Britain – Northern Ireland was exempted – were required to complete two years of National Service between 1950 and 1963 (18 months between 1947 and 1950). Recruitment ceased in 1960. Basil would have been born between 1930 and 1935 so was eligible to serve in the Korean War (1950-53). John Cleese was exempt as from 1957 it was agreed that those born on or after 1 October 1939 did not need to serve – his birthdate is 27 October 1939.
6. *From Fringe to Flying Circus*. Methuen, 1980.
7. *And Now For Something Completely Different*, 1999, Chameleon/Andre Deutsch.
8. Noun: A wild, reckless, or quarrelsome person. Adjective: Characterised by a wild, unruly, or rakish manner or attitude. Both work for Basil.
9. Born 1952, writes scifi-fantasy with a high level of farce.
10. Born 1955, Atkinson is best known for *Blackadder* and *Mr Bean*.
11. https://www.gq-magazine.co.uk/culture/article/rowan-atkinson-interview
12. 1859-1941, a French philosopher and Nobel Laureate in Literature.
13. Interview with the author 2024.
14. https://www.eruditorumpress.com/blog/pop-between-realities-home-in-time-for-tea-22-fawlty-towers-the-hitchhikers-guide-to-the-galaxy
15. https://en.wikipedia.org/wiki/Michael_Apter

16. Journal of Popular Culture, 1982.
17. 1935-2022
18. *Mrs Slocombe's Pussy*, Flamingo/Harper Collins, 2000.
19. Greenall, Annjo K. "Gricean Theory and Linguicism: Infringements and Physical Violence in the Relationship between Manuel and Basil Fawlty." *Journal of Pragmatics* 41.3 (2009).
20. The unfair treatment of an individual or community based on their use of language. https://en.wiktionary.org/wiki/linguicism#English https://onlinelibrary.wiley.com/doi/abs/10.1002/9781405198431.wbeal1460
21. https://tomsalinsky.co.uk/blog/index.php/2011/07/12/the-why-of-funny-3-just-a-flesh-wound/
22. *Class and Other Hotel Matters in Fawlty Towers* in Kamm, Juergen and Neumann, Birgit. *British TV Comedies: cultural concepts, contexts, and controversies*. Palgrave Macmillan, 2015.
23. FTRO.
24. Random House, 2014.
25. Usually made of metal, so a futile gesture.
26. Cleese and Booth went to see Feydeau farces, as well as modern British theatrical farces, in the first years of their married life in London. Cleese has also written a stage farce and appeared in more than one film farce.
27. At the time, the only magazine allowed to print BBC TV and radio listings. The 13-19 September 1975 issue featured a number of pieces on the first episode of *Fawlty Towers*.
28. BBC2 Wed 20 June 1979, 21:25. (After 11 episodes of *Fawlty Towers*, but before the first broadcast of *Basil the Rat*.)
29. FTRO.
30. Quoted in https://www.independent.co.uk/arts-entertainment/arts-to-hell-with-basil-1619527.html
31. 1989 film based on Jones' own children's book.
32. Cleese provides the voice of the theatre announcer at the start of the play and the interval.
33. Born 1939, Weston-Super-Mare, another seaside town in the west of England.
34. A pre-Python sketch show co-written with Tim Brooke-Taylor (shortly to found *The Goodies)*, Marty Feldman, and Graham Chapman. Bill Oddie (Goodies) and Eric Idle (Python) would also appear. The children's show *Do Not Adjust Your Set* (1969) would feature Terry Jones, Eric Idle, Michael Palin and artwork by Terry Gilliam, and is sometimes bundled as "the other half" of the group's pre-Python TV work. Cleese (and Chapman) were keen fans.
35. https://en.wikipedia.org/wiki/I%27m_Sorry,_I%27ll_Read_That_Again
36. Tim Brooke-Taylor, Bill Oddie, and Graeme Garden were all series regulars.

37. John Cleese, Eric Idle, and Graham Chapman contributed material to the show.
38. https://en.wikipedia.org/wiki/Bang_Bang!_(play)
39. In 1963-4, when the Fawltys got married, the average age of a newlywed couple was 21 (women) and 23 (men). Sybil and Basil would have been around 28 by then. Even allowing for Basil's National Service delaying their plans a little, if they had married immediately after he left the army they would have been married for around 20 years by the events of series 1.
40. Multiple interviews including FTRO and her biographer, Teresa Ransom; the details differ but the gist of the exchange is the same in all tellings.
41. Born 1949. Co-creator, with Laurence Marks, of sitcoms 1980-date. Titles include *Goodnight Sweetheart, Shine On Harvey Moon, The New Statesman, Birds of a Feather* (including stage adaptation, 2012).
42. Interview with the author 2024.
43. FTRO.
44. https://www.independent.co.uk/arts-entertainment/arts-to-hell-with-basil-1619527.html
45. He admits he did this with both Connie Booth and Graham Chapman.
46. Interview with the author 2024.
47. Born 1932 in Surrey; married to actor Timothy West from 1963 until his death in 2024.. Their son Samuel is also an actor. Scales was diagnosed with vascular dementia in 2014 and retired from TV in 2019.
48. https://www.theguardian.com/stage/2015/feb/03/bridget-turner
49. Diary, 22 May 1978.
50. *Open house with Gloria Hunniford*, Thames TV. 25 Feb 2000.
51. *So You Want To Be An Actor*, Prunella Scales and Timothy West, 2005 Nick Hern Books.
52. Ransom, Teresa. *Prunella: the authorised biography,* John Murray, 2005.
53. https://www.youtube.com/watch?v=Pkau8btnlJg
54. Kate Starling, 44 episodes 1963-6; Sarah France, 34 episodes on BBC radio 1985-89, 38 episodes on ITV 1988-92. Sybil, 12 episodes.
55. "A new category of privilege was created for the European nationals who had formed the bulk of the work of the Immigrations Service for the preceding 50 years. This represented a dramatic change in Freedom of Movement from one that was previously ethnically diverse that included nations from Africa, Asia, Americas, Caribbean and Pacific to white only European nations. Membership of the European Community, now the European Union, encompassed the freedom of movement of workers within member states." Wikipedia.
56. Or his five mothers and four aunties, if you listen to him when he is drunk. S1e3 *The Wedding Party.*

57. *Sidekick Stories* BBC4, 2010.
58. https://www.spectator.co.uk/article/perfecting-the-art-of-rudeness/ 15 December 2007, review of Graham McCann's *Fawlty Towers* book.
59. Adapted from his 1975 novel *The Death of Reginald Perrin*. Perrin is perhaps what Fawlty might have become if he had had a loving wife and a mundane office job.
60. While Rik Mayall and Adrian Edmondson had developed their style of harsh slapstick in comedy clubs in the late 70s, after *Fawlty Towers* the post-Fawlty acceptance of slapstick in TV comedy allowed them to bring it to their sitcom work. By the time Rik Mayall starred with Greg Davies in *Man Down* (2013), other comedies would be shying away from slapstick violence but Mayall had been 'grandfathered in'.
61. 2010.
62. Born 1946. Baldrick and Manuel would have a lot to discuss.
63. Disturbingly for Manuel, "being carried about and dumped in a hamper" also describes the hotel's treatment of a corpse (Derek Royle in *The Kipper and the Corpse*). Royle was a former acrobat who was easily manhandled; Sachs was not.
64. 1930-2016. Born Andreas Sachs in Berlin, his family moved to Kilburn in 1938. Raised in London from the age of 8, after his part-Jewish family fled Nazi Germany in 1938.
65. Cleese's company, which makes training films.
66. £5282 in 2024.
67. Sachs continued to appear in the stage show while recording the first series of *Fawlty Towers*.
68. https://www.independent.co.uk/arts-entertainment/arts-to-hell-with-basil-1619527.html
69. Initially written as a philosophy student, this plot point was rewritten after filming.
70. Interview with the author 2024.
71. Interview with the author 2024.
72. Born 1940, Indianapolis, Indiana.
73. 20 February 1968 to 8 September 1978, after separating in 1976.
74. https://www.chortle.co.uk/news/2009/03/23/8590/polly_speaks
75. FTRO
76. St Peter's Preparatory School, Weston-Super-Mare.
77. *So, Anyway*.
78. National Service effectively prevented Cleese from going straight to university – although he was too young to be required to complete it, those leaving at 20 taking up deferred and new university offers meant there were fewer places

available for 18 year olds. Cleese effectively did two years 'service' as a teacher, instead. Basil Fawlty, being older than John Cleese, did have to do National Service.
79. https://www.fawltysite-net.icerasemi.com/people/ballard_berkeley.htm
80. Operation Overlord. https://en.wikipedia.org/wiki/8th_Army_Group_Royal_Artillery
81. https://x.com/hantscricket/status/1840047564198162474
82. An entirely fictional address.
83. Known in the 1970s to viewers as 'The English Riviera', it offers one of the warmer climates in the UK. During the run of *Fawlty Towers* British citizens were just starting to holiday "on the continent" – currency restrictions imposed at the outbreak of World War II would not be fully lifted until October 1979 and so holidaying abroad was expensive and difficult to arrange for many. The lifting of the ban, combined with the late 70s/early 80s boom in cheap flights, would contribute significantly to the decline of the English seaside hotel. https://en.wikipedia.org/wiki/Exchange_controls_in_the_United_Kingdom
84. S1e4 the inspectors say 26 rooms, 12 with bathroom.
85. S1e1 *A Touch of Class*.
86. 7.30-9.30 according to Basil in *The Psychiatrist* but he also notes that the chef leaves at 9pm, which makes sense of times quoted in *The Anniversary* and *Waldorf Salad*, and the inflexibility of certain meals.
87. A very popular bitter, 1931-1979.
88. In *The Hotel Inspectors* Mr Hutchinson requests the hire of a TV but this cannot be accommodated; Basil does agree to reserve BBC2 for him but we do not find out where he will watch this.
89. S1e4 *The Hotel Inspectors*.
90. Polly, Manuel, and at least two chefs are seen. A previous maid/assistant named Elsie has left, and a new one will start (unseen) during s2.
91. Their wedding day was Friday 17 April 1964, established in s2e5.
92. S2e3 *Waldorf Salad*.
93. S1e4 *The Hotel Inspectors*.
94. S2e3 *Waldorf Salad*.
95. S2e4 *The Kipper and the Corpse*.
96. S1e2 *The Builders*.
97. S2e4 *The Kipper and the Corpse*.
98. s2e4 *The Kipper and the Corpse*.
99. s2e6 *Basil the Rat*.
100. A duvet intended to be used without a cover.
101. S1e2 *The Builders*.

102. https://www.thepoke.com/2014/08/21/have-you-seen-this-lego-fawlty-towers-hotel/ As part of the Lego Ideas programme fans can submit plans for future sets and *Fawlty Towers* has been submitted, but not approved to date. Fan-built models can be found online and occasionally at Lego events.
103. https://cstonline.net/inside-fawlty-towers-by-marcus-harmes/
104. https://tvstudiohistory.co.uk/bbc-tv-centre/the-television-rehearsal-rooms/
105. An 'Easter egg' on the DVD and Blu-ray releases shows the aftermath of the fire – broken and boarded up windows, missing roof, burned beams – but the hotel facade is still recognisable. The front door was almost undamaged. The end of the short film, made by Philip Dee, Stuart Fyvie, and Robert Greenwood, shows the building site and some of the new houses.
106. A blue plaque has been put up by the Torbay Civic Society.
107. Various sources describe the scripts as being twice the length of regular TV sitcom scripts, and often longer than the allotted thirty minutes. Each episode took Booth and Cleese six weeks to write.
108. Interview with Teresa Ransom 2005.
109. The Sunday recording was dictated by Andrew Sachs's theatre role – the show should have been recorded on Thursdays but Sunday was his only free evening.
110. *So You Want To Be An Actor*.
111. *Pointless* 18 March 2010.

FIRST BROADCAST 19 SEPTEMBER 1975 – A TOUCH OF CLASS

1. Unlike subsequent shows, which would mostly be recorded shortly before broadcast, this was recorded on 23 December 1974, with external footage shot on 16-17 December and additional material added in summer 1975. The show's theme tune was recorded on 19 December.
2. Born 1943. Simeon would, like many other cast members, appear in A Fish Called Wanda.
3. Basil does not consider this to be important, however. This is a direct reference to the Python team's experience at the 'real life Fawlty Towers', the Gleneagles Hotel run by Donald Sinclair. The anecdote is variously ascribed to Michael Palin and Eric Idle; Palin does not explicitly mention it in his diary entries dealing with Gleneagles.
4. https://www.britmovie.co.uk/forum/cinema/actors-and-actresses/extras-aa/2177-fawlty-towers-uncredited-speaking-parts
5. 1929-2023. Wheeler, like many who appeared in *Fawlty Towers,* was a seasoned character actor.
6. Conoley will appear again as Mr Johnstone in *Waldorf Salad*, s2e3.

7. Peters would appear in the first episode of *The Fall and Rise of Reginald Perrin*; Conoley was a series regular.
8. Born 1942, Robin Ellis was about to hit the big time as Ross Poldark in the original TV adaptation of the *Poldark* novels by Winston Graham; he appears again in the remake 2015-19.
9. 1916-76. Gwynn was a Hammer Horror and TV actor. He would appear in *Poldark* and thriller *State of Emergency* before his premature death, only 4 months after this episode aired.
10. 1914-88.
11. Also listed at https://www.britmovie.co.uk/forum/cinema/actors-and-actresses/extras-aa/2177-fawlty-towers-uncredited-speaking-parts
12. Good old Dolly! 1931-2011. England cricketer from South Africa, he was the first non-white player in county cricket.
13. Dating the show from the outset – newspapers are no longer *de rigeur* in hotels and the Major would get his news online today.
14. Ballard Berkeley and John Cleese would regularly discuss cricket during the filming of both series.
15. Another dated reference. Printed magazines do still exist – including *Country Life* – but businesses like Fawlty Towers are no longer reliant on ads. Today this would be an online ad or affiliation with an umbrella booking organisation. In 1975 this would have been a very big deal indeed for the hotel, however, as word of mouth is not going to get the Fawltys many recommendations.
16. A print magazine, founded in 1897 and still in print today (2024). It is aimed at an upper class (and aspirational upper middle class) readership, containing articles on rural life, sports, architecture, arts, and gardening, among other topics.
17. Email to the author, 13 Aug 2024. Many thanks to Lucy Khosla and team.
18. Average price checked with booking.com for October 2024.
19. The equivalent of £420.50 in 2024 – so half the price of the cheapest ad.
20. Ellis does not, and learned the lines by rote. https://robin-ellis.net/2015/09/19/fawlty-towers-forty-years-old/
21. "A week's TV work just before Christmas after three years earning peanuts in the theatre was very welcome. But it involved recording in front of a studio audience–something I'd *never* done–and I was nervous!" https://robin-ellis.net/2015/09/19/fawlty-towers-forty-years-old/
22. For modern readers, this may be more baffling than intended. Before the proliferation of ATMs and the decline in cheque usage, cashing a cheque avoided the need to visit an open bank branch. Hotels would have been a good place to – legitimately – cash a cheque, as they could pay it in with their takings (storing and carrying less cash as a result) while giving the cash to

the guest, saving both parties some effort. However, Melbury is asking for a lot of money: more than most banks would allow in an over-the-counter transaction, even for a legitimate customer who is visiting their own home branch. As he is clearly committing fraud, we can assume that the cheque will be rejected – bounced – by the bank. The deception relies on Melbury being long gone with the cash by the time this happens. Fraud via cheque cashing is revisited in *The Fall and Rise of Reginald Perrin* a year later (Sept 76).

23. S2e1 *Communication Problems*.
24. Filmed in Cookham in Berks, not Torquay. No filming for the show would ever be done in the resort itself.
25. A green Austin Maxi MkII NOA288M – built 1973 in Oxford, registered 29 August 73 and at time of filming, taxed until March 1975 (and offroad since June 1985, now presumed scrapped). This car was part of the British Leyland press fleet, lent to TV and film productions as well as to journalists for review.
26. Conservative MP and then-Deputy PM Michael Heseltine was described thus by Chief Whip Michael Jopling, though the quip is often ascribed to Alan Clark MP, who did inherit his furniture. Clark merely recorded it in his diaries.
Alan Clark *Diaries: In Power 1983–1992* (Wednesday 17 June 1987) Weidenfeld & Nicolson, 1993.
27. Sotheby's was founded in 1744 and remains a pre-eminent auction house and broker of fine arts.
28. Criminal Investigation Department: detectives, often in plain clothes like Mr Brown.
29. In a brand-new Rover 3500, an expensive car. So much for Basil's 'tatty' theory, although the AA awarded this car the title of "*worst new car in England*" in August 1975.
30. The tone of this rant will be familiar to fans of *Monty Python's Flying Circus*, where Cleese indulged in similar rants – e.g. The Architects Sketch in s2e4 *The Buzz Aldrin Show*.
31. *John Howard Davies: A Life in Comedy* 7 Jan 2012 BBC2
32. In the middle of things. We don't need to see how the Fawltys met, found the hotel, hired the staff. We just need to accept that all of those things happened, and not ask too many questions about *why*.
33. Audio recording for LP/subsequent audio releases.
34. Specifically, a Playout Director – making sure TV programmes go out on time with correct links, subtitles, etc.
35. https://www.dirtyfeed.org/2023/05/project-no-1144-3361/#more-22581
36. Published as *The Complete Fawlty Towers Scripts*, Cleese & Booth.
37. Both shows written by Dick Clement (1937-) and Ian le Frenais (1937-).

FIRST BROADCAST 26 SEPTEMBER 1975 – THE BUILDERS

1. The studio recording took place on 3 August 1975, under the working title '*O'Reilly*'.
2. Another character actor with a long CV in UK television. Lee appears again in s2.
3. 1929-2012. Irish actor Kelly would appear in a lot of UK shows after Fawlty Towers, eventually appearing in Hollywood films in old age.
4. "*Who is man with beard?*" Man with beard is Michael Cronin, best known to Generation X as Mr Baxter, the PE teacher in Grange Hill.
5. 1923-2014. Like Michael Gwynn, Appleby was a familiar character actor.
6. Judy Rodgers.
7. 76-138. Emperor 117-138. Famously had a wall, not just a pile of bricks.
8. 1918-97. English cricketer.
9. A fictional road; the original Gleneagles hotel was in Asheldon Road in Wellswood, a rather well to do area of Torquay. Rob Hurley, Torquay resident, confirms that there is no hint of a sea view there. Conversation with the author 2024.
10. Contemporary viewers would have been familiar with the PG Tips chimps from adverts.
11. Although the red Austin Countryman is already in the car park, as Basil drove it back. Sybil gets out of a yellow Ford Cortina, and has clearly been driving it – Audrey is in the passenger seat. Is it Audrey's car that Sybil is driving, perhaps due to Audrey's recent hysterectomy?
12. Compare with s2e5 *The Anniversary*.
13. Rolled steel joist, also known as an I-beam. Vital for supporting walls.
14. Sellers, Robert. *Raising Laughter: How the Sitcom Kept Britain Smiling in the '70s* (new ed), The History Press, 2023.
15. 13 May 1979 (after series 2, though before the recording of *Basil the Rat*). https://www.dirtyfeed.org/2024/09/unsolved-fawlty-towers-mystery/
16. FTRO.

FIRST BROADCAST 3 OCTOBER 1975 _ THE WEDDING PARTY

1. Recorded 10 August 1975, under the title '*Morality*'. https://www.radiotimes.com/tv/comedy/fawlty-tours-april-walker-exclusive/
2. 1931-2018. Gilan was another TV character regular; she later became a motivational speaker. Her son was the TV critic A A Gill.
3. Uncredited at the time, but the *Radio Times* in 2021 named him as Mark Allington, with confirmatory photographs. https://www.radiotimes.com/tv/comedy/fawlty-towers-rare-photos-from-the-radio-times-archive/

Endnotes

4. 1946-2000. Adams starred in *The Fall and Rise of Reginald Perrin* a year later.
5. Born 1943. Walker was a regular in sitcoms, and the original choice for Sarah Jane Smith in *Doctor Who*.
6. 1925-2016. Philips was the original TV William Tell and appeared in many films.
7. 1918-86. A sitcom regular, King had played Scales's mother-in-law in *Marriage Lines*.
8. Sachs wrote in his autobiography that the rehearsal pan was padded; Cleese picked up the wrong one. Cleese told him it was always intended to be a metal pan, just not as heavy a blow. Cleese offered Sachs "*a Babycham and a big kiss*".
9. Cleese coined "*machine-gunning a seal*" about Booth's natural laugh, dropping the line into the episode as well.
10. A peignoir is a dressing gown or negligee.
11. John Howard Davies was very proud of casting Yvonne Gilan for this part, praising her accent and looks in the DVD commentary (2009). Gilan herself thought later that the accent sounded more Hungarian than French (FTRO).
12. In 1975, the companies of Ricard and Pernod Fils, the two largest French aniseed aperitif producers and fierce competitors merged creating the Pernod Ricard Group, which now produces and distributes Ricard. https://en.wikipedia.org/wiki/Ricard_(liqueur)
13. 1965 US black comedy with Jack Lemmon and Virna Lisi.
14. He is already 6ft5 and in his 40s – our first hint that the Ladies may be a little senile themselves.
15. Cleese, however, on the DVD commentary, seems to relish this scene rather too much. "*I was married to that.*"
16. Trevor Adams had worked with Cleese before, as had April Walker, so Cleese cast them himself.
17. We know Basil did National Service; it is strongly implied he was sent to Korea as part of this. As this would have been between 1950 and 1953, we can comfortably assume that Fawlty is over the age of 40 by 1975. Cleese, who was only 35, was made up to look older. Scales was 43, playing her own age. (Booth was also 35.)
18. Another surprise to 21st century viewers who are used to being able to buy condoms openly in shops and supermarkets.
19. Another sign of the times, both the specification of electric razors and the lack of shaver sockets in the hotel.
20. JHD says this was Cleese's own choice – appropriate bedtime reading when sharing a room with Sybil.
21. JHD notes that it makes it harder and harder to follow his lines here.
22. Cleese notes in the commentary that Basil wouldn't necessarily know that the couple are connected, as he doesn't see them together, but it doesn't hurt the plot.

23. The window in this room is also on the wrong wall, when we attempt to rationalise the landing layout and the view of the other bedrooms. The door and wall wobble when he shuts it, and it's notable that the wallpaper is also peeling and badly applied.
24. The previous establishment of a heatwave means he has to help her open the window. It's also very typical of Basil to not yet have done something he was asked to do, of course.
25. The classic *Monty Python* sketch illustrating a range of sexual euphemisms.
26. Interview with author, 2024.
27. JHD claims credit for this line.
28. Uncomfortably for Sachs. JHD says Cleese talks about it being better if they'd used a rubber pan for this reason but claims it's much better with metal. The clang is obvious.
29. 218-201BC, the Punic wars were fought between Rome and Carthage. This reference is even gloomier than Sybil's "1485" when asked about the length of the Fawltys' marriage.

FIRST BROADCAST 10 OCTOBER 1975 – THE HOTEL INSPECTORS

1. Recorded "27 August 1975" according to Cribbins, although this was a Wednesday. 17 August is the correct date. https://www.dirtyfeed.org/2023/04/the-unexamined-sitcom/ The working titles included *The Inspector, Hotel Inspector*.
2. Written for Richard Briers, then offered to Leonard Rossiter before Cribbins was cast.
3. 1928-2022. Much-loved British character actor.
4. 1933-1997. Known to many as Jimmy, he was a popular repertory theatre actor and character actor on TV and film.
5. *"A crucial member of the team"* – JHD. Bob Spiers also rates him highly.
6. 1923-2023, United States secretary of state from 1973 to 1977 and national security advisor from 1969 to 1975, in the presidential administrations of Richard Nixon and Gerald Ford. Not especially funny.
7. *"Leader of the Blackfoot Indians in the 1860s."* Cleese and Booth appear to have invented him. His name may be an allusion to Kicking Bird, a Kiowa leader in the 1860s and 70s.
8. Named after Alan Hutchinson, a Cambridge friend of Cleese's. DVD commentary.
9. Named after Nicholas Walt, a shopkeeper in Covent Garden and another friend of Cleese's.
10. It suggests that at some point during plotting and scripting, lines may have been switched between characters.

11. For 1975 BBC2, quite rude really.
12. The hotel does not have a visible television set but since the Major also reports watching TV, and Basil doesn't turn Mr Hutchinson down, we can assume it's either in the bar/lounge, or there is a separate TV room somewhere.
13. Different rooms are allocated different tables according to a daily rota, presumably to take advantage of window views etc. On Wednesdays room 7 is table 5, not table 1…
14. Bernard Cribbins says that he had to ask John Cleese to ease up a bit – he was a *"young, powerful man"*. FTRO.
15. John J Hoare notes that Cleese makes an error here: the script says *"Good afternoon. And what can do I for you three gentlemen?"* but Cleese adds a second 'gentlemen' after 'afternoon', making the final line irritatingly repetitive. https://www.dirtyfeed.org/2023/01/too-much-duck/#fn2-19905
16. 1928-2022.
17. 1973-75; stop motion series based on the books by Elisabeth Beresford.
18. Cribbins read stories on a record 114 programmes between 1966 and 1991, including excerpts from *Charlie and the Chocolate Factory, James and the Giant Peach, The Wizard of Oz, Alice's Adventures in Wonderland and Alice Through the Looking Glass, The Hobbit*, and stories by Joan Aiken.
19. *Right Said Fred; The Hole in the Ground.*
20. *Carry On Jack* (1963) and *Carry On Spying* (1964); he would later appear in *Carry On Columbus* (1992), the last in the series.
21. *Casino Royale*, 1967.
22. Mascot of the Post Office, then British Telecom.
23. *Bernard Who? 75 Years of Doing Just About Everything*, 2018, Constable.
24. https://www.raycooney.co.uk/ray-cooney-jottings-the-rules-of-farce
25. Born 1932. Actor and playwright, he was a long-time friend of Sachs and played in Whitehall farces with him under Brian Rix before writing his own plays.
26. Anne Elk appears in s3e5 The All-England Summarize Proust Competition; Mr McGough – named for poet Roger McGough – in s3e11 episode *Dennis Moore*.
27. For younger readers, travelling salesmen may be a bit of a mystery. It was a popular profession until the internet age – visiting retailers and factories with samples of goods or at least, information about them. Mr Hutchinson has samples of spoons with him, but Mr Walt, who sells outboard motors, only has brochures. The phrase "travels in [goods in question]" was a standard way of referring to such salesmen – and they were mostly male – which leads to jokes like "he travels in women's underwear".

FIRST BROADCAST 17 OCTOBER 1975 – GOURMET NIGHT

1. Recorded 7 September 1975; external filming 22-23 July 1975. Working title: '*Duck's Off*'.
2. 1920-2015. Familiar to younger viewers from *Rentaghost*, 1978-84.
3. We'll see her again in series 2. Benson was married to BBC producer Douglas Argent, who produced series 2.
4. Born 1960. Child actor Page went into the Navy. https://www.dailymail.co.uk/femail/article-3240286/
5. According to the script book.
6. 1926-2021. French-born actor who appeared in a diverse range of productions, from the *Pink Panther* films and *Doctor Who* to *Bonjour Francaise* and other BBC French educational programmes.
7. 1913-1994. Plytas was a Greek character actor born in Turkey and based in the UK.
8. 1920-1988. An Australian actor who often played military men in UK productions.
9. 1915-1993. Another *Jackanory* reader, Way also appeared in *Clockwise* with Cleese.
10. Possibly named after Kenneth Twitchen, a BBC sound engineer. His son John commented on a VHS collection site: https://bbc-video-uk.fandom.com/wiki/Fawlty_Towers_-_The_Kipper_and_the_Corpse
11. 1908-1995. Calidcot's voice was familiar to contemporary audiences from his long-standing role in *The Navy Lark* on BBC Radio. He and Sachs were both appearing in *No Sex Please, We're British* at the time of recording.
12. 1911-93. Another repertory actress and opera singer.
13. In the episode it is Leslie, in the published script it is Lionel.
14. WLG 142E. 1967. An incongruous car for a 6ft5 man to drive, of course. JHD: "*28mph top speed, 0-60 in 1hr 17 mins.*"
15. Cleese notes that he plays this scene in the accent of Mr Praline, the *Monty Python* character from the *Dead Parrot* and *Crunchy Frog* sketches.
16. Compare with s1e1 *A Touch of Class*.
17. Cleese says that he named the cancelled diners after some guests who failed to turn up for dinner with the Cleeses, "*as a reminder*".
18. It's tempting to read 'dry' as a sexual joke with modern eyes but more likely it refers to her character, as a synonym for dull. While slipping jokes past informal or formal censors has always happened, this one probably isn't an example.
19. Stalwarts of TV comedy, Ronnie Barker and Ronnie Corbett, who had both worked with Cleese in the 1960s. The phrase 'rook's off' – pronounced 'orf' – is the groanworthy punchline to a long and involved restaurant menu joke.

Endnotes

20. This scene was filmed – we can hear the audience reaction – but was edited to avoid showing vomiting in broadcast versions of the episode. This scene does not appear in any version, although it is clear from the preceding scene that the actor has something in his mouth and we hear part of the audience reaction. It is absent from the 'remastered' DVDs and Blu-ray, and so we can probably assume that the footage no longer exists.
21. Actually filmed in Harrow – 294 Preston Road. Now Wings Chinese Restaurant. André's number is Torquay 9120. Cleese mentions in the commentary that this was a valid phone number at the time.
22. Compare with The Two Ronnies 'Rook restaurant' sketch.
23. https://www.dirtyfeed.org/2023/01/too-much-duck

FIRST BROADCAST 24 OCTOBER 1975 – THE GERMANS

1. Filmed 31 August 1975, as '*Fire Drill*'.
2. 1925-2010. A character actress who played a long string of wives and nurses in TV.
3. 1938-2020. Mahoney was a long-standing campaigner for racial equality within the acting profession, as a member of the Equity Afro-Asian Committee (previously called the Coloured Actors Committee until he renamed it), founding Performers Against Racism to defend Equity policy on South Africa, and as co-creator, with Mike Phillips and Taiwo Ajai, of the UK's Black Theatre Workshop in 1976.
4. 1915-2002, Bowman was born in Berlin and often played German characters in UK shows, including *Colditz* and *Secret Army*.
5. 1915-93, a British actress.
6. Born 1937.
7. 1938-99.
8. He would appear in the first episode of *The Fall and Rise of Reginald Perrin* with Annet Peters, another *Fawlty Towers* alumna.
9. Do they really need annotation?
10. The BBC paid Andrew Sachs damages after this stunt went wrong.
11. Accurate statistics for 1975 are hard to obtain, as the Office for National Statistics had been recording people's places of birth rather than ethnicity; there was some work put in to start to record ethnicity in the 1981 census for England and Wales, but in the end it did not happen until 1991. The earliest government statistic available is from 1966, when an estimated 1 million non-white people lived in Britain, rising to 3.3 million by 1995. The total population of the UK in 1975 was 56 million.
12. India v. Surrey at the Oval. He quietly says "*Surrey had to get 33*" at the end of the scene.

13. In 1975, chips were usually cooked in a large pan of oil or a deep fat fryer, both of which are regrettably easy to set on fire. AirFryers and oven chips would have revolutionised 1970s catering.
14. A now-iconic image, often seen in memes, comes from this section: Basil, shaking his fist at the heavens, thanks God *"so bloody much"* for everything he is faced with.
15. https://www.independent.co.uk/arts-entertainment/arts-to-hell-with-basil-1619527.html
16. Morris Bright & Robert Ross, BBC, 2001.
17. Sections 130, 86 and 86a of the German criminal code, among others. There is an exception for artistic, educational and journalistic works, so the episode is exempted. Basil himself, however, could be facing prosecution for his behaviour in the wrong circumstances.
18. The arm gesture Basil performs before he begins to goose step.
19. 1968-77, Jimmy Perry and David Croft. An extremely popular show about an English Home Guard unit who almost never see enemy action. The majority of German characters in the show are Luftwaffe airmen with very little to say – if they are seen on screen at all – and the captured crew of a U-Boat. None are portrayed as stereotypical Nazis, only as opposing military forces.
20. 1974-81, Jimmy Perry and David Croft. Set in an Entertainment unit in India and Burma, it has been criticised for its use of white actors in make-up ('brownface'), racism, pro-imperialism, and homophobia, but it was very popular at the time.
21. 1972-74, created by Gerard Glaister and Brian Degas. It was a loosely fictionalised narrative of the prisoner-of-war camp at Colditz Castle, 1940-45.
22. Another BBC drama created by Gerard Glaister, 1977-79, about a Belgian Resistance unit. The sitcom *'Allo 'Allo* (1982-92, written by Jeremy Lloyd and David Croft until 1989, Lloyd and Paul Adam 1991-92), started as a direct spoof of *Secret Army* – even featuring many of the same actors – and would finally introduce bumbling comic, even sympathetic Nazi characters to UK TV, almost two decades after the US show *Hogan's Heroes* – 1965-71 – did it. *Hogan's Heroes* has been shown occasionally in the UK in the 1990s, and 2010s, but is not well-known.
23. https://www.theguardian.com/media/2009/may/06/television-john-cleese
24. *I Know Nothing*.

BETWEEN THE WARS

1. Ceefax actually started in September 1974 but very few viewers could access it as it required a text-capable set. It was switched off in 2012 and replaced by the Red Button service.

2. https://www.radiotimes.com/tv/comedy/fawlty-tours-april-walker-exclusive/
3. *TV Zone* issue 151.
4. *When Love Turns Sour at Fawlty Towers*, Daily Mirror 2 June 1976.
5. https://www.independent.co.uk/arts-entertainment/arts-to-hell-with-basil-1619527.html
6. Video Arts was formed in 1972 with Antony Jay, whom Cleese had met while Jay was writing for *The Frost Report*. Peter Robinson (film and tv director) and Michael Peacock (previous controller of BBC2) also joined. They produced films for industry and retail trades, combining instruction with entertainment. Stars such as Ronnie Barker and Angharad Rees worked for them, and Cleese wrote many early scripts himself. Michael Palin and Terry Jones would similarly write for e.g. the Midland Bank: Palin discusses "how to use a cheque book" in his diary, June 1970.
7. Cleese sold in 1989 for £43m.
8. Andrew Bonar Law was Prime Minister of the UK 1922-1923. For a modern equivalent consider: *The Liz Truss Story*.
9. Swann was Chairman of the BBC 1973-80.
10. *From Fringe to Flying Circus*.
11. That and the fact that many sitcoms would produce a Christmas special – and still do. Lars Holger Holm's odd book *Fawlty Towers: A Worshipper's Companion* claims to have the script for the 13th episode but it is his own creation.
12. Around £500,000 in 2024.
13. Around £119 in 2024.
14. *I Know Nothing*.
15. FTRO.
16. https://www.bbc.co.uk/news/articles/c90z18q2egpo

FIRST BROADCAST 19 FEBRUARY 1979 – COMMUNICATION PROBLEMS

1. Recorded 28 January 1979 as '*Mrs Richards*' and also known as '*Theft*'. 12.9 million tuned in for this episode.
2. 1932-2017. Shannon was a former boxer who was best known for playing gangster Harry Flowers in the cult movie *Performance*.
3. 1914-93, another repertory and character actor.
4. 1912-92. Sanderson would later play Prunella Scales' mother in *After Henry,* 1985-89 on radio, 1988-92 on TV.
5. 1931-2010.
6. 1910-83 or 1914-83. Trinidadian-British piano player, Atwell was the first black artist and (to date) the only female instrumentalist to have a number 1 single in the UK.

7. An 1890 one act opera by Pietro Mascagni.
8. For younger readers: cheques could be written without a guarantee card but would bounce if the bank refused to pay them e.g. if the account was empty; the guarantee card meant businesses could take cheques without risk. See *A Touch of Class*.
9. As Exeter is the closest racecourse to Torquay, this can be considered a more plausible tip than most – Mr Firkin may have an inside tip.
10. National Hunt racing – jumps – takes place between October and April each year, flat racing between April and October. There *are* occasional races during the summer months at Exeter so charitably we can assume Mr Firkin meant one of those.
11. VAT for hotel rooms in spring 1979 was 8% so she is paying £7.77½ per night, unless Basil is rounding the halfpenny up to £7.78. This is equivalent to £37.18 in 2024, so she is getting a bargain, and as we will shortly see, she can afford it.
12. £358 in 2024.
13. https://tomsalinsky.co.uk/blog/index.php/tag/fawlty-towers/
14. Any seemingly irrelevant and forgotten line or plot element that comes back at the very end, like a brick thrown away in one joke that hits a character in another joke, to great effect.
15. Polly covers with "*it got off to a flying start*".
16. He adds "*one of those, you know*", implying homophobia. Another example of the Major not embodying Cleese's own views.
17. 1572-1637, Jonson popularised the 'comedy of humours' in satirical plays.
18. 1564-1616. Shakespearean comedy is often farcical with a lot of wordplay, and can be played with as much physical humour as *Fawlty Towers*.
19. A show which today we would recognise as dealing with depression, burnout, and mental health issues.
20. Barker did not stutter himself but regularly used speech impediments such as Spoonerism and stammering for comic effect.

FIRST BROADCAST 26 FEBRUARY 1979 – THE PSYCHIATRIST

1. Recorded 4 February 1979 as '*Sex*'.
2. 1945-2019. Cleese often asked Henson for casting tips and called him to ask who to cast for a character to whom he planned to be really abusive. Henson, a good friend of Cleese, agreed to play the role himself as he could take the abuse in his stride. Henson wore his own clothes for the episode.
3. Born 1952.
4. 1918-90. A busy theatre and TV actor.

5. 1929-13. Elspet Gray was married to Brian Rix, an old hand at theatrical farces. She may be more familiar to younger audiences as the mother of Prince Edmund in *The Black Adder*.
6. 1946-2017. Peters appeared in a significant number of Hammer Horror films.
7. 1906-99. Delamain was 72 during filming.
8. William Ewart Gladstone, 1809-1898, 4-time Prime Minister of the UK between 1868 and 1894.
9. Field Marshal Douglas Haig, 1st Earl Haig, 1861-1929. Military commander of British forces in the First World War.
10. Robert Baden-Powell, 1st Baron Baden-Powell, 1857-1941. Founder of the Scout and Girl Guide/Scout movements.
11. Narrowly missing Sachs, who mistakenly attributes this scene to *The Wedding Party* in his autobiography.
12. There *is* an Orchard Street, Torquay, but it is residential and an unlikely place to find a French restaurant.
13. For younger viewers, in a time before mobile phones and digital watches, ringing the Speaking Clock to get the correct time was not uncommon – the hotel's grandfather clock is likely to lose time if not wound and set correctly.
14. Luan Peters plays her as Australian but the actress was British.
15. A pun on Bleak House, and an improbable cuisine for a Torquay restaurant.
16. The Spanish Armada of 1588, which was intended to help Spain overthrow Queen Elizabeth I and occupy England.
17. Bob Spiers points out that as Basil opens the bedroom door we can see Manuel crouching to the left of it. He appears to be picking something up. He may be retrieving ice cubes dropped in the previous scene.
18. Modern viewers may be more familiar with Brylcreem, a similar product.
19. *"You'll have to sew 'em back on first."* Basil acknowledges that Sybil has him by the mind and balls.

FIRST BROADCAST 5 MARCH 1979 – WALDORF SALAD

1. Recorded 21 January 1979, as the first episode of the series, and under the working title 'USA'.
2. 1926-2011. Another *Poldark* cast member.
3. 1910-85. Best known as Mrs CJ in *The Fall and Rise of Reginald Perrin*.
4. 1908-95. Many of the smaller parts in *Fawlty Towers* have unusual names; this pair suggest the graverobbers *Burke* and Hare.
5. 1924-2005.
6. 1925-2012. Tanner appeared in a huge list of sitcoms and shows from *Sykes to EastEnders*.

7. 1928-2021. Another character actor who appeared in many 70s and 80s shows.
8. 1930-2004. Boa often played 'the token American' in UK productions, and appeared in *The Empire Strikes Back*.
9. Born 1937.
10. Tinned fruit cocktail was ubiquitous in 1970s cuisine. It is still available but not, thankfully, on hotel menus.
11. In 1979, the section that the Hamiltons would have used was less than a decade old.
12. Their route will have been M4 to Bristol, M5 to its terminus at Exeter, 24 miles north of Torquay.
13. $27 at the February 1979 exchange rate, or around $117 adjusted for inflation, not far off the UK equivalent.
14. Orange juice and vodka, as the Hamiltons will explain. Basil can be forgiven for not knowing this term as the British drank 'vodka and orange' – Mrs Hamilton knows this and could have made things easier by ordering one in the first place!
15. A 22 mile stretch of the South Devon coast, from Maidencombe to Brixham, also known as Torbay. Torquay is near the northern end of this bay, with a sheltered harbour.
16. At least it wasn't powdered orange juice, which was very common in homes at the time.
17. Very popular 1970s romantic novelist.
18. This rather implies that he did not in fact drive himself from London, or is planning to simply abandon his hire car. The 21st century reading, that he would not drive after one vodka and orange, is less likely in the "have a drink, have a drive" 1970s. It also suggests the Ladies and the Major would be leaving, when we know they will not.
19. Get out, scram!
20. https://en.wikipedia.org/wiki/Waldorf_salad
21. Venture into Reddit if you dare: r/fawltytowers and r/BritishTV are a good place to start if you do.
22. *It's all bottoms, isn't it.*
23. Rationing did not create a good impression of British food.
24. https://www.bristolpost.co.uk/news/bristol-news/man-gobsmacked-after-discovering-original-8217259

FIRST BROADCAST 12 MARCH 1979 – THE KIPPER AND THE CORPSE

1. Recorded 11 February 1979, working title '*Death*'.
2. 1914-2006; primarily a comic repertory actress. She often played upper-class or aristocratic women.

Endnotes

3. 1926-2015. A regular in *Z-Cars* and sitcoms.
4. 1928-90; younger viewers might recognise him as the second M. LeClerc in *'Allo 'Allo*. A slight man, Spiers notes that he was easy to carry around, and Sachs adds that he had been an acrobat so the physical nature of the role was easy.
5. 1927-2020. A big name for the show, like Bernard Cribbins, Palmer had been a comedy character actor for some time and was known to contemporary viewers from *The Fall and Rise of Reginald Perrin* and *Butterflies*. He would go on to appear in *A Fish Called Wanda* with Cleese in 1988.
6. 1920-90. Producer and actor.
7. Born 1932, she was a dancer and *"...the possessor of the longest legs in show business"* in the 1950s.
8. Born 1939.
9. Born in 1946, writer and actor McKeown was a frequent collaborator with the Pythons, and Terry Gilliam in particular.
10. Modern viewers may not be familiar with kippers, which are smoked herring. As they are dried and smoked, they may well be edible past an arbitrary best before date.
11. A play on 'a woman's work is never done' – Sybil is rarely seen *doing* any work, only delegating it to others.
12. This means that Mr Leeman went to bed and died almost immediately – it was past 9pm the previous night when he went to bed and is now just past 8am, 11 hours later.
13. 1940-2021. Known as Aitch, his book *Extra! Extra!* details the location shoot a fortnight before the studio recording.
14. http://www.turnipnet.com/aitch/aitch/1979.htm
15. 1946-2007.
16. https://alt.obituaries.narkive.com/ET3QTLZL/andrew-leeman-introduced-tacos-and-margaritas-to-london
17. https://www.telegraph.co.uk/news/obituaries/1561472/Andrew-Leeman.html
18. https://www.dirtyfeed.org/2020/01/two-dead-twenty-five-to-go/

FIRST BROADCAST 26 MARCH 1979 – THE ANNIVERSARY

1. Recorded 18 March 1979, a very short turnaround.
2. Iain McLean, a crossword fan, was tasked with creating the anagrams. He told JHD that they couldn't use this one as it was *"a little vulgar"*. JHD and Cleese assured him they'd find a home for it.
This is the only true anagram in the show, and McLean says she did not look for more. FTRO.

3. 1932-2003.
4. 1941-2008. Writer, actor, and experimental theatre director, Campbell was a friend of Cleese, and also appeared in *A Fish Called Wanda*.
5. 1937-2021. Model, actress, dancer and TV personality, Stubbs had been married to Nicky Henson until 1975, and knew Cleese and Booth well. Contemporary viewers knew her from *Till Death Us Do Part*, *Give Us A Clue* and *Wurzel Gummidge*; younger audiences from *The Worst Witch* and, most recently, *Sherlock*.
6. Born 1944. Son of comedian Stanley Holloway, he appeared in a number of *Carry On* films.
7. 1931-2003. A regular in *Dixon of Dock Green*, Arnold was married to June Brown, who played Dot Cotton in *EastEnders*.
8. 1933-2013. Keen would work with Cleese again in *Clockwise*.
9. 1940-96. Hume was a radio actor as well as TV, appearing regularly in *The Archers* 1988-96.
10. Born 1931.
11. The 2024 equivalent of £634. Presumably she already has some of the money she needs, or this is a very cheap car.
12. Average manual wage for women in the South West UK April 1979 was £50.45 – Hansard https://hansard.parliament.uk/commons/1979-04-03/debates/a2bbe635-766b-47c7-9ed5-1ec2ad6ff487/Wages We can assume Polly is not being paid anywhere near this figure, as she gets bed and board, and Basil is not likely to be a generous employer.
13. *An die Freude* by Friedrich Schiller. He is humming Beethoven's tune and not singing any of Schiller's words, but presumably thinks Polly would already know that. He cannot score a point over her if he asks her something too well-known.
14. Oil prices were in crisis in 1979.
15. 25 October 1415
16. 21 October 1805
17. 26 August 1346
18. 19 September 1356
19. If referring to the Jewish religious day of Yom Kippur, the day of atonement, this falls in September or October; if to the Yom Kippur war, October 1973. As all Basil's other references are to battles we can assume this is a battle reference too, a thinly veiled reference to his marriage. None of these battles occur in or near April.
20. The second most offensive word in the show – previously used in *The Germans* by the Major – and unusual for Terry, who normally seems to like Manuel.

21. Basil Brush is still amazingly popular for a tatty stuffed fox, in 2024, and younger readers may be aware of his catchphrase: Boom boom!
22. Wilde's dying words were reportedly *"My wallpaper and I are fighting a duel to the death. One or other of us has got to go."*
23. The Fawltys' bedroom moves between series; in *The Wedding Party* we see that Basil is on the left, closest to the door, and Sybil is on the right, with the window behind her. This room has a door on the opposite side, and the window is to the right of what we must presume is Sybil's bed.
24. Email to the author 2024.
25. Email to the author 2024.

FIRST BROADCAST 25 OCTOBER 1979 – BASIL THE RAT

1. Eventually recorded 20 May 1979.
2. Cleese notes that this is the most appropriate anagram, although it is missing a W.
3. Mr Carnegie is named after a genuine health inspector at the Royal Borough of Kensington council, who provided an enormous amount of help to Cleese and Booth while they were writing the episode.
4. 1929-2019. Another rep and character actor.
5. 1927-2015. Another Brian Rix alumnus, who appeared in *Dad's Army* and other sitcoms.
6. Can be seen occasionally playing slightly posh young men in TV comedy for the next decade or so.
7. Born 1954.
8. Andrew Sachs's wife, Melody Lang was a repertory actress and dance teacher. She died in 2017.
9. Born 1940. English Test Cricketer.
10. 1889-1951. Austrian philosopher.
11. 1903-1950. English novelist.
12. 1892-1975. Head of State in Spain 1936-1975.
13. OYF747R. This is the same colour as their previous Countryman, and appears to have been a BBC Production vehicle rather than a loaned press car.
14. Cleese notes that there was a generation who believed depression was a personal failing, but of course sadness and depression are healthy (in moderation) and normal.
15. Cleese says they initially attempted a pun with "*gerbil*", but it didn't really work.
16. George Burns (1896-1996) and Gracie Allen (1895-1964), a married couple, wrote and performed comedy together from 1924-58.

17. Bob Spiers complains that this cat is not a good actor. *"I think the trainer forgot to bring the trained one in. You can see he does not want to be in show business – he's a non-show business cat."* Cleese, who didn't have to deal with the technical side of filming, praises the cat hugely in his commentary.
18. Polly later claims it is Japanese.
19. Scenes with the live rat were pre-recorded and inserted in the edit, both to make the animal handling easier and to avoid scaring the audience members.
20. Another inserted scene.
21. A fake rat on a nylon line.
22. Controlled from underneath by Connie Booth.
23. Andrew Pixley, *TVZone* 152, 2002.
24. https://tellyspotting.kera.org/2015/11/24/1979-the-year-fawlty-towers-crossed-paths-with-not-the-nine-oclock-news
25. A PUNCH UP BLACKS OUT TV SHOW. This story was published on Friday 9 March 1979 after *Songs for Europe* was blacked out the previous evening. Rigger-driver Terry Ryan and transport manager John Cater were involved in a fight outside a BBC club in Acton, and Ryan was dismissed. His union, the Association of Broadcasting Staff, objected. The action cost the BBC a reported 170K in lost filming – the 2024 equivalent is more than £660K.
26. 1979-82, three series. It was a satirical sketch show featuring found footage and songs as well as more traditional comedy sketches.
27. The BBC generally avoids political comedy during the run-up to any general election. Once the election was called, after the sitting Prime Minister James Callaghan lost a vote of no confidence on 28 March, politically slanted shows were pulled or postponed until after the election on 3 May 1979.

MEMORIES

1. https://www.independent.co.uk/arts-entertainment/arts-to-hell-with-basil-1619527.html
2. Reportedly relaxed during the 1991 Gulf War by watching *Fawlty Towers*.
3. Jackson worked on *The Young Ones, Red Dwarf,* and *Girls On Top* among other shows. https://www.theguardian.com/tv-and-radio/2022/nov/12/the-young-ones-40-years-lise-mayer-nigel-planer-alexei-sayle-chrisopher-ryan-interview
4. https://tvtropes.org/pmwiki/pmwiki.php/Main/BritishBrevity
5. https://legacy.aintitcool.com/node/38030
6. Interview with the author 2024.
7. Interview with the author 2024.

8. It is easy, in the 21st century, to forget just how difficult it was to re-watch a show before the advent of home video – three channels, no VCRs so no tapes, few repeats, and not even full-day broadcasting until the 1980s. Even with live broadcasting, there was always a risk of a phone call, power cut, or something significant being on BBC1 at the same time.
9. Interview with the author 2024.
10. Fforde's novels are largely based on surreal concepts – what if rabbits were human-sized and spoke? What if humanity hibernated, or couldn't see colour? Very Pythonesque.
11. Interview with the author 2024.
12. 37 years, 1973-2010.
13. https://rts.org.uk/article/steven-moffat-his-cancel-culture-drama-douglas-cancelled
14. FTRO. Very understated, as Palmer often was.
15. FTRO
16. FTRO
17. https://www.gq-magazine.co.uk/culture/article/rowan-atkinson-interview
18. Writers of the sitcom *Father Ted. Father Ted: Unintelligent Design*, Channel 4, 1 Jan 2011.
19. Actor. British Comedy Awards 2012
20. 1940-80, former Beatle. BBC Radio 1 interview recorded in New York with Andy Peebles, 6 December 1980, two days before Lennon's murder. https://www.youtube.com/watch?v=aaTy3kSxyoo
21. https://www.theguardian.com/tv-and-radio/2022/nov/12/the-young-ones-40-years-lise-mayer-nigel-planer-alexei-sayle-chrisopher-ryan-interview
22. 1928-2009. Gelbert co-wrote comic Broadway musicals and films such as *Tootsie,* and created the TV version of *M*A*S*H*. *Newsday* 10 July 1980.
23. *Newsday* 10 July 1980.
24. *Newsday* 8 July 1982.
25. https://www.telegraph.co.uk/tv/0/david-mitchell-interview-stay-away-edgier-jokes-now

CRITICISM OF FAWLTY TOWERS

1. 1943-23. Film critic and co-writer, with Cleese, of *Fierce Creatures.*
2. 1923-1998.
3. https://www.theguardian.com/culture/interactive/2013/oct/12/fawlty-towers-bbc-rejection-letter

4. https://www.express.co.uk/celebrity-news/1772143/John-Cleese-Fawlty-Towers-rejection-letter-Instagram
5. https://www.telegraph.co.uk/culture/tvandradio/11858008/How-the-BBC-almost-turned-down-Fawlty-Towers.html
6. FTRO.
7. Born 1951, Lloyd has been instrumental in writing and producing many influential radio and TV comedies. He was a contemporary of Douglas Adams at Cambridge, and another Footlights member.
8. FTRO
9. Tony Pratt would later recant and write of series 1: *"Only six shows were made, but they were of such quality that they remain fresh in viewers minds."*
10. 12 October 1975.
11. Contemporary of Cleese, born Dec 1939. Son of Sir VS Pritchett, writer; father of cartoonist Matt, Pritchett has written TV criticism for the Daily Telegraph, Evening Standard, and The Oldie among others.
12. 22 Sept 1975.
13. 1923-1993. Journalist and broadcaster whose TV career was derailed by the Sex Pistols in 1976.
14. 1926-94, journalist and novelist. Daily Telegraph TV critic from 1966-mid 80s.
15. 1931-2022. Son of Poet Laureate Cecil Day-Lewis, older brother of actor Daniel Day-Lewis.
16. Lassen, Henrik, and Roy Sellars. "The Fawlty Rhetoric of National Character." European journal of English studies 13.3 2009.
17. NB the article calls Gill "a young teen" at the time of recording but he was actually 21 in summer 1975.
18. https://www.standard.co.uk/lifestyle/aa-gills-sober-truths-the-critic-on-his-lost-years-his-missing-brother-and-why-hes-a-fan-of-jeremy-corbyn-a3129021.html Hermione Eyre 3 December 2015
19. 1928-2016.
20. 1953-2016.
21. Born 1942.
22. FTRO.
23. https://www.theguardian.com/tv-and-radio/tvandradioblog/2013/jan/23/fawlty-towers-isnt-racist-major-gowen-is
24. *The Joke's On Us: Women in Comedy from Music Hall to the Present Day*, 1987, Pandora/Routledge.
25. Born 1961, Banks has written and appeared in a wide range of TV shows.
26. First on BBC Radio 4 1988-92, and then on ITV 1991-8 (the first four TV series were directly adapted from the radio scripts).
27. 1999-2001

28. 1963-2016. Aherne was very influential in 90s and 00s comedy.
29. 1998-2012
30. 2017-2020
31. https://www.independent.co.uk/arts-entertainment/arts-to-hell-with-basil-1619527.html
32. The Exchange Control Act 1947 capped the amount of money British citizens could take out of the UK. Harold Wilson set the amount at £50 (foreign currency) and £15 (British currency) in 1966, and this limit remained in place until October 1979. This had an obvious impact on the holiday industry and led to the growth of package holidays – which could be paid for in the UK.
33. Interview with the author, 2024.
34. https://www.dailymail.co.uk/news/article-7767363/Unedited-Fawlty-Towers-episode-containing-N-word-broadcast-Britbox.html
35. https://www.thetimes.com/culture/tv-radio/article/john-cleese-forces-bbc-u-turn-over-ban-on-fawlty-towers-f5gwkczvl
36. https://news.sky.com/story/fawlty-towers-john-cleese-hits-out-at-stupid-removal-of-episode-12005118
37. HARDTalk 29 June 2020.
38. https://www.dailymail.co.uk/news/article-7767363/Unedited-Fawlty-Towers-episode-containing-N-word-broadcast-Britbox.html
39. Kamm, Jürgen, and Birgit Neumann, eds. *British TV Comedies: Cultural Concepts, Contexts and Controversies*. Palgrave Macmillan, 2015.
40. 1728-74. Anglo-Irish writer.
41. https://www.stewartlee.co.uk/written_for_money/political-correctness-gone-mad/
42. https://www.theguardian.com/tv-and-radio/tvandradioblog/2013/jan/23/fawlty-towers-isnt-racist-major-gowen-is
43. https://uk.news.yahoo.com/bbc-airs-edited-fawlty-towers-the-germans-103619272.html
44. Gillespie, Nick. Reason magazine January 2023. https://reason.com/2022/12/18/john-cleese-on-how-wokeness-smothers-creativity/
45. https://faroutmagazine.co.uk/john-cleese-obsessed-woke-culture/

CULTURAL INHERITANCE

1. 1955-76, BBC TV.
2. Interview with the author 2024.
3. Basil calls Polly a 'cloth-eared bint' in *The Builders*.
4. Interview with the author 2024.

5. University of Indiana Knowledge Base, now archived; many similar documents can be found in internet archives.
6. Reddit.
7. Only slightly shorter than Cleese, at 6ft3, and of similar build. Born 1952, Barrymore was a very popular impressionist in the early 80s, with an act based on stars such as Cleese and Norman Wisdom.
8. https://en.wikipedia.org/wiki/100_Greatest_(TV_series)
9. https://en.wikipedia.org/wiki/Britain%27s_Best_Sitcom
10. https://www.chortle.co.uk/news/2012/06/03/15518/blackadder_the_best_show_ever
11. UKGold, now U&Gold. https://www.bbc.co.uk/news/entertainment-arts-38507022
12. Like the Oscars, industry peer awards can sometimes feel out of step with the popular vote, but not on this occasion. https://en.wikipedia.org/wiki/BFI_TV_100
13. http://news.bbc.co.uk/1/hi/uk/480720.stm
14. Andrew Pixley, *TVZone* 152, 2002.
15. Andrew Pixley, *TVZone* 152, 2002.
16. *From Fringe to Flying Circus,* 1980.
17. *"Video Arts was born out of the belief that people learn very little when they are bored and nothing when they are asleep... Using hilarious scripts, famous faces and TV-quality production, what started as actual VHS films (remember those?) has transformed into ... e-learning that engages learners and improves organisational performance."* https://www.videoarts.com/the-video-arts-story/
18. https://www.chortle.co.uk/review/2008/01/01/35679/rhod_gilbert_and_the_award-winning_mince_pie
19. https://www.comedy.co.uk/fringe/2012/rhod_gilbert
20. https://letterboxd.com/man_out_of_time/film/rhod-gilbert-the-man-with-the-flaming-battenberg-tattoo/
21. Published since 1979. Dury has been contributing since 1985.
22. Email to the author 2024.
23. FT.com 2017.
24. https://www.theguardian.com/business/shortcuts/2013/nov/08/michael-o-leary-33-daftest-quotes
25. vol. 349. 1998.
26. Black, Ian and Arle, Sophie. *The Guardian* 4 July 2003. https://www.theguardian.com/world/2003/jul/04/pressandpublishing.media
27. Paton, Suzie. *"Those Basil Fawlty Moments." Farmers Weekly* 2008.
28. Ezard, John. *The Guardian – Fings Ain't What they should be at* Fawlty Towers. 9 Feb 1995.

Endnotes

29. Wright, Malcolm, and Armstrong, J Scott. IDEAS Working Paper Series from RePEc (2007).
30. *Times Higher Education Supplement*, 4 February 2000.
31. https://campaignbrief.co.nz/2016/10/31/fawlty-towers-and-the-art-of-p/
32. 1946-2014. Political columnist.
33. https://www.theguardian.com/politics/2008/jan/19/politicalcolumnists.comment
34. https://www.tripadvisor.co.uk/Hotel_Review-g312659-d9837752-Reviews-Fawlty_Towers_Afari_Lodge-Cape_Town_Central_Western_Cape.html
35. https://www.tripadvisor.co.uk/Hotel_Review-g34145-d636136-Reviews-Fawlty_Towers_Motel-Cocoa_Beach_Brevard_County_Florida.html
36. https://www.hotelfawltytowers.com/
37. https://www.tripadvisor.co.uk/Hotel_Review-g303712-d1143715-Reviews-Fawlty_Towers_Hotel-Yangshuo_County_Guangxi.html
38. 11 June 2021.
39. https://www.theguardian.com/commentisfree/2019/apr/09/brexit-basil-fawlty-towers-sitcom
40. Cobb, Neil (Durham Law School) in *Social & Legal Studies*, 2009.
41. Payne, Stewart. *Gay Couple's Hotel Break like Fawlty Towers, says Judge, Daily Telegraph*, 24 February 2006.
42. Ewen, Shane. University of London Press, 2023.
43. https://www.churchill-living.co.uk/news/retirement-property-news/blue-plaque-unveiled-at-site-of-former-fawlty-towers-hotel/
44. https://www.youtube.com/watch?v=72DOLhLHIKw
45. https://en.wikipedia.org/wiki/Don%27t_Mention_the_World_Cup
46. 2001 BBC documentary series written by Cleese.
47. https://www.youtube.com/watch?v=n9tSN0178Us A related interview: https://www.youtube.com/watch?v=iRdldNfUXNM
48. https://fb.watch/v9jNZPaI0x/
49. https://www.youtube.com/watch?v=Lu0QHxEw8Ss
50. 1987. The Amnesty International event was co-founded by Cleese in 1976.
51. Named for comedian Dick Emery.
52. An American comedy tradition from 1949, it is not common in UK comedy.
53. Beloved fox puppet from children's TV. Boom boom!
54. A daily regional newspaper with a very credible history of Pulitzer Prize wins and nominations.
55. 1929-23. TV critic, humorist, and Pulitzer Prize nominee, Kitman wrote for *Newsday* for 35 years.
56. *The Marvin Kitman Show, Newsday.* 25 September 1996.
57. https://www.interactivetheatre.com.au/

58. https://www.interactivetheatre.com.au/news/ft-timeline/
59. https://www.huffingtonpost.co.uk/amp/entry/que-my-evening-as-a-guest-at-fawlty-towers_n_7373968/ 2013
60. *Travel trade gazette UK and Ireland* 2006. Superbreak holiday firm.
61. https://www.warringtonguardian.co.uk/local-events/search/?_evDiscoveryPath=/event/2304499-fawlty-towers-weekend-22-06-2024
62. https://comedy-dining.co.uk/
63. https://www.warble-entertainment.com/the-fawlty-towers-show
64. *Fawlty Towers: Fully Booked.*
65. *Basil the Rat,* s2e6.
66. https://www.radiotimes.com/tv/entertainment/how-to-choose-the-perfect-specialist-subject-on-mastermind/
67. https://metro.co.uk/2018/01/30/mastermind-banned-fawlty-towers-blackadder-father-ted-specialist-subjects-list-7271803/
68. https://www.theguardian.com/tv-and-radio/2018/jan/30/fawlty-towers-among-subjects-banned-by-mastermind-as-questions-run-out
69. https://www.bbc.co.uk/news/uk-42871651
70. 2013-14 season e5, 2 Jan 2014; 6 points; came 4th.
71. 2010-11 season e1, 19 Nov 2010; came 2nd.
72. s20 e4, 26 Feb 2022; came 2nd.
73. https://lifeaftermastermind.blogspot.com/2012/08/mastermind-heat-1.html 10 August 2012, the first episode of the 2012-13 series.
74. A tobacconist.
75. Noriega, Toynbee, Thorndike, Rathbone are forenamed, respectively, Manuel, Polly, Sybil, and Basil. Kudos to the Extras, 12 August 2017.
76. https://www.writebetterpoems.com/articles/how-to-write-haiku
77. Cleese's former colleague David Jason, in *Only Fools and Horses* (1981-2003).
78. Ricky Gervais in *The Office* (2001-03).
79. Richard Wilson in *One Foot in the Grave* (1990-2000). Andrew Sachs had auditioned unsuccessfully for the role and believed that the overpopularity of Manuel probably cost him the part.
80. Harry H Corbett, the Son in *Steptoe and Son* (1962-74). Steptoe is also in many ways the 'father' of Basil Fawlty, a man with frustrated aspirations and a thwarted desire to improve his life.
81. Leonard Rossiter in *The Fall and Rise of Reginald Perrin* (1976-79, 1996), contemporary with *Fawlty Towers.*
82. https://lithub.com/turns-out-1980s-midwesterners-didnt-want-their-sitcoms-set-in-boston-bars/
83. As he died in the first episode he will never get the chance to be one (though his actor has inevitably aged).

Endnotes

84. A 1980s Cosgrove Hall production, *Count Duckula* features a vegetarian vampire duck (voiced by David Jason) who dislikes blood and much prefers carrot juice.
85. HBO, 2021-date. Armond is only in s1.
86. https://thewhitelotus.fandom.com/wiki/Armond

FAWLTY TOWERS – THE PLAY

1. http://rowneygreenplayers.co.uk/fawlty-towers-2006/
2. Licences to perform plays are controlled in the UK by Samuel French Ltd; there are usually regional restrictions on shows that are currently being put on by professionals, preventing any performance within 50 miles of the West End, for instance. At time of writing the original *Fawlty Towers* scripts are not licensed for performance anywhere in the UK.
3. https://amdram.co.uk/fawlty-towers-15/
4. https://www.noda.org.uk/show-reports/fawlty-towers-17
5. National Operatic and Dramatic Association.
6. Dubbo, New South Wales, is around 250 miles from Sydney.
7. https://www.youtube.com/watch?v=dWa6d7pIA_4
8. Sydney, Australia
9. https://www.stagewhispers.com.au/news/fawlty-towers-live-stage
10. https://en.wikipedia.org/wiki/Spamalot The show would, however, cost the Python team nearly a million pounds in royalties and legal fees after the producer of the original film sued for royalties.
11. https://www.chortle.co.uk/news/2016/08/22/25601/fawlty_towers_live_deemed_a_hit
12. https://tvtonight.com.au/2016/08/fawlty-towers-live-reviews.html
13. https://www.telegraph.co.uk/comedy/what-to-see/fawlty-towers-live-roslyn-packer-theatre-sydney-review/
14. Quoted in the Chortle roundup and https://tvtonight.com.au/2016/08/fawlty-towers-live-reviews.html. The original is no longer online.
15. https://www.theguardian.com/stage/2016/aug/21/fawlty-towers-live-review-fun-but-pointless-adaptation-screen-to-stage
16. 18 August 2016. "*A really terrific performance from our Aussie cast tonight, earning a prolonged standing ovation, with cheering. Hard for anyone to hatchet...*"
17. https://www.theguardian.com/tv-and-radio/2018/jun/04/father-ted-only-fools-and-horses-rise-sitcom-musical
18. https://en.wikipedia.org/wiki/Uncanny_valley
19. https://www.dailytelegraph.com.au/entertainment/sydney-confidential/fawlty-towers-live-show-proves-a-hugely-fun-and-funny-romp/news-story/587cf6fd084f1c51891505441c56fc47

20. *"A commercialised machine raking in dollars"* https://www.theguardian.com/stage/2016/aug/21/fawlty-towers-live-review-fun-but-pointless-adaptation-screen-to-stage
21. Apollo Theatre 4 May 2024-28 September 2024; extended to 4 January 2025 and then 1 March 2025 during the writing of this book.
22. https://www.telegraph.co.uk/theatre/what-to-see/john-cleese-basil-fawlty-towers-west-end 26 April 2024
23. https://www.youtube.com/watch?v=xrfXDY0Z5XQ
24. Spoiler: The Major reacts to the commotion by shooting one of the inspectors.
25. https://www.dailymail.co.uk/tvshowbiz/article-13363193/Reclusive-Connie-Booth-sneak-watch-Fawlty-Towers-stage-launches-West-End-getting-writing-credit-ex-husband-John-Cleese-likes-low-profile-days.html
26. https://www.bbc.co.uk/news/articles/czk0y318d8ko
27. https://www.youtube.com/watch?v=xrfXDY0Z5XQ
28. https://www.youtube.com/watch?v=g2CD8Tfgw_M
29. https://www.broadwayworld.com/westend/article/Review-FAWLTY-TOWERS-THE-PLAY-Apollo-Theatre-20240516
30. 1990-98 Channel 4 sitcom based on a TV station, featuring the news in the week of transmission.
31. https://www.youtube.com/watch?v=BoIW-ImUIPE
32. https://www.spectator.co.uk/article/fawlty-towers-the-play-is-the-best-museum-piece-youll-ever-see/
33. https://www.chortle.co.uk/review/2024/05/15/55633/john_cleeses_fawlty_towers%3A_the_play

ADAPTATIONS AND REVIVALS

1. https://metro.co.uk/2009/05/15/john-cleeses-fawlty-towers-movie-122006/
2. 7 episodes, broadcast from 8 October to 31 December 1976.
3. Collaborators on *Bless This House, Love Thy Neighbour,* and other shows.
4. Born 1947.
5. https://tvenradiodb-nl.translate.goog/index.php/22562/hotel-de-botel.html
6. Episode 3: https://www.youtube.com/watch?v=HcoZ8FRb0W8
7. In the 1970s and early 80s the USA had successfully remade *Steptoe and Son (Sanford and Son), Man About the House (Three's Company);* the UK had remade *Good Times (The Fosters), Maude (Nobody's Perfect).* Later successes include *The Office, Shameless, The Upper Hand/Who's The Boss.* The list of infamous failed attempts includes *Red Dwarf, The Golden Girls, Coupling,* and *The IT Crowd* which, like *Fawlty Towers,* had at least three failed attempts.
8. 24 June 1978 to be precise. Viacom.

9. AKA *Chateau Snavely*. It can be watched at https://www.youtube.com/watch?v=XxPUpq-vV54
10. 1927-2008. Korman worked extensively with Carol Burnett and Mel Brooks.
11. 1922-2021. Doyenne of US comedy, she had starred in *The Mary Tyler Moore Show* and many quiz and talk shows by 1978; she is probably best known to UK viewers as Rose in *The Golden Girls*.
12. Frank LaLoggia, born 1954.
13. Deborah Zon.
14. Ivor Francis, 1918-86.
15. George Pentecost, 1939-2003.
16. FTRO
17. *In the Picture – Remade in America. Northern Echo,* Darlington. 20 September 2003.
18. 1982-90.
19. 1929-2024. Stand-up comedian and comic actor.
20. https://www.rollingstone.com/tv-movies/tv-movie-features/bob-newhart-interview-1235063501/ Nov 6 1986.
21. 10 February to 26 May 1983. Available in full on YouTube.
22. Tony Rosato.
23. Natalie Core. 1919-2011.
24. Fred McCarren.
25. Simone Griffeth.
26. 1927-2020. Veteran of many US sitcoms and films. Father of Ben Stiller.
27. 1914-86. Musical theatre and film star.
28. Gore-Langton, Robert. *John Cleese: And Now for Something Completely Different*. Chameleon/Andre Deutsch, 1999.
29. alt.fan.pratchett 11 Aug 2003.
30. *Daily Express*, 9 Jul 1993.
31. John Laroquette. Born 1947, he was a regular on sitcom *Night Court* and a number of major dramas.
32. JoBeth Williams, born 1948.
33. Rick Batalla, born 1962.
34. Julie Benz, born 1972, and much better known for playing Darla in *Buffy the Vampire Slayer* at the time.
35. 15 March to 28 April 1999. *The J Edgar Hoover Pin Story, Sexual Intercom, Whatever Happened to Baby Payne?, Gossip Checks In and a Cat Checks Out, Pacific Ocean Duck, Trouble in Room 206, I Never Forget A Face-Lift, Wedding Fever,* and *Pacific Ocean Duck* (unbroadcast). Only *Pacific Ocean Duck* is a direct adaptation of an original *Fawlty Towers* script – *Gourmet Night*.

36. 1957-2011. Prolific actor, writer, and director.
37. In conversation with John Hooper https://www.theguardian.com/culture/2001/jul/10/artsfeatures2
38. An island in Schleswig-Holstein.
39. Also playing the David Brent character in the German version of *The Office, Das Amt,* in the same year.
40. Busse: born 1941.
41. https://lostmediawiki.com/Hotel_Zum_letzten_Kliff_(partially_found_German_reboot_of_Fawlty_Towers;_2001)
42. 1986. Written by veteran farce creator Michael Frayn.
43. John Ferguson, unknown date, but after 1988. https://en.wikipedia.org/wiki/Clockwise_(film)
44. https://cultfollowing.co.uk/2021/07/08/clockwise-review/
45. 1988.
46. https://www.dailymail.co.uk/tvshowbiz/article-1179168/John-Cleese-blames-ex-wifes-divorce-demands-delay-Fish-Called-Wanda-musical.html
47. From 5 September.
48. The following week's issue correctly credits Ken Campbell, so must have gone to press after 11 March.
49. Albeit at 11.40pm. But a slot on BBC1 on Christmas Day is a major compliment.
50. Aspden, Peter. "*From* Fawlty Towers *to* Frasier – *the Tricky World of TV Reboots"* The Financial Times, 2023.
51. https://www.theguardian.com/culture/2023/may/27/alan-carr-interview-i-used-to-say-awful-things
52. https://www.theguardian.com/tv-and-radio/2023/feb/08/why-the-fawlty-towers-remake-is-a-truly-nauseating-idea-john-cleese
53. Scales was diagnosed with vascular dementia in 2014, but is still working in a very limited capacity, aged 91, as of 2024. https://www.theguardian.com/stage/article/2024/may/13/prunella-scales-returns-to-role-of-queen-victoria-for-edinburgh-fringe-show
54. https://www.dailymail.co.uk/tvshowbiz/article-11819037/Fawlty-Towers-John-Cleese-ex-wife-Connie-Booth-not-told-return.html

BIBLIOGRAPHY

1. https://www.bbc.co.uk/sounds/play/p0093xyx
2. https://www.bbc.co.uk/sounds/play/p00944v0
3. https://www.bbc.co.uk/sounds/play/m0010p13
4. BBC Radio 4, 2021.

Dear Reader,

We hope you have enjoyed this book, but why not share your views on social media? You can also follow our pages to see more about our other products: facebook.com/penandswordbooks or follow us on X @penswordbooks

You can also view our products at www.pen-and-sword.co.uk (UK and ROW) or www.penandswordbooks.com (North America).

To keep up to date with our latest releases and online catalogues, please sign up to our newsletter at: www.pen-and-sword.co.uk/newsletter

If you would like a printed catalogue with our latest books, then please email: enquiries@pen-and-sword.co.uk or telephone: 01226 734555 (UK and ROW) or email: uspen-and-sword@casematepublishers.com or telephone: (610) 853-9131 (North America).

We respect your privacy and we will only use personal information to send you information about our products.

Thank you!